The Music of Britten and Tippett

Michael Tippett and Benjamin Britten (January 1964). An informal double portrait by permission of Erich Auerbach FRPS.

The Music of Britten and Tippett

Studies in themes and techniques

ARNOLD WHITTALL

Cambridge University Press

Cambridge

London   New York   New Rochelle

Melbourne   Sydney

Published by the Press Syndicate of the University of Cambridge
The Pitt Building, Trumpington Street, Cambridge CB2 1RP
32 East 57th Street, New York, NY 10022, USA
296 Beaconsfield Parade, Middle Park, Melbourne 3206, Australia

First published 1982

Printed in Great Britain by the
Cambridge University Press

Library of Congress catalogue card number: 81-38554

British Library Cataloguing in Publication Data
Whittall, Arnold
The music of Britten and Tippett.
1. Britten, Benjamin   2. Tippett, *Sir* Michael
I. Title
780' .92'4   ML410.B853
ISBN 0 521 23523 5

Contents

Acknowledgements

I wish to thank the editors of *Music and Letters* and the Council of the Royal Musical Association for permission to employ and adapt material.

I am most grateful to the following, who have helped me in various ways: Sally Cavender of Boosey & Hawkes Music Publishers Ltd, David Stevens and Sally Groves of Schott & Co. Ltd, and Martin Kingsbury of Faber Music Ltd, London, willingly supplied scores and tapes; Rosamund Strode of the Britten–Pears Library at Aldeburgh answered queries and showed me some of the fascinating material which the library contains; Meirion Bowen, Ian Kemp, Colin Matthews and Donald Mitchell all provided the stimulus of ideas and insights often refreshingly different from my own. I owe particular debts to Peter Evans, who read my completed typescript, and to my wife Mary, without whom the book could scarcely have been begun.

The music examples are reproduced by permission of the following publishers.
Boosey & Hawkes Music Publishers Ltd: exx. 4, 5, 9, 10, 12, 13, 16, 19, 20, 21, 22, 23, 24, 27, 28, 31, 33, 34, 35, 36, 39, 40;
Faber Music Ltd, London: exx, 2, 3, 41, 43, 44, 45, 46, 47, 48, 49, 52, 53, 54, 57, 58, 59, 60, 61;
Oxford University Press: ex. 6;
Schott & Co. Ltd: exx. 1, 7, 8, 11, 14, 15, 17, 18, 25, 26, 29, 30, 32, 37, 38, 42, 50, 51, 55, 56, 62, 63, 64.

The quotation from Britten's diary is © The Britten Estate. All quotations from Britten's previously published diaries, letters, speeches, articles and interviews are used by permission of the Britten Estate, and are not to be reproduced without the written consent of the executors.

Extracts from Michael Tippett, *Moving into Aquarius*, are reproduced by permission of Routledge & Kegan Paul Ltd, and the extracts from *Music of the Angels. Essays and Sketchbooks of Michael Tippett*, selected and edited by Meirion Bowen, are reproduced by permission of Ernst Eulenburg Ltd.

A.W.

Prologue

Benjamin Britten and Michael Tippett have already been the subject of several separate studies, the number of which can confidently be expected to increase with some rapidity. For this reason alone, it might seem sound economic sense to compress two books into one. Nevertheless, my intention is to offer one book about two composers, rather than two books in one, since I believe that Britten and Tippett complement and illuminate each other in striking and distinctive ways.

Precedents for such a double portrait, as a means of focusing on matters of similarity and contrast, are not hard to find, though the result, at least in studies of composers, has often run the risk of either diluting or exaggerating both the differences and the similarities. One of the most successful examples of the genre can be found outside music altogether: George Steiner's *Tolstoy or Dostoevsky. An Essay in Contrast*.[1] My own title refers to Britten *and* Tippett, rather than Britten *or* Tippett, because my principal concern is with their responses to similar and, at times, identical situations and circumstances. And yet it may ultimately appear that my two subjects, for all their similarities, represent significantly different aspects of that 'relation to tradition' which no composer can wholly escape. As a result, the critic may come to develop a strong preference for one or the other. But the analyst may well feel a less pressing need to evaluate or discriminate: for him, the definition and interpretation of a composer's means and methods is a sufficiently demanding (and rewarding) task.

Comparisons – and judgements – are only too easy. But those compared and evaluated must be important and interesting enough, as well as sufficiently similar and different, to justify the kind of focused treatment which detaches them from their contemporaries and precursors, and yet implies that there is something special about their 'historical' significance. Steiner's choice was made in the belief that Tolstoy and Dostoevsky 'are the two greatest of novelists',[2] and his discussion centres on one crucial difference between them – what he calls at one point 'an inherent antagonism'.[3] Tolstoy, like Homer, is essentially an epic artist: Dostoevsky, like Shakespeare, essentially a dramatic artist. As Steiner elaborates the point, therefore, the two 'stand in contrareity', and this justifies his decision 'to consider their achievements and define the nature of their respective genius through contrast'.[4]

1

Steiner's claims on behalf of his subject are contentiously but plausibly extreme. I would not claim that Tippett and Britten are 'the two greatest' of composers. But I do believe that they are the two best British composers of that first twentieth-century generation, born between 1900 and the outbreak of the First World War, and among the best of all composers born in the first two decades of the twentieth century. That, perhaps, is sufficient to justify the enterprise – if not to the composers themselves.

Evaluations, comparisons – the whole apparatus; does it mean anything to you? It doesn't to me, much . . . We have known each other now for more than twenty years; we have been very close often, at other times we have seemed to be moving in different directions. But whenever I see our names bracketed together (as they often are, I am glad to say) I am reminded of the spirit of courage and integrity, sympathy, gaiety and profound musical independence which is yours, and I am proud to call you my friend.[5]

In this tribute to Tippett on his sixtieth birthday, Britten expressed his intense dislike not only of criticism, but of the critical medium – words. 'Criticism likes to separate, to dislodge, to imply rivalries, to provoke jealousies', he wrote. And although Tippett has been far less wary about plunging into verbal expression, his greeting to Britten on the latter's fiftieth birthday similarly complains of 'the inability of so many music critics and others to distinguish between the facts of public acclaim and the pretensions (and maybe necessity) of value judgements'.[6] Britten's belief that 'criticism likes to separate' could well have arisen in part because the bracketing together of 'Britten-and-Tippett' was so often undertaken, even by enthusiasts, more from the desire to point up obvious differences than to explore more complex similarities. Perhaps the emphasis on contrast was encouraged by the common knowledge, from the early 1940s, that both men were pacifists. In one such early comparison, Edward Sackville West remarked that Tippett's music 'has none of the vivid colour, the immediate dramatic effectiveness, the winning sensuous beauty, of Britten's best work. Its strength is that of consistency and rational construction informed by an emotional and intransigent nature.'[7] At much the same time, Eric Blom described Tippett as 'perhaps the only one among the outstanding modern creative musical Englishmen who shows none of the leaning towards romanticism or nostalgia for the past discernible more or less clearly in others of similar standing, even in Britten, when all is said'.[8] And Wilfrid Mellers, while admitting that 'Britten approaches the setting of his native language with a sensitivity that rivals Tippett's', thought that

it would hardly be an exaggeration to say that Britten's development has been exactly opposite to Tippett's. Tippett started very tentatively and his career has been a continual probing outwards, an exploration intended to comprehend and reconcile ever more elements of his complex personality. Tippett's work is based on a struggle between spontaneous creativity and the modern self-consciousness in which each side must be accorded its rights. In Britten's work there is no struggle. He early acquired a virtuoso command of many – one nearly said all – stylizations; in his development he has learned to purge his language of extraneous elements, to make the stylization subservient to the musical purpose.[9]

Such summary judgements were rather easier to formulate in the 1940s than in later years, of course. And it has since become easier to observe certain common features; for example, Arthur Hutchings has noted that

despite the disparity of their ages, Tippett and Britten have temperamental affinities. They read more widely than most musicians and are interested in other arts than music. They differ greatly as composers yet are both attracted by subjects (in songs, operas or cantatas) dominated less by the expression of the primitive passions than by the pity, fear, disgust or amusement with which we contemplate their survival or perversion among supposedly civilized men.[10]

Direct comparison of the two is, no doubt, all the easier if the object is simply to observe parallels between personal circumstances – middle-class background, pacifism, sexual orientation – and the subject-matter of their compositions. Starting with the fact that, as David Matthews has put it, 'the two dominating English composers of our time were brought up within 40 miles of each other in the same county'[11] and were born a mere eight years apart, they can be shown as responding creatively and consistently to the various personal, national and international events which occurred in their lifetimes. On the technical level alone, these responses are of the greatest interest, and it is to matters of technique that this study is primarily addressed. Yet at the same time I have attempted to produce a reasonably comprehensive narrative, rather than a series of separate analytical commentaries. Although not every work by each composer is discussed in detail, and some are not even mentioned, the presentation tends more to the chronological than the generic, and the discussion is by no means exclusively 'analytical': hence the distinction in my title between themes and techniques. There is a certain amount of aesthetic comment and biographical information, even some literary criticism. But such elements form a background to the main area of discussion, and that area itself can be defined through some consideration of the ways in which technical developments in music during the late nineteenth and early twentieth centuries can best be verbally explored.

The principal change in the language of music during this period has been variously described, but the two principal and often interacting tendencies are, respectively, 'harmonic' and 'thematic': they refer either to a 'breakdown' in the tonal system, or to a shift of emphasis from harmonic to thematic organization in compositional technique. One of the effects of the advance of Schoenberg and others into 'atonality'

3

around 1908 was to make possible a distinction between composers who believed that the structural and expressive potential of tonality had been exhausted – that music must be transformed or die: and those who believed that it was still possible to continue technically, or even technically *and* stylistically, along the paths of those nineteenth-century composers who had enriched traditional harmony to the extent that certain fundamental structural features of the tonal system were enhanced rather than undermined. Something of this enrichment and enhancement can be understood by the concept of 'extended tonality', which features prominently in what follows.

It was inevitable that attempts by musicologists to define 'tonality' should lead to attempts to subdivide it. And since the systematic study of the properties and potential of tonality was something which really got under way only after Fétis in the second half of the nineteenth century, it is hardly surprising that a central concern of theorists has been the distinction between what Ernst Kurth identified in *Tristan* as 'a clinging to the basic paths of tonality', and a complementary 'striving for expansion and disintegration'.[12] The variety and complexity of the terms devised by later theorists to reflect the various types of procedure which they have observed in tonal music can be imagined. But all agree that what is involved after Wagner is a shift of emphasis in which the traditionally strong association between a tonic and its close relatives, especially at cadence points, is reduced by techniques which bring the more chromatically remote areas of the tonal system into a relationship with that tonic which is not merely arbitrary in effect and momentary in significance. A leading practitioner of 'atonality', and of music which proceeded primarily through the developing variation of its basic motives, Schoenberg was also a leading harmonic theorist, and by the time he had completed his *Structural Functions of Harmony* in the late 1940s he had arrived at a view of what he termed 'extended tonality'. For Schoenberg, to extend tonality by moving beyond the diatonic degrees into distant chromatic regions, was not to disrupt or destroy it. He argued that 'remote transformations and successions of harmonies were understood as remaining within the tonality', and that the progressions which extend the tonality 'function chiefly as enrichments of the harmony'.[13] For Schoenberg there was no theoretical problem about extended tonality because there was no aesthetic problem: 'the ear of the contemporary musician is no longer disturbed by far-reaching deviations from diatonic harmonies'.[14] And this echoes a statement he had made many years before in the *Theory of Harmony*: 'a piece can also be intelligible . . . even when the tonality is kept, so to speak, flexible, fluctuating. Many examples give evidence that nothing is lost from the impression of completeness if the tonality is merely hinted at, yes, even if it is erased.'[15]

4

Several points arise in considering the connection between these general technical issues and the music of Britten and Tippett. To ask, technically, of any twentieth-century composer, 'what kind of music did they write?' seems to invite, at least as a preliminary answer, the single word 'tonal' or 'atonal'; and it is certainly in the field of tonal and harmonic organization that the most fundamental distinctions between the achievements of Britten and Tippett may emerge. Perhaps the most interesting contrast is in the sense that, while Britten remained faithful to the first principle of musical modernity, the emancipation of the dissonance, to the extent that this was consistent with the retention of an essentially hierarchic view of harmonic organization and tonal structure, Tippett advanced to what I would describe as the emancipation of the consonance; the structurally significant use of chords – they will be called 'higher consonances' – which, while giving some priority to triadic elements, no longer require the exclusive presence of those elements in any privileged contexts: their function is mediation rather than resolution. The final bars of Tippett's String Quartet No. 4 (1978) offer a good example of the nature and function of such harmony in his later music (Ex. 1). The work is not 'tonal', since the initial emphasis on E flat and the final arrival on A are both too local to acquire the larger functions of genuinely tonal relations; yet tonal procedures have not totally been lost sight of. The music is not merely textural or colouristic, and the sense of hierarchic procedures being called on occasionally rather than consistently is appropriate in view of the fact that such procedures can easily acquire a stronger focus in later Tippett, as the Triple Concerto witnesses.

Ex. 1 Tippett, String Quartet No. 4

As for Britten, the music of his last decade did show distinct signs, under the influence of totally chromatic and twelve-note techniques, of shaking itself free of the continuous presence of a tonic triad as a structural pivot: but it remained focused on tonics whose relevance is to establish certain large-scale connections, even when the effect of the music is more to threaten than to confirm any single tonic. The ending of Britten's String Quartet No. 3 (1975) shows how near to a pure, triadic E major harmony the composer could come, and the effect is compounded both of the implications the music sets up with respect to such a close, tangible background, and of its actual contradiction and evasion of those implications (Ex. 2).

The limitations of such summary comparisons will be obvious. Yet it is clear that there is much more in common between the early Britten of the Phantasy Quartet (1932), with its non-tonic, tonal ending (see Ex. 5, p. 21) and the late Britten of the Quartet No. 3, than between the tonal affirmations of early Tippett and the use of higher consonance to control the essentially atonal tendencies of his later works. Only very rarely, even when surface features of thematic manipulation and rhythmic patterning seem to be carrying the argument, might one form the opinion that the vertical aspects of Tippett's textures are devoid of all harmonic significance.

To focus the discussion of any two composers on the same technical issue naturally invites distortion and dangerous selectiveness, but to avoid any focus at all invites vagueness and imprecision. The differences between Britten and Tippett are indeed obvious and not to be obscured: but even if we acknowledge that Tippett was a composer whose 'indifference to functional harmonic progression is well attested',[16] and that an essential aspect of Britten's development is the sense in which his pre-

Ex. 2 Britten, String Quartet No. 3, Recitative and Passacaglia (finale)

sentation of the 'symbolism of conflict . . . moved from the tonal plane to
the motivic, even intervallic',[17] it remains essential to determine the
extent to which vertical relationships, and the function of harmonies,
chords, or 'aggregates' are anything more than the inevitable but arbitrary consequence of writing more than one note at a time. Little of technical value can be discerned in music unless the nature and significance
of vertical combinations is determined, and even if the music is monodic,
the linear implications and relations retain a 'harmonic' dimension (see
the discussion of the 'Lamento' from Britten's first suite for solo cello,
p. 221). However accidental or unintentional the composition of such ele-

ments may appear to be, they have an innate capacity to relate and to generate; to conflict, contradict, clarify, resolve, integrate, and, in the world of extended tonality, to imply – by allusion and association.

The technical discussion which follows will certainly not exclude matters of rhythm, theme or motive, nor shun the dangerous generalities of the traditional formal categories, since these never cease to be relevant to either composer. Nevertheless, these are the aspects which have already been well aired by other commentators in studies with more pretensions to completeness than mine. The world embracing both extended tonality, still defined by the presence of a tonic, and the kind of harmonic allusiveness in which focused higher consonances perform a pivotal but not all-pervading role is a rich and complex one, and there is a corresponding richness and openness in the music of Britten and Tippett, even when the effect is spare and concentrated, which gives the lie to glib comments about austerity and meagreness.

Even if it is accepted that a consideration of the music of these two composers which is primarily tonal and harmonic is of value in focusing on the extent to which such relationships are indeed 'essential', there nevertheless remains the large question of how a discussion of extended tonality and 'higher consonance' (whether alongside other features or not) should be conducted. The difficulty here is considerable, since there is little sign of consensus even with respect to the 'mainstream' tonal-harmonic music of the eighteenth and nineteenth centuries. It was Heinrich Schenker who, during the first three decades of the twentieth century, provided the most fundamental and far-reaching insights into exactly how Kurth's 'basic paths of tonality' functioned in the music of those composers from Bach to Brahms whom Schenker regarded as the bearers of the Great Tradition. However, composers who seemed to be 'striving for expansion and disintegration' were anathema to Schenker himself, and none more so than Schoenberg with his yearning to be 'the godfather of new chords' and his heresy, argued in the *Theory of Harmony*, that there were no such things as 'non-harmonic tones'.[18] As his theoretical works and textbooks indicate, Schoenberg's preferred technique for the presentation of harmonic analysis of tonal music of all kinds remained, in essence, that of identifying and labelling chords according to their relationship to the tonic of the work in question. Certain hierarchic distinctions emerge automatically in this way, simply through the degree of distance from that tonic, but the more subtle and far-reaching distinctions of function and level which the voice-leading techniques of Schenkerian method make possible are not in evidence. It was one of Schenker's pupils, Felix Salzer, who began the attempt to adapt and extend the master's analytical methods in order to reveal structural principles in much earlier and much more recent music. Salzer's examples range from chant to Stravinsky, and other analysts, notably Roy Travis, have carried the extension further, into 'atonal' music itself, arguing that it is possible to identify a 'dissonant tonic sonority' which assumes a position of hierarchic pre-eminence in the structure.[19]

Of course, the difference between Schenker and Schoenberg was not simply one of analytical technique but of analytical emphasis: as Carl Dahlhaus has put it,

it is manifest that Schenker, when speaking of coherence, meant primarily tonal coherence, whereas Schoenberg thought of motivic coherence . . . Schenker's *Ursatz* is a formula for the passage from the tonic to the dominant and back to the tonic. In Schoenberg's musical thought, on the other hand, the central category . . . is his concept of the developing variation.[20]

Since it follows that Schoenberg's preferred analytical technique, as opposed to his preferred method for teaching the 'structural functions' of harmony, was concerned with thematic transformation, it seems inescapable that any serious discussion of structural harmonic issues should seek to make use of the insights consequent on the application of Schenkerian methods. Yet the most radical aspect of those methods is not the conclusions they draw about harmonic relationships in music, but the fact that they demand presentation in graphic, non-verbal form: they therefore tend to the rejection of the book 'as we know it'. Such analyses, at their fullest and most authentic, need to be the subject of detailed discussion and study by those familiar with the graphic techniques concerned. Yet in the case of 'extended-tonal' music the codification of those techniques is still a matter of much debate, even among those who accept the principles of such analysis, and will probably remain so for some time. So, in a commentary which is concerned as much if not more with the general developments through a great number of individual compositions, some of which have moved beyond the limits of the most tenuously extended tonality, it is still necessary to retain the 'word' as the prime means of communication.

Although the term 'extended tonality' occurs frequently in this study, I should nevertheless stress that my 'words' are more the result of contemplating the post-Schenkerian debate about matters of line and level than the consequence of pursuing Schoenberg's ideas about harmony. In fact, as should soon become clear to the reader, I do not apply a 'theory' to the music of Britten and Tippett; still less do I demonstrate in detail how every structural level functions in every piece. But I do comment on how certain features which I regard as crucial to structure and expression establish contacts between the particular qualities of the individual piece and those more general aspects of hierarchic musical structure which Schenker and his successors have placed in high relief.

Most analytically orientated writing retains the traditional concern with unity as the overriding aim of the artist and the one vital aesthetic and analytical criterion of the listener, critic and musicologist. In a sense, the shift of emphasis from harmonic to motivic processes in Schoenbergian thought is a means of retaining that emphasis. But it is more difficult to talk about harmonic or tonal unity in music where a single tonal or chordal construct does not rule throughout, however strong the sense may be of 'progressive' tonality in which a tonic is ultimately unveiled. 'Unity' may well be more evident through consistent harmonic elements and procedures, however: and music which is less unified than under the 'rules' of traditional tonality may be no less coherent, even if motivic considerations are not brought into play at all.

The value, and appeal, of ideas about unity and coherence is precisely that they seem to bridge the gulf between the aesthetic and the analytic. Once again, however, it should be admitted that the more technical the discussion of music, the less likely the composer himself is to approve:

> What is important . . . is *not* the scientific part, the analysable part of music, but the something which emerges from it but transcends it, which cannot be analysed because it is not *in* it, but *of* it . . . it is something to do with personality, with gift, with spirit. I quite simply call it – magic.[21]

> Music, in my opinion, should speak to us so far as possible immediately, directly and without analysis.[22]

It would be doubly parasitic to engage in a one-sided debate with these remarks of Britten and Tippett, and I would not deny for a moment that what music expresses should be felt – *must* be felt, rather than merely described. Yet if 'the analysable part of music' is not the 'expression' itself, it is the basis, the cause of that expression. To analyse should be to enhance the understanding, or at least the intensity, of feeling. If analysis inhibits emotional response, it should be abandoned. But it should not be automatically assumed that music might not speak to us *more* directly after analysis than it does before.

The real trouble with technical commentary is not in what it says about the music's structure but in what it implies about how the music was actually composed. In his *Theory of Harmony*, Schoenberg made a characteristically blunt distinction between pupil and master, student and composer, which could usefully be applied to analyst and composer: 'the pupil should think; but the artist, the master, composes by feeling. He no longer has to think, for he has reached a higher kind of response to his need for self-expression.'[23] If, as Schoenberg asserts, the essence of the act of composition is feeling rather than thought, then it is not surprising that the analyst can say little about how the music actually came into being: but he can and should comment in detail on the actual result of the compositional process, for without that there would be no 'magic'. Of course, there is no law against speculating about precisely what 'decisions' the composer made along the road from initial inspiration to first performance, and the study of sketches and drafts is a fascinating if dangerous aid to such activity; nor is there any prohibition of the kind of speculation of writers who, following Adorno, see twentieth-century composers as responding to a unique set of historical circumstances, and inescapably reflecting and reacting to them in specific, if usually depressing, ways. One interpretation of those circumstances is Freud's: 'the meaning of the evolution of civilization is no longer obscure to us. It must present the struggle between Eros and Death, between the instinct of life and the instinct of destruction, as it works itself out in the human species.'[24] It is certainly by no means essential for a composer to be involved in 'progressive' music in order to respond significantly to that struggle. Even if Britten and Tippett do seem essentially 'conservative' or 'neo-classic' according to the harsh criteria of the post-war avant-garde, they offer a sense of relation to the Freudian struggle no less immediate than that of their avowedly more radical contemporary Elliott Carter, who has written:

Before the end of the Second World War, it became clear to me, partly as a result of re-reading Freud and others, and thinking about psychoanalysis, that we were living in a world where . . . physical and intellectual violence would always be a problem, and that the whole conception of human nature underlying the neo-classic esthetic amounted to a sweeping under the rug of things that, it seemed to me, we had to deal with in a less oblique and resigned way.[25]

No doubt one could conclude from this perspective that, while Tippett became less oblique and less resigned during the post-war decades, Britten became more so. But neither could be accused of the kind of evasiveness which 'sweeping under the rug' implies; both 'thematically' and 'technically' they confronted the essential issues and provided memorable solutions.

Whether our reasons for admiring and studying them are primarily 'thematic', relating to their preferred subject matter and connections with the world beyond the manuscript paper, or 'technical', and focused on such issues as tonality and harmony, form and structure, it is through a conjunction of the two aspects that their identities and achievements will emerge in fullest focus and sharpest relief.

I THE THIRTIES AND THE WAR

1 Britten: Four early works (1931-3)

When Benjamin Britten began to compose a String Quartet in D major on 8 May 1931, he was seventeen years old and had been a student at the Royal College of Music in London since the previous September. He had already written a vast amount of music by that date, much of it since becoming a pupil of Frank Bridge in 1927, and Bridge continued to be his most valued and stimulating mentor throughout his student years: hence Britten's remark, 'I studied at the R.C.M. from 1930-1933 but my musical education was perhaps more outside the College than in it.'[1] In later years, Britten explained that

Bridge never wanted to influence me too strongly too young; and yet he knew that he had to present something very firm for this stiff, naive little boy to react about.... In everything he did for me, there were perhaps above all two cardinal principles. One was that you should try to find yourself and be true to what you found. The other – obviously connected with it – was his scrupulous attention to good technique, the business of saying clearly what was in one's mind.[2]

Bridge was that very rare phenomenon, a good composer who was also a good teacher and, although any teacher is likely to have found Britten a rewarding pupil, Bridge seems to have been the only one to have offered him something rewarding in return.

For Britten, trying to find himself, and achieving the crucial transition from prodigy to mature composer, involved at least one very decisive change of emphasis.

When I was very young, my music was inclined to be hectic, to rely on exciting crescendos and diminuendos, on great climaxes, in one word, to rely on 'gestures'. At this time I was absorbed in the music of Beethoven. But for myself, I felt the danger of this technique, so I turned away from that great pillar of music, turned to another – to Mozart, the most controlled of composers, who can express the most turbulent feelings in the most unruffled way.[3]

And Britten commented elsewhere on his early reaction against still earlier enthusiasms:

Between the ages of thirteen and sixteen I knew every note of Beethoven and Brahms. I remember receiving the full score of *Fidelio* for my fourteenth birthday. It was a red letter day in my life. But I think in a sense I never forgave them for having led me astray in my own particular thinking and natural inclinations.[4]

Michael Tippett's response to Beethoven and Mozart was very different. Tippett has admitted that

when I was a student I submitted entirely to the music of Beethoven. I explored his music so exhaustively that for a long time later on I listened to every other music but his. But as a student I was fascinated by his music and his personality, though I had also a very catholic taste, to which little was foreign. I doubt if in adolescence one can be absorbed by Beethoven and have a real understanding of Mozart. In so far as I have acquired that it has come later.[5]

Beethoven, whom he described in an early article as 'the great master' of 'the artistic use of the tonal system',[6] has always remained central for Tippett. Turbulent feelings must be expressed turbulently, and Beethoven may even be quoted if such quotation serves the purpose, as it does in Tippett's Symphony No. 3 and String Quartet No. 4. But for Britten the early change of emphasis, and taste, was permanent and profound even if other composers to whom turbulence was by no means foreign – Mahler, above all – were to affect him in ways the more classical, less lyric Beethoven failed to do.

The general sense of Britten stressing the 'braces' of control and Tippett the 'relaxes' of turbulence can be usefully associated with these different attitudes to Beethoven. But in Britten's early flight from turbulence, Mozartian control has to be interpreted in the light of those more modern technical developments which he encountered as a youth. He heard his first Bridge at the age of eleven, and

by the time I was thirteen or fourteen I was beginning to get more adventurous. Before then what I had been writing had been sort of early nineteenth century in style; and then I heard Holst's *Planets* and Ravel's string quartet and was excited by them. I started writing in a much freer harmonic idiom.[7]

That idiom, reaching from Wagner through Strauss to Debussy and Ravel, can be clearly heard in the Four French Songs with orchestra of 1928. Later, the still 'freer' procedures of Bartók, Stravinsky and Schoenberg would have their effect. But a full study of Britten's stylistic evolution will involve examination of all his juvenilia, and that task is not even begun here. What is significant is not that all traces of the 'hectic' suddenly disappear from his works of the early 1930s, but that the way those traces are controlled and directed reveals the basis of a truly 'good technique'. The D major Quartet, though flawed, provided the immediate background to the rapid attainment of technical mastery in the Sinfonietta, Phantasy Quartet and the choral variations *A Boy Was Born* during 1932 and 1933. By May 1933, before his twentieth birthday, there could be no doubt of Britten's ability to say clearly what was in his mind, even if it is true, as he himself stated in later years, that he did not shed all the 'bad influences' of the RCM until the early 1940s.

Britten's three early instrumental works were produced over a brief period of some eighteen months, between May 1931 and October 1932. But the development they chart is remarkable, and only a few fundamental issues of form, thematic process and harmonic structure can be dealt with in the discussion which follows.

The D major Quartet is a substantial work of some 19 minutes duration, but it apparently occupied Britten for less than a month: 8 May to 2 June 1931. A little more than a year later he composed his 'official' op. 1, the Sinfonietta for chamber orchestra, and although this too was written down with some speed (between 20 June and 9 July 1932) the stylistic and structural contrasts with the Quartet are of no small significance, and confirm the rapidity of the young prodigy's development during his second year at the College. The Sinfonietta is not only more economical – shorter and denser – than the Quartet, but also more controlled and more complex. It carries further the tendency of the 1931 Quartet to run its three movements together. But the Phantasy Quartet for oboe, violin, viola and cello, written three months after the Sinfonietta during September and October 1932, is a fully integrated single-movement structure, which also employs the framing thematic recurrences of its two predecessors. Both the Sinfonietta and the Phantasy Quartet eventually received professional premières, the latter at the ISCM Festival in Florence in 1934: both were to be published. But the String Quartet disappeared until its revision at the end of Britten's life, in 1975.

The gestures which the 1931 Quartet makes in the direction of integration and unity are obvious and effective. The first movement leads into the second, preparing its opening idea, and the finale ends with a return to the first movement's first theme. But even with the various cuts and revisions made by Britten in 1975, the work still tends to sprawl. The extended tonality appropriate to Britten's 'freer harmonic idiom' lacks sufficient focus, with too much of the kind of triad-shunning 'wrong-note' writing often found in the work of Britten's British seniors at this time. Admittedly, it is difficult to demonstrate conclusively where bad, 'wrong-note' harmony ends and good, extended tonality begins. But it is primarily a matter of deflecting the impression that triads (though strongly implied by the thematic ideas) are being avoided simply because of their embarrassing associations. In 'wrong-note' harmony one senses that diatonic writing has been altered by piecemeal shifts from bar to bar: extended tonality creates the sense of broader, more purposeful perspectives, of expansion rather than alteration.

The emphasis in the 1931 Quartet is firmly on conscientious thematic working, on filling out and rounding off, and so the concluding reminder of the material with which the work began is appropriate and effective.

15

In British music before Britten the most memorable examples of such climactic recurrence probably occur in Elgar, notably the Symphony No. 1. The final paragraph of Britten's quartet – *ff, largamente* – is very much of this Elgarian type. The first thirteen bars of the work are restated with only the slightest change, but the continuation is then reworked to prepare an augmented assertion of the main subject's last two bars. The diatonic dominant, A, is at last allowed to hint at its most powerful cadential function, but it remains unharmonized and, in the concluding 'tonic triad' to which it leads, thirds are replaced by seconds (Ex. 3).

Such a device, placed as the coda to both the finale and the whole work, can serve more of a rhetorical than a genuinely organic function unless, as here, it is effectively prepared and presented. In classical symphonic works, motivic relationships between separate movements may often be detectable: but when the work's coherence and unity are most essentially expressed through unambiguously hierarchic tonal schemes, which give the greatest prominence to closely related tonalities, the re-establishment of the tonic key is less likely to be so obscured or delayed in the finale that its eventual emergence needs to be associated with the actual thematic material from the very opening of the work. Such thematic 'framing' is most effective when, as here, it provides long-delayed tonal closure as well as clinching thematic reminiscence: a memorable model from the world of chamber music, though Britten may well not have known it in 1931, is Schoenberg's String Quartet No. 1 op. 7. But a composer seeking concentration as well as unity might well desire to dispense with one of the more expansive effects of late Romanticism and make a stronger point of integrating thematic cross-references into the main body of the work. This is what Britten does, both in the third movement of the Sinfonietta, and in the multi-sectioned single movement of the Phantasy Quartet.

Like the String Quartet, the Sinfonietta may be more memorable for the effectiveness of its integrating processes than for the sheer quality of its ideas, but the presence of a fiery spirit not too remote from that of the early Schoenberg – turbulence is controlled rather than repressed – indicates how rapidly Britten had outgrown the tendency to allow his passion for vocal polyphony to infiltrate his instrumental textures: Bridge had criticized the early Quartet in this respect.[8] Like the Quartet, the Sinfonietta ends with a fast 6/8 movement: but the most striking difference between the expansive Quartet and the economical Sinfonietta is at once apparent in the way the Sinfonietta begins, rejecting the plain octave doubling of the Quartet's first statement, and its ample rhythmic contours, in favour of the sharply focused contrast between a dissonantly accumulating 'background' and a 'foreground' of terse motivic

16

Ex. 3 Britten, String Quartet in D major (1931), third movement (finale)

generation. This fusion of 'background' and 'foreground' will be developed further in the first section of the Phantasy Quartet: there, however, the roles are in a sense reversed, since it is the thematically less significant 'background' which is the more rhythmically active of the two elements.

In the first 17-bar paragraph of the Sinfonietta, the background is provided by the motivically essential, tonally ambiguous accumulation of sustained B flats and As in the strings. The foreground consists of a sequence of four related thematic statements which demonstrate just how richly the young composer could already employ the technique of small-scale variation within a paragraph. The brevity of the motives, and their tonal ambivalence, creates the impression of intense argument from the outset, and the variation techniques both within and between the sub-phrases, though they can also be found in the earlier Quartet, are used with greater assurance: free and exact inversion, free and exact transposition, extension by repetition or rhythmic addition and truncation are all employed. Yet this first paragraph is introductory to the second (bars 18-39) in the sense that the thematic components of the second are much richer, more fully realized. Nor are there any separate clues to the tonal basis of the second paragraph, no accompanying pedal notes or chords: tonal tendencies must be deduced from the combined thematic lines themselves.

The second paragraph is, in the broadest sense, a variant of the first: it elaborates and extends the same basic material without radically changing (or clarifying) its tonal orientation. It is more of a variant than a development, however, because of the parallels between the two. Both end climactically with intensifying repetitions. Both are highly unified, yet both have a basic duality: their backgrounds move in longer rhythmic values than their foregrounds. As befits the early stages of a work, the similarities are very important: but the differences are of the kind that it will take the rest of the composition to work out.

The synthesis of material which takes place at the end of the Sinfonietta is none the less triumphant for being predictable, given the rather transparently counter-subject-like nature of the Tarantella-finale's main theme. Britten compressed the first movement's recapitulation by the simple device of superimposing the two principal strands of material over a dominant pedal: recapitulation and coda are also conflated, and maintain doubt as to whether the dominant may not rather be some kind of tonic. The brevity of the final section of the first movement (from Fig. 19, bars 180–211) is all the more notable in view of the fact that the central development is slightly longer than the exposition: the 32-bar recapitulation is, roughly, only a third of the length of either, or a seventh of the movement as a whole. In the Tarantella, by contrast, the development (78 bars) and recapitulation (76 bars) are virtually the same length and, combined, they are not very much longer than the extended exposition (141 bars).

When the first movement's principal material does begin to steal into the Sinfonietta's finale (from four bars before Fig. 20), variants are projected on to the background of the original presentation. The horn theme seems willing to become absorbed into the prevailing Tarantella rhythm, but in the end it is the most basic shape of all, the half or whole step, ascending or descending, whose influence over all the essential material is asserted as the tonic D is revealed unambiguously for the first and only time (Ex. 4). The climactic reminiscences of earlier material in this recapitulation (including a second-movement theme at Fig. 19) effectively clarify the sense of progress into resolution which makes this so exciting an apotheosis, and override any alternative tendencies to an ending which matches the opening with more symmetrical exactness.

Ex. 4 Britten, Sinfonietta: Tarantella (finale)

Nevertheless, such an ending was to prove both necessary and highly effective in Britten's very next work, the Phantasy Quartet.

The Phantasy Quartet and *A Boy Was Born* both make richer use of the structuring processes of thematic derivation and formal variation evident in the Sinfonietta. The single-movement Phantasy is an elaborate arch, *A Boy Was Born* is a set of six variations on a theme which is itself a miniature set of variations. The Phantasy, which has more or less the same duration as the Sinfonietta (14½–15 minutes), is also the first of Britten's mature works to end with music which is recessional in character (Ex. 5). The use of the idea of procession and recession to provide a musical as well as dramatic frame would be most distinctively evident in the Church Parables thirty years later. But the Phantasy, with its fusion of variation and sonata schemes around a central slower

Ex. 5 Britten, Phantasy Quartet

21

episode, is already a formidable technical achievement, not least because of the instinctive rightness of its proportions.

Detailed comparison of the outer sections of the Phantasy reveals a blend of economy and expansiveness which had been hinted at in the thematic processes of the D major Quartet, and was implicit in the Sinfonietta's clear demarcation of simultaneous yet distinct levels of activity. In the first section of the Phantasy the superimposed contrast does not occur immediately, but almost halfway through, with the entry of the oboe at Fig. 2 (bar 24 of the 57-bar section). The march material which provides the active background up to this point is presented in three phrases of eight, six and ten bars, each variously subdivided: we might in any case think of the first phrase as containing only seven bars, in view of the empty first bar. These subdivisions are dictated by the staggered entry of the strings, but Britten avoids academic fugato: the cello's material is a single interval whose alternations are given a different rhythmic pattern for each bar, until bars 9 and 10 repeat bars 7 and 8. The inversion of the interval in bar 5 announces an interchangeability confirmed by the violin's entry at Fig. 1. But the viola has so far provided only a repeated E with a grace note, and the E does little to clarify any possible tonal or triadic connotations which the F sharp and A may have. On its own, the cello line in bars 10–12 favours G major, but the force of this preference is reduced by the viola's E. The master of tonal ambiguity is already apparent in such strategies.

Independently of the oboe, the strings' march pursues its own small-scale variation scheme, the related phrases forming a ternary design:

$$a \text{ (bars 1-24): } a^1 \text{ (bars 25–40): } a^2 \text{ (bars 41–57)}$$
$$\text{total bars: } 24 \qquad 16 \qquad 17$$

Two of the most notable events within this scheme are, first, the way the viola E returns to persist virtually unbroken through the central subsection (a^1) and, second, the replacement of the thematic minor thirds by seconds when the main march material returns at Fig. 3. The sub-sections are neatly dovetailed together, and the harmony avoids pure triads, but the crisp march-rhythm helps to minimize any sense of invertebrate, 'wrong-note' modality. As for the oboe, its five phrases also relate through similar variation techniques – extension, abbreviation, transposition; in particular, the third phrase (bars 37–41) has both a sequential and a quasi-mirror relationship to the second (bars 29–35).

Since the section as a whole is progressive, the degree of metric homogeneity, expressed through a uniformity of principal accents in the various instrumental lines, increases with the oboe's last two phrases, and it is the reassertion of the two-bar unit (two bars before Fig. 32) which is both the climax of the work as a whole and the beginning of the recessional final section. The quasi-mirror relationship between this final section and the first is clear enough. There is no question of literal, palindromic reversal, but rather of letting the particular phrases, or relatives thereof, be heard in reverse order. What is really important in Britten's first fully integrated use of a symmetrical frame form is that it enables variation processes, as unifiers, to become particularly explicit, while also rejecting the convention of the tonally resolving end (Ex. 5). In the Phantasy, there is dissolution rather than resolution, and although Britten was to continue to find fresh ways of employing both kinds of endings they were, invariably, the natural conclusion to the particular formal scheme as a whole. Both types of ending, 'resolving' or 'dissolving', would enable Britten to explore relationships and tensions between diatonic and chromatic harmonic elements, and it is often in these endings that his sensitivity to ambiguities which blend frustration and satisfaction is most fully apparent. In Britten's music, ambiguities are positive structural features, to be exploited and controlled. They are never evidence of indecision, but rewarding responses to a series of technical perceptions about tonality and formal conventions: a response to tradition.

For all its stylistic uncertainty, therefore – most evident in the pastoral melismas which would be subliminally recalled a decade later in the Serenade's framing fanfares – the Phantasy demonstrates Britten's vital ability to control and direct lyric flow: vital, since Britten would never be drawn to concentrated utterance as an end in itself. He sensed that the power of extended tonality depended on its not being regarded as a licence to meander. However restrained the lyricism, there must be progress, direction. A song could no more afford to be static than a symphony.

After the remarkable progress revealed in the Sinfonietta and the Phantasy Quartet, Britten's impulses did not immediately direct him away from instrumental forms. A phantasy for string quintet which was first performed in London on 12 December 1932 and broadcast on 17 February 1933 has not so far been unearthed. And a year later, on 11 December 1933, three movements of an unfinished suite for string quartet called 'Go play, boy, play' were heard. The critic Frank Howes responded in what was already becoming a representatively frigid tone to Britten's youthful music, which might well have seemed at the time to be rejecting the hard-won seriousness and strength which such iconoclasts of the 1920s as Bliss and Walton had at last acquired. According to Howes, Britten 'exploited the styles of a march, a waltz and a burlesque with that steely efficiency and heartless wit proper to the young men of an age that is at once disillusioned and mechanically minded'.[9] Britten never finished the suite: nor did he return to the quartet medium until 1941. But the march from 'Go play, boy, play' was employed six years later in the eighth movement, 'Parade', of *Les Illuminations.*

Britten's major work of 1933 was his first substantial vocal composition, and a remarkable début it was. The Sinfonietta was a textural as well as formal *tour de force,* with its confident handling of ten instrumental lines: the Phantasy Quartet was a brilliant piece of structural organization, which blended elements of strictness and freedom with instinctive flair. Yet it is in the choral variations *A Boy Was Born* op. 3, begun a month or so after the completion of the Phantasy Quartet, in November 1932, and finished six months later in May 1933, that Britten's virtuosity of textural handling and richness of formal imagination come together for the first time in a work of substantial dimensions: the variations are about as long – some thirty minutes – as the Sinfonietta and the Phantasy Quartet put together. Simply in terms of stylistic originality, Britten may not transcend all those elements of Englishry which he had perforce to employ until his own sharper, more purposeful harmonic idiom and well-focused extended tonality came to maturity. But the skills of the musical dramatist, blending various texts into satisfying formal schemes, are already startlingly assured.[10]

The tripartite theme of the work is itself a set of variations on a major-second/minor-third motive which seems to step straight out of the 1932 instrumental works. So pervasive is this basic shape in Britten's music that it will be referred to here in shorthand integer notation as the 0,2,5 trichord, the numbers representing the distance in semitones between the three notes of the motive: if D is 0, E is 2, and G is 5. The expansion of this motive into a major-second/perfect-fourth shape – the 0,2,7 trichord – is crucial to the material of the Phantasy, and provides the ultimate transformations at the end of stanzas 2 and 3 of the theme of *A Boy Was Born.* The variation techniques within the theme are simple but strictly applied: transposition and rhythmic manipulation, with repetitions which are either exact or sequential. There is a clear distinction between the theme as such (whether in the soprano or bass parts) and the surrounding harmonies, whose sheer unpredictability balances the high degree of motivic invariance in the theme itself. While the theme as a whole is in no sense 'all-motivic', it does provide a clear procedural basis for what follows in its sparing, climactic use of pure consonance – there are no full triads – and its balance of 'chords' of bare fourths, fifths and octaves with the richer, tonally less explicit blends of seconds and sevenths.

Of the nine chords, excluding transpositions, which contain four different pitches, six derive from the same basic tetrachord (0,2,5,9), which provides the characteristic 'secondary seventh' sound; two employ a tetrachord which contains the harsher semitone clash (0,1,5,8); and one is a 'fourth chord' (0,2,4,7). It may seem preferable to speak primarily of linear motions in the four separate vocal lines of the theme, but its harmonic flavour, however 'accidental', cannot be set aside, and like any other aspect of a masterwork, gains from being precisely, systematically described.

The linear structure of the theme also deserves close study. In the first stanza the gradually ascending sequences of the melody – statements on D, E and G sharp – are the means whereby an overall octave ascent is achieved, only to be countered by the concluding fall of an octave back to the initial D; the main difference is that this final D is supported by a B in the bass. The second stanza, where the bass initially has the theme, passes through three principal stages: at the end of the first phrase, the upper D is restored in the top voice, and is now supported by a D in the bass; the next phrase unfolds an ascending minor third in both voices to reach F natural; and the stanza ends with the progression on to G in the upper voice and E in the lower, a perfect fourth higher than the interval which ends the first stanza.

In spite of the octave drop at the end of the second stanza, the third begins in the higher register reached before that drop. Moreover, the third stanza begins with the upper voice an octave higher than in the first. The second phrase initiates the complementary process of descent, and the first 'Alleluya' restores the original octave position in all the voices, with a bass outlining a descent from tonic to dominant. The concluding minor third is a fourth below that which ended the first stanza, and a seventh below that which ended the second stanza. The fact that there is no drop of an octave may be ascribed solely to the nature of the human voice: but its absence certainly facilitates a smooth transition to the first variation.

Variation I ('Lullay Jesu') is the most complex in form of the six apart from the finale, and is texturally in many respects the richest of all. The theme has employed harmonically elusive homophony, with the strongest contrast between the invariant motivic trichord and the shifting perspectives of its transpositions and expansions. Variation I employs a greatly extended range of contrasts between four layers of material, and each layer or type is varied independently of the others; the whole process is absorbed into a ternary scheme which itself reflects the theme's own original form. These principal formal divisions occur at Figs. 8 and 13, and represent the main points of departure and return. Yet it is in the detailed treatment of the four types of material, their progressive inter-actions and transformations, that the skill and subtlety of this movement lie. The first element is the rocking fifth or fourth which flows like an undercurrent throughout. It provides a background for Britten's fa-voured texture of contrapuntal superimpositions of different thematic elements, and its more rapid changes in the central section help to ensure greater instability of both texture and tonal direction. The second element is the thematic melisma on the word 'Jesu', using the 0,2,5, trichord: this generates subsidiary lines and its own contrapuntal textures, often in association with the 'Lullay' material.

These two elements together use only the two words of the text which provide the title of the variation. The third element is that which carries the main text – beginning 'so bless'd a sight it was to see' – and the fourth, an offshoot of the third, is the refrain for boys' chorus. Since all these elements are varied texturally as well as technically, with their shape and size modified in various ways, the complexity is considerable. Yet all is blended into an effortless flow which shows a perfect balance between the handling of details and the control of the totality.

For all their extreme difference of texture, the theme and Variation I are linked by a common formal basis. And so are the equally contrasted pair formed by Variations II and III, since they both contain four principal sections. Variation II, 'Herod', is much more fragmented in texture and dramatic in mood than Variation I. But it retains an element of refrain-like repetition – 'Noel' in place of the 'Lullay' of Variation I – and this is much associated with the basic thematic interval of the minor third. 'Herod' has an introduction which incorporates a direct reminisc-ence of the text as well as the melodic outline of the original theme: and there is a distinct element of the rondo about the form, with the refrains in as specific a relationship of variation to each other (and therefore to the theme) as are the verse episodes themselves. The concluding reference to the 'Noel' refrain is nevertheless too brief to meet the normal require-ments of 'true' rondo. The form is, in a sense, cut off before its natural completion to provide a more effective lead-in, attacca, to Variation III.

Variation III is the shortest and slowest of the set, returning to the homophonic texture of the theme itself, but draining out melodic connections and allowing the basic intervals to re-emerge only in the brief melismatic refrains which link the end of each section to the start of the next. In spite of this 'a-melodism', however, with the soprano line re-taining a pedal B throughout, the harmonic character clearly recalls that

26

of the theme itself. This variation may be the still centre of the work, but it contains its own evolutionary process, with each phrase after the first a variant of its predecessor, and the relative identity between the first and last of the four providing an element of closure.

Variations IV and V, apart from being distinctively characterized by their very different treatment of the principle of a recurrent background ostinato, draw further formal conclusions from the contrast between three-part and four-part schemes. Variation IV, 'The Three Kings', will be seen as tripartite if the end of the first section is located at the point of departure from the initial tonic area (five bars before Fig. 33) and the end of the second at the point of return to that area (four bars after Fig. 35). On the smaller scale, however, sub-sections are defined by the wave-like ascents and descents of the quaver ostinato (the 0,2,5 trichord), and for the most part these remain distinct from the superimposed lines of text, except for the climax at the start of the third section.

Superimposition of distinct yet related ideas is still more intensely evident in Variation V, 'In the Bleak Mid-Winter', where the four stanzas of the Corpus Christi carol are floated by the boys' choir on to an icy bed of rotating thematic fragments. Here, apart from the formal division into two parts, signified by the return of the opening material at Fig. 44, there are symmetrical parallels between the beginnings and endings of both layers, and a strong sense that each phrase of the Corpus Christi stanzas is a variant of its predecessor (a permutation of the 0,2,5 trichord). The clashes between B flat and A are as determining in harmonic function here as in the Sinfonietta, and in spite of the clear favouring of the B flat by the Corpus Christi carol, the ending reaffirms the irreconcilable opposition of the two pitches.

The finale, Variation VI, at once releases the tension of Variation V, but its opening phrases are deceptively artless in their transparent contrasts between sustained pedal backgrounds and active, thematically derived foregrounds. The 'Noel' refrain recalls Variation II, but the refrain technique is central to the whole work, so it is appropriate that here it receives its most thorough-going treatment. A large first section (to Fig. 52) which is itself rich in variants but economical in its basic material, leads to the first episode ('Good day, good day'). This episode is also variationally elaborate in its own right, and provides strong contrast before the return of the 'Noel' material seven bars before Fig. 58. The section which follows is, naturally, a variant of the finale's first section, and includes references to the first episode: the process of synthesis has begun. The second episode, which begins eight bars after Fig. 63, reduces the new material to a patter-like background for the broad thematic phrases of the boys' choir. There is a climax as the original material returns for the second time, centred on the dominant A:

more new material is sown in, the scalic lines contrasting neatly with the oscillations denoting the main theme. The virtuoso contrapuntal accumulation ensures that great harmonic emphasis is placed on the thematic intervals, but Britten avoids a conventional dominant preparation on A, so that the assertion of the pedal D at the beginning of the coda is, at least to a degree, 'unexpected'. There is a gap, which is all the more effective dramatically when so much else in the finale is so skilfully expanded and prolonged.

The coda has several functions, all brilliantly realized; tonal resolution, with the initially asserted D gradually moved away from to recall previous tonal motions, but finally restored by increasing employment of its hitherto much-avoided dominant; thematic synthesis, with dramatic reminders of previous variations impinging on, and provoking fuller elaborations of, the final variation of the theme itself; and formal completion, as a finely proportioned conclusion to the finale and to the whole work. Example 6 contrasts the final phrase of the theme as initially presented (Ex. 6a) with its triumphant transformation in the coda (Ex. 6b). The strength and fulfilment of the final phrase are in strong contrast to the mirror-recessional form employed in the Phantasy. But the way in which the coda formally parallels, varies and enriches the initial thematic statement shows that the balance between recall and resolution, cumulation and synthesis, found at the end of the Sinfonietta is even more powerfully present here.

Britten's productivity in 1932 and 1933 had been as remarkable as his progress. But his next major work, the symphonic cycle for high voice and orchestra *Our Hunting Fathers,* was not begun until May 1936, virtually three years after the completion of *A Boy Was Born.* Not surprisingly, therefore, Britten saw it at the time as his 'real' op. 1.[11] In many respects, and not least in its use of a solo voice, *Our Hunting Fathers* was a new start. But its effect was not such as to deprive its predecessors of all significant influence on Britten's later development.

Ex. 6a Britten, *A Boy Was Born* (theme)

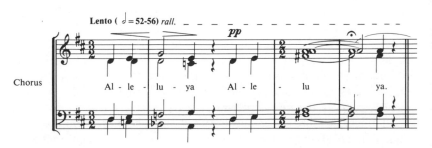

Ex. 6b Britten, *A Boy Was Born*, Variation VI (finale)

2 Tippett: String Quartet No. 1, Piano Sonata No. 1 (1934-7)

The first concert performance of *A Boy Was Born,* in December 1934, was the occasion on which Tippett remembered seeing Britten for the first time:

I had no intuition then that the slim figure walking down the gangway to take his bow before the public would become so decisive and beloved a personality in my life. But I have an unusually vivid mental picture of that moment. The aural memory is much vaguer. It is really only of the Brosa Quartet madly counting quavers in the finale of my first quartet, also a première![1]

In fact, Tippett has confused the December 1934 Macnaghten–Lemare concert, at which the Britten was performed, with the December 1935 event when his own quartet was played – his first professional London performance.

Tippett's first quartet was the fruit of a very long apprenticeship. He had spent five years studying composition, piano and conducting at the RCM (1923–8), and had worked for a further two years as a private pupil of a College professor, R.O. Morris. Those two years – 1930–2 – were also Britten's first at the College, but the two did not actually meet until shortly after Britten's return from America during the war.

Since Tippett was already twenty-five in 1930 one would expect many of his musical predispositions to have emerged by then. He worked on fugue, rather than Renaissance polyphony, with R.O. Morris, but his teacher's belief in the continued relevance for composers of the techniques of sixteenth-century counterpoint may well have given a decisive stimulus to Tippett's sense that the true tradition of British music lay in the still largely unexplored and under-appreciated works of Byrd, Gibbons and Purcell, rather than in the late-Romantic synthesis of Elgar, or the new nationalism of Holst and Vaughan Williams. The possibility of reconciling aspects of their techniques with the spirit of his beloved Beethoven may have seemed remote, however, and one reason for the relative slowness of Tippett's development during the thirties could have been a tendency to intellectualize about musical issues to the extent that intuitive impulses were inhibited. There was a nervous crisis, too, and an experience of Jungian psychoanalysis in 1938 which soon led to a period of intense self-analysis. Gradually the composer learned to

31

interpret his own dreams, and to understand the psychic mechanisms of integration in such a way that his creativity could be directly and positively involved. It may be an exaggeration to argue that Jung was a greater influence on Tippett's development as a composer than any musician, but it certainly seems true that Tippett's exploration of, and understanding of, Jungian ideas opened the way for, and participated in, the purely musical achievements which followed.

The String Quartet No. 1 was far from being the thirty-year-old composer's first attempt at a quartet; between 1928 and 1934 he had completed several substantial orchestral, instrumental and vocal works, including a symphony, two string quartets and two ballad operas. But it remains his first acknowledged work, and the last two movements provide the earliest accessible examples of his formally mature, stylistically still developing music. The first two movements were replaced by a new, single movement in 1943 because, in the composer's words, 'I think I felt the first two movements of this original version to be potentially successful in complement and contrast to the two that followed: but I felt them to be failures in themselves. (. . . I was quite right as to the second movement, but less right as to the first.)'[2] Yet, even though the revision may not have solved all the problems of the work, it is worth examining the finale both as a convenient antecedent of much that is most characteristic in Tippett's later work, and as a fascinating solution in its own right to some of the contrapuntal and harmonic issues which Britten had tackled so ambitiously in his earliest mature compositions.

The movement, marked 'Allegro assai', is, Tippett says, 'a fugue harking less back to Bach in feeling than to Beethoven'. Its bounding energy originally led him to head it with a quotation from Blake, 'damn braces, bless relaxes', which could easily function as a motto for his entire approach to rhythm and accent, provided only that 'relaxes' has the connotation of exuberant freedom rather than lazy relaxation. It has become a cliché of writing about Tippett to comment that the bar-lines in such movements are included solely for the convenience of the performers, and not as a guide to metric organization. Yet the notation of the first four bars of this movement shows clearly that the placing of bar-lines and the changes of time-signature have a distinct and positive compositional function. The first phrase, played by the viola and cello in octaves (Ex. 7(i)), could have been notated as seven bars of 3/8, in which case the first beat of every bar save the last but one would be occupied by an attack (Ex. 7(ii)). Tippett's notation, with its reliance on syncopation, suggests strongly that there is only one principal accent after the first, at the beginning of the first 3/4 bar (Ex. 7).

Through such relaxations of regularity are his typical tensions created. Nor are the tensions purely rhythmic, for the main subsidiary accent is

Ex. 7 Tippett, String Quartet No. 1, third movement (finale)

placed on a C natural, and the whole of the second part of the phrase – the two 3/4 bars – balances the first by seeming to question its simple assertion. The phrase as a whole spans the ascending dominant–tonic interval E to A, and ends with a simple descent from the upper dominant to the tonic. Yet even if the basic shape is read as an ascent from E to E through B, followed by a descent on to A, the emphasis on C and F naturals is of more than merely colouristic significance. Tippett could hardly have failed to learn from his studies of Renaissance polyphony, and of the modern British pastoral school, that a simple modality could provide the composer with a good basis for flowing lyricism: the first two movements of his next work, the Piano Sonata No. 1, show his awareness of this. But dramatic tension had to be created by other means. Modality might occupy the background for a foreground–background conflict with chromaticism in just the same way as 'pure' diatonicism might. But it was most important to ensure that the balance between the conflicting elements was handled so that a vital sense of direction and propulsion could be maintained.

The sheer speed at which the finale of the quartet moves, and the persistently polyphonic textures, ensure that tonal ambiguity can be maintained – not to the extent of leaving the actual tonic in doubt, but giving its appearances and disappearances a healthily unpredictable character. Still more striking, however, is the sense in which ambiguity is used as a positive formal device. It is not difficult to accord to variation the prime form-building role in the movement: but to describe its large-scale form in terms of anything other than departures and returns is to risk combining prescription with over-simplification.

The importance which Britten attached to the superimposition of dissimilar strands of material in his early works has been noted. The young Tippett may have had a more conventional view of counterpoint in that he tended to combine similar strands; consequently, large structures like the finale of the Quartet No. 1 demand a high degree of developmental continuation, as well as an appropriate admixture of contrasting material. This movement has a splendid passage of sustained humour in the middle when the main contrasting idea (in the first violin at Fig. 36) is selected for the only extended demonstration of conventional fugal exposition. Even in this moment of literalness, however, Tippett cannot exclude all allusion, since there is a hint of the earlier thematic idea in the course of a theme which has been described as 'a direct result of Tippett's interest in Stravinsky's Violin Concerto of 1931'.[3] The first part of the movement, by contrast, has made great play with hinting at fugal orthodoxy, most obviously at the very beginning, where the four-bar 'subject' is 'answered' both by its own continuation, and by the distorted version of itself which is combined with it.

This opening section can be divided into four sub-sections – one 'statement' and three variations. The initial statement, to Fig. 28, preserves rhythmic homophony and has the instruments playing almost entirely in octave doubling, with increasing emphasis given to the final descent of the initial four-bar statement. The second sub-section (to Fig. 29) introduces more independent part-writing, but is essentially a transposition of the first up a perfect fifth, so the overall motion is from B to F sharp, as that of the first sub-section was from E to B. After a short transition in which A is asserted as central pitch, the third sub-section therefore uses the material of the first a fifth *lower* (in basic pitch-class terms), but again with variation, and although the fourth sub-section is launched with the main material at its original level, the continuous increase in polyphonic activity gives the whole of this first part of the movement an evolving continuity which is intensely exciting.

It may be that the central part of the movement, from Fig. 39, where stretto-like treatment of the basic motive is projected through a rather self-consciously wide-ranging tonal scheme, is at once too unyielding and too episodic to avoid all sense of effort; but the way in which the final section, from Fig. 45 onwards, compresses the first part by further variation shows Tippett's confidence in his powers of control on the largest scale. This finale lacks the kind of broad, lyric subsidiary melody which appears in the Concerto for Double String Orchestra some four years later. It is unremitting, for all its ingenuity and wit, recalling nothing so strongly as the fierce finale of Beethoven's last Sonata for cello and piano op. 102 no. 2. Yet composing it helped Tippett to master the art of projecting an elaborate thematic process through an extended structure of great rhythmic energy and tonal diversity, while at the same time not permitting basic factors of tonal and harmonic cohesion to lose pertinence and power.

Tippett's first string quartet was followed by his first piano sonata (1936–7). Like the quartet, this was subject to later revision, in 1942 and

34

again in 1954. Like the quartet, it seems relatively tentative and un-
focused when placed beside the blazing confidence of its immediate
successor, the Concerto for Double String Orchestra. But it confirms the
contrapuntal predispositions of the quartet since, although there is no
fugue, there is a tendency to prolong single chords rather than to
compose in 'progressions'. The linear motion around the chords is what
matters, even when cadential definition is relatively clear.

The two middle movements are the most interesting. The Andante
tranquillo alludes to a folk tune, 'Ca' the yows', but its figuration intensifies thematic discipline so effectively that even a 'retoricamente' climax
admits nothing of rhapsody: the pastoralisms remain under firm contrapuntal control. The Presto third movement has the unbuttoned vigour of
the first quartet's finale, and offers a skilled demonstration of 'goal-
directedness' in the postponed assertion of its B minor tonic. The
movement contains a 'singing' counter-theme (Ex. 8) of the kind which
would soon be given a still stronger role in the finale of the Double
Concerto. That masterpiece is also hinted at in the subsidiary material of
the sonata's rondo-finale; and there is even a suggestion of the folk-like
music which opens Act III of *The Midsummer Marriage*.

Ex. 8 Tippett, Piano Sonata No. 1, third movement

Tippett has remarked that the work was first called 'Fantasy Sonata', and this might seem to indicate an even closer contact with prevailing British ideas about the forms of folk-influenced 'abstract' works than he would have cared to admit even a few years later. But such tendencies are more than offset by such elements as the 'unequal beat rhythm of that variation in the first movement which derived from recordings I heard at that time of Indonesian music on gamelan gongs' and the 'hints in the rondo theme of an interest in American popular music, as heard always through the ears of someone whose ancestors took English, Scottish, and Irish songs with them to the new land'.[4] The sonata itself may not be a completely satisfactory synthesis of its diverse sources and stimuli, but it indicates that the need to achieve such a synthesis was a pressing one, and that the materials were at hand. Tippett's next work would lift his music on to a new plane of individuality and achievement. It would set a standard of excellence which he would often find difficult to match in the future, but one which might never have been possible at all without the long, self-searching apprenticeship of the 1930s.

3 Britten: *Our Hunting Fathers* to the Violin Concerto (1936–9)

Throughout the 1930s Tippett lived in a cottage at Oxted, within striking distance of London, and was much involved with music-making in the capital, both at Morley College and with two amateur choirs of which one, sponsored by the Royal Arsenal Co-operative Society, had strong left-wing associations. Tippett had joined the Communist Party briefly in 1935, but his essentially Trotskyite sympathies were scarcely compatible with the party's central beliefs, and his commitment to Trotskyism itself faded as its impotence in face of the tyrannies of both Left and Right became more apparent.

From 1935 to 1939 Britten was also in contact with left-wing ideas, but at this stage of his career he was much more the young professional composer seeking to make a living through his work than the journey-man musician prepared to turn his hand to as many different varieties of teaching, writing and performance as came his way. If, after leaving the Royal College in 1933, Britten had immediately retired to Suffolk to do nothing but compose, his development would doubtless have been very different, and possibly a good deal more consistent. But the precocious student who could so effortlessly outshine his teachers in the artificial environment of a conservative academic institution needed to make a living from music, and neither then nor at any later stage did teaching in an academic institution, conservative or not, attract him in the least. Soon, therefore, there was less time for serious composition: and possibly some doubts about the value of complex works of relatively limited appeal like the Sinfonietta, the Phantasy Quartet and *A Boy Was Born*. A period of consolidation was doubtless inevitable and essential after the startling achievements of that final student year. But Britten was not simply a young composer looking for work in the theatre, films and radio: though he would not have realized it at the time, he was a member of 'the Auden generation'[1] and needed to respond and adapt to the social and political conditions of the mid-1930s.

The poets, dramatists and film-makers of the Auden generation often seemed able to express serious concern about major social issues only through a mask of self-consciously clever simplicity. It was necess-ary to instruct through entertainment, and the avoidance of conspicu-ous artfulness itself became an art: the best chance of saying something serious was to adopt an air of nonchalance. As a result, middle-class paternalism blended with youthfully earnest over-simplification in a manner potentially disastrous for all concerned. Fortunately, the bracing antidote of abrasive bitterness, and an increasingly fatalistic pessimism, cut the archness and the superficiality down to size. Donald Mitchell believes that Britten never came to share Auden's eventual view that 'art . . . is powerless to change the world'.[2] But it was increasingly difficult to 'advance democracy' in the Age of Anxiety, and few talented creative artists were good at sinking the best of themselves into the collective, the popular and the propagandist.

From 1935 until his departure for America in 1939, Britten was kept busy composing film, theatre and radio scores. (His earliest commission came from the GPO Film Unit in 1933.) Most of the films were stronger in simple documentary virtues than in social comment, though one at

37

least – John Grierson's *Coal Face* (1936) – was forthright in its presentation of the peculiarly hazardous nature of mining, implying that the public at large too easily ignored the 'special case' of the colliers. But it was in the theatre that Britten's contacts with radical thought can be most clearly traced, initially in connection with the communist writer Montagu Slater (later to provide the libretto of *Peter Grimes*), for whose *Easter 1916* (Phoenix Theatre, 1935) and *Stay Down Miner* (Westminster Theatre, 1936) Britten provided incidental music. In 1939 Britten dedicated *Ballad of Heroes* op. 14 to Slater and his wife.

During 1936 Britten had collaborated with Auden on the best known of the GPO films, *Night Mail,* and Auden had also compiled and part-written the text for *Our Hunting Fathers,* first performed at the 1936 Norwich Festival. Then, on 26 February 1937, came the first performance at the Mercury Theatre of Auden and Isherwood's *The Ascent of F.6,* for which Britten provided a substantial score whose forms and idioms, often popular, as in the 'Cabaret Jazz Song', look forward to their second main collaboration, *On the Frontier* (Arts Theatre, Cambridge, November 1938), and ultimately to the operetta *Paul Bunyan,* composed in America during the winter of 1940-1. In his memoirs, Christopher Isherwood has provided a brief sketch of Britten at this time, 'pale, boyish, indefatigable, scribbling music on his lap then hurrying to the piano to play it'.[3] There were other Auden settings of course: the Two Ballads of 1937 comprise a haunting setting of Slater's 'Mother Comfort' and a characteristically pointed treatment of Auden's 'Underneath the Abject Willow'. The first cycle with piano, *On This Island*, which uses texts by Auden, was completed in October of that same year, and the separate setting of 'Fish in the Unruffled Lakes' was made in November. A little later, *Ballad of Heroes* also uses texts by Auden and the communist writer Randall Swingler: it was first performed at a Festival of 'Music for the People' on 5 April 1939.

In these circumstances it seems remarkable that Britten was able to find any time for composing concert music during these years, and it was some while before anything ambitious was completed. Between December 1933 and June 1935 he wrote three suite-like instrumental works: *Simple Symphony* op.4, *Holiday Diary* op.5, and Suite for violin and piano op.6, as well as the two *Insect Pieces* for oboe and piano. For the voice the most extended piece is the diligent exercise in *Gebrauchsmusik,* the twelve songs *Friday Afternoons* op.7, for the children of his brother's Prestatyn preparatory school. So the commencement of *Our Hunting Fathers* on 13 May 1936 marked a significant return to substantial serious work. Britten later described it as his most successful collaboration with Auden;[4] it is an ambitious, large-scale score, more radical in style than the earlier pieces, and in it he tackles for the first time as a fully mature composer the building of forms in a cycle for solo voice. *Our Hunting Fathers* op.8 is a work of its time in that its text displays full consciousness of persecution as the ultimate social evil. But the text does not preach, and the music blends brilliance and seriousness in a way which enhances the positive essence of its ambiguities.

By labelling the finale of op.1 'Tarantella' Britten had shown the attraction for him of instrumental movements built from regular rhythmic patterns, and the Suite op.6 had provided more recent evidence of his ability to bring off formidably witty, energetic genre pieces of this kind: March, Moto perpetuo, Waltz. The symmetrical plan of *Our Hunting Fathers* profits from this predisposition by placing two fierce scherzos (a March and a Tarantella) on either side of the central lament, 'Messalina', and the scherzos in turn are flanked by a Prologue and Epilogue.

Britten began work with the march 'Rats Away', and its orchestral introduction in contrapuntal style, with a simple stepwise motive, recalls the procedures of the Sinfonietta. Yet the presence of a single voice is an important new feature, making it possible to argue that *Our Hunting Fathers* is indeed the work in which Britten 'found himself': his 'real' op.1, as he thought of it at the time. From now on, the solo voice dominates Britten's forms and textures, with the crucial consequence that the kind of polyphonic equilibrium so prominent in the earlier pieces is less frequently appropriate. With the tendency to polarize vocal line and accompaniment comes a more explicit tonal-harmonic focus, and less inclination to irradiate entire textures with motivic elements, at least until the less triadic music of later years. By definition, accompaniments must not detract from the supremacy of the vocal line, but they will still tend to control its form and contour.

'Rats Away' also indicates that Britten's ability to control the relation between large and small structural elements has not been lost during the three relatively fallow years. The introduction, while modally 'pure' in its use of the D major scale, avoids any clear harmonic assertion until at its climax (a dominant emphasis) the main, motto theme of the cycle is heard, outlining the tonic triad and moving inwards on to the minor third, F natural, thereby announcing the main alternative tonal centre, used in the march-like second section. A prominent motive here (in essence the 0,2,5 trichord in retrograde inversion) links into a third, developmental section centred on C, but after the return to D at Fig. 13 the final section is increasingly bombarded with the scalic features of the introduction. The coda uses a recapitulatory assertion of the motto to promote a dissolving, modally ambiguous ending.

Apart from the medium, there is nothing particularly new about 'Rats Away'. But the Prologue to the whole work offered a new challenge, and it is perhaps not surprising that Britten should have tackled its composition last: he began it on 26 June 1936 and, after some reworking of 'Dance of Death', the whole cycle was complete by 23 July. Auden's enigmatic text is prose, with a syntax complex enough to make musical elucidation difficult, and concepts too abstract to evoke obvious illustrative parallels. The appropriate 'form', evidently, is accompanied recitative, but knowledge of Britten's later, arresting examples of this kind of opening gambit (pre-eminently in *The Turn of the Screw*) should not diminish appreciation of the problems faced and solved in this first attempt. As a form, recitative is at the opposite extreme from unified dance-type movements. In its simplest manifestation it amounts to little more than heightened speech, a narration punctuated by chords and cadences of no particular thematic import. But it is possible to build the chords, however detached in time, into a continuous progression, using colour and register as the means of connection. Further unity will obviously result if the vocal phrases centre on the same pitches as the chords: such unity is likely to be inherent in most tonal recitative anyway. What is less inherent is the positive, evolutionary interaction of voice and instruments: in the Prologue of *Our Hunting Fathers* such an interaction provokes a climax in which the motto of the work is heard for the first time in the orchestra, and its own modal ambiguity makes the brief allusion to the original C minor tonality in the final bars seem even less secure than it did at the outset.

Throughout his career Britten was to offer a variety of answers to the question of how unified a song cycle should be. Is a general stylistic consistency sufficient? Or should there by an all-embracing tonal plan, coupled perhaps with thematic interconnections? Since individual songs are usually likely to be relatively simple in form it might indeed be self-defeating to devise too elaborate a formal scheme in purely musical terms. And, as his first substantial orchestral score of any kind, as well as the only one which he gave the ambitious, hybrid label 'symphonic cycle', *Our Hunting Fathers* achieves a satisfactory balance between the needs of overall coherence on the one hand and separate, sectional characterization on the other. There are 'attaccas' between all the movements except the last two, but Britten is not concerned to provide transitions between movements. The only direct connection is the sustained D joining 'Messalina' and 'Dance of Death'. (The tolling pedal D in the orchestral coda to this central movement anticipates the beginning of the *Sinfonia da Requiem*.)

With the absence of strong, binding transitions goes the avoidance of the degree of symmetry which the presence of a framing Prologue and Epilogue might make possible. In *Ballad of Heroes*, written three years later, the sections with these titles contain the same music. In *Our Hunting Fathers*, however, the text of the Prologue is prose, that of the

Epilogue verse, so identical music could scarcely be contemplated. Instead, Britten achieves a strong sense of contrast between the decisive yet unstable chords of the Prologue and the integrating ostinatos of the Epilogue, his first 'dissolving' ending since the Phantasy Quartet. But the Epilogue is also an intensification. The vocal line is an impassioned arioso, making the recitative of the Prologue seem almost matter-of-fact by comparison, while the orchestral accompaniment is much richer in thematic detail and harmonic density, showing that the polyphonic lessons learned in the Sinfonietta continued to pay dividends. Tonal ambiguity also increases; the xylophone ostinato appears to support the C of the Prologue, the final statements of the motto theme cadence on a D which was certainly the most important pitch during the middle movements of the cycle, and the bass remains coldly neutral, vanishing altogether before the end (Ex. 9). Appropriately, given the conflicts between 'civilized' and 'uncivilized' modes of behaviour referred to in the text, the ending is irresolute. Yet Britten has succeeded in expressing concern with compassion, not just through sardonic distancing. Whether he or Auden decided on the juxtaposition of 'German' and 'Jew' near the end of 'Dance of Death' is not known: they are not so juxtaposed in the original Ravenscroft poem. But Britten was to remain haunted by images of intolerance and persecution, and by the special expressive quality of representing such images with a directness all the more disturbing for the degree to which it flirted with the superficial, the sardonic. Often enough, as in *Our Hunting Fathers* and *Ballad of Heroes*, the dances

Ex. 9 Britten, *Our Hunting Fathers*, Epilogue

were to be dances of death, the marches funereal. The search for peace was so central, so obsessive because war, tension, conflict, were so inescapable, so real.

After the première of *Our Hunting Fathers* in September 1936 Britten plunged again into his film and theatre work: only one other concert piece belongs to that year, the *Temporal Variations* for oboe and piano. But in May 1937 he made two settings of poems by Auden which would form part of his first cycle with piano, *On This Island* op.11. Then came a last-minute commission for the Salzburg Festival, and the *Variations on a Theme of Frank Bridge* op.10 were written in the remarkably brief period of ten days at the beginning of June 1937. In October Britten returned to the Auden texts and set three more poems from *Look! Stranger* to complete the cycle.

The two Auden settings which preceded the composition of the Bridge Variations, 'Nocturne' from *The Dog Beneath the Skin* (dated 5 May) and 'Now the Leaves are Falling Fast' from *Look! Stranger* (27 May), were placed as Nos. 4 and 2 in the completed cycle. There is an eloquent plainness about 'Nocturne', as if Britten was attempting to find a precise musical equivalent for the idea expressed in Auden's epigraph to *Look! Stranger*:

> What can truth treasure, or heart bless,
> But a narrow strictness?

There is indeed a very basic simplicity about the opening of 'Nocturne', with repeated tonic triads of C sharp minor in the piano and an arpeggiated tonic triad in the voice. Yet such a rudimentary start makes the later modifications the more impressive and effective, since they never contradict the song's basic mood or material. The sombre elegance of the music has a 'conceit' perfectly appropriate to Auden's restrained yet fanciful verse, in which the 'meaning' is as much in the metrical smoothness as in the sense of individual words and phrases. There is, as a result, a characteristically modern disturbance of reality, which makes its effect through understatement, and the gentle irregularities of the music again provide a perfect match.

There are four stanzas of text, and in the first half of the song Britten provides precisely the same music for the first two stanzas. The second half of the song is, broadly speaking, a variation of the first half, but stanzas 3 and 4 have strikingly different music. Stanza 3 develops each of the main thematic elements of the song in turn, and loses tonal stability as the bass begins to crawl in anxious steps towards the remote triad of F minor. In the final stanza, the vocal line is at first reduced to a monotone, and the accompaniment, though keeping a firm grip on the A flat and C which relate to F minor, offers no reminders of the song's

43

principal thematic idea: only its rhythm remains related. The initial idea and the C sharp minor tonality eventually return, but the pure tonic triad is not regained until the final syllable of text.

'Nocturne' suggests that Britten had gained a new simplicity without all loss of formal subtlety. Indeed, the challenge of working with the most apparently conventional material (also evident in the much less sophisticated *Friday Afternoons* songs) centred on how best to modify and transform scales, arpeggios and regular rhythmic pulsation without loss of coherence and clarity: how to express an individual personality through such simple conventions?

The second song of *On This Island,* 'Now the Leaves are Falling Fast', also has a developmental second half, as well as a coda which recalls and extends the brief introduction, providing a final transformation of the main material. Of the songs written in October, No. 1, 'Let the Florid Music Praise', also falls, for textual reasons, into two distinct halves: however, the second is scarcely a development of the first, though they are linked by transformation of the 'fanfare' motive. No.3, 'Seascape', and No.5, 'As it is, plenty', each have three main sections in an evolving, variational relationship, the third section restoring the tonal centre of the first. *On This Island* does not employ thematic cross-references between songs, nor, apparently, is there any overall tonal scheme. The fact that the first and last songs have the same tonality – one which Britten used a great deal in his earlier works – provides a frame within which there is freedom of movement, rather than a sequence of fixed, logically related centres.

It is probably easier to hear the original, personal qualities of this first cycle with piano today than it was when it was new. Certainly such things as the Stravinskian touches to which Peter Pears has drawn attention[5] now seem less derivative, more connected to Britten's own distinctive harmonic procedures as they became more clearly defined over the years. Most importantly, *On This Island* is full of drama, even though it avoids the more dramatic vocal forms. It has melisma, but no recitative; it has a touch of pastiche, but none of the freely flowering ariosos which distinguish many of the later cycles. As for the attempt at a popular style in the last song, this may now seem like one of the miscalculations of immaturity. It shows that Britten was likely to find it easier to be simple than to use popular idioms in his 'serious' compositions – unless in 'popular' we include the folk songs which became so fruitful a source of ideas for him after more commercial, modern manifestations had lost their appeal.

By 1937 Britten had already amply demonstrated his ability to compose quickly and to order, and never was sheer speed more essential than with the *Variations on a Theme of Frank Bridge.* Yet the variety of moods in the work is remarkable, and there is a particularly impressive finale which, like the finale of *A Boy Was Born,* generates such tension that a large coda is required which is not only a further variation in itself, but a resolution, an apotheosis. This coda reflects Britten's new 'plainness' of style in avoiding polyphonic elaboration, but the way in which harmonic tensions are shaped and controlled around the eloquent melody anticipates the skilled handling of harmonic motion in later symphonic and dramatic works.

Britten had already dedicated one work to Bridge – the Sinfonietta. It was appropriate, therefore, that in choosing Bridge's Idyll No. 2 (1911) as theme for the variations five years later he should select a piece which, nonchalant and unassuming though it is, enshrines those very elements of internal derivation and relation which Britten's own music had so precociously explored. The four phrases of the theme (with prominent 0,2,7 trichord) each have their own sequence of four statements, and each phrase has a relationship of variation to each other phrase. Add the elusive harmonic character, and its appeal to Bridge's most eminent disciple is understandable. Britten's variations naturally vary in form and degree of tonal ambiguity. There is no broadly based 'symphonic' tonal continuity, though the final D major goal is prefigured in the 'March' (Variation II), the 'Bourrée Classique' (Variation V) – which has a variation in A (the 'Aria Italiana') to prepare it – and in the 'Moto Perpetuo' (Variation VII).

As an extended suite of movements, the variations work so well because the various dances and formal prototypes, many of them Britten 'specialities', are treated with affection as well as, where appropriate, with a more astringent touch of parody. Even a fugal exposition which is guyed to the extent of turning into a 'monody' does not seem too irreverent. But the more striking, general formal characteristic of the work is its mixture of similarity and contrast to avoid a single curve of intensity. Such schemes always run the risk of becoming mere sequences of episodes, and they are more likely to be the stock-in-trade of the opera composer than the more unremittingly goal-directed structures of the tonal symphonist. But Britten got the balance between contrast and cumulativeness right in the Bridge Variations, and the loss of some of the intense concentration of the Sinfonietta, or of the finely judged transitions of the Phantasy, are not so serious as to make the music seem either trivial or thinly spread.

The first variation grows almost imperceptibly out of the Introduction and Theme. The second variation ('March') is an extreme contrast. The next five variations, the core of the 'dance suite' aspect of the work, proceed by contrast, but the 'Funeral March' and 'Chant' are similar in character. The fugue begins as an extreme contrast, but this time – the only time in the work – there is a transition. It leads into the finale, and is achieved simply by focusing on a sustained unison E in all the instruments except the double basses. This moment is the climax of the composition, for what might have been an ascent to a still bigger climax at Fig. 42 is made part of the 'running down' before the final cadence. The fugue and finale provide the most symphonic, complex music of the variations, but they form a suitably majestic crown to the work without retrospectively trivializing the earlier parts of it.

Britten's international success with the Bridge Variations confirmed his professional ability to work well, and rapidly, to commission. Not surprisingly, others came his way, and the demand for instrumental music may explain why he was relatively slow to follow up the more individual formal and textural features of *Our Hunting Fathers*. His next pair of large-scale instrumental compositions, the concertos for piano and violin, are as different in structure from the Bridge Variations as they are related to it in style. Both concertos were subject to later revision, the Piano Concerto receiving a new third movement in 1945, and the Violin Concerto being modified in 1950. Each lasts over half an hour: indeed, the 'official' duration of the Piano Concerto made it Britten's longest work to date. The four-movement Piano Concerto retains in three of its movement titles – Toccata, Waltz, March – a link with the earlier suite-like instrumental compilations, while some thematic cross-reference and clear tonal closure bring a degree of overall unity. A few years later, the concerto provoked a rare 'Auden generation' analogy in one reviewer, who found 'something of the masochism of Isherwood's Mr Norris' in the March: 'but perhaps the thought was engendered by the whip sounds of the slap-stick orchestration'.[6]

The Violin Concerto, completed in September 1939, is more ambitious and original both in its evolving tonal scheme and in its formal exploitation of textural and dramatic tension between the lyric and rhetorical gestures appropriate to a work in this form. It was dedicated to Henry Boys, who had recently published a perceptive and by no means uncritical article on Britten. This is of particular interest in that it seeks to provide some technical explanation for what many reviewers of Britten's work regarded as its principal failing: as Edmund Rubbra put it in a note on the Bridge Variations, 'emotionally the music lives in a vacuum'.[7] Boys wrote:

it is a tribute to Frank Bridge as a teacher that Britten's music is quite unlike his own; nor is there any obvious debt to John Ireland. Britten's very spare harmony looks as though it might be a reaction against English lushness: as a matter of fact . . . it keeps a semblance of tonality without the organic function of tonality, thereby becoming empty.[8]

Boys went on to argue, with no little foresight in view of what happened to Britten's music after 1950, that the composer should turn away from tonality towards the twelve-note system: 'He is one of the few who are technically capable of making good use of this system, as it is to this system that those compelling his deepest admiration have turned. Should he himself turn to it, he would be able to integrate much in English music which badly needs integrating.'

Boys's views on the twelve-note system are certainly of interest, but in characterizing Britten's steadily evolving use of extended tonality as inorganic and 'empty' he seemed to be striking a blow at the composer's most necessary basis of communication. In this context the Violin Concerto, whether or not it was written at least in part as a response to Boys's criticisms as well as in acknowledgement of his friendship, can be seen as a particularly important and highly personal testing of the formal coherence and expressive power of which such extended tonality was capable. Reviewing the première, which took place in New York on 28 March 1940, Elliott Carter saw it as

an English counterpart of recent Prokofiev and Shostakovitch music. A composition of this kind has an autobiographical air about it; its appeal lies, I think, in its disarming frankness. The varying feelings of the composer appear to be projected with such intense directness as to make the listener forget the great disparity of styles. Prokofiev succeeds sometimes in creating this effect. Britten's work was a little too artificial and contrived. Yet at almost every moment, nobody could fail to be impressed by the remarkable gifts of the composer, the size and ambition of his talent.[9]

By any standards, certainly, the finale is a most impressive achievement. What is most vital to its success is the composer's skilful control of the form to postpone and prepare clarification of the essential tonal issue of the work; this process is on a grander and more ambitious scale than is evident even in *A Boy Was Born*. Simply because he is working with long-range tonal tensions, his polyphony is of a rhythmic simplicity in stark contrast to Tippett's flamboyant flexibility in the Concerto for Double String Orchestra of the same year. And Britten's finale, far from clarifying the formal and tonal relationships of the first movement, elaborates them by means of a radically different form.

The first movement, Moderato con moto, is a notably simple structure which plays off lyric against dramatic material in a three-part form. Tonally, it moves from a less-than-wholly stable F major, in which root position triads are avoided, to a more secure D major at Fig. 8. The scherzo which follows is predominantly allusive rather than assertive in matters of tonality, and this helps to lend interest to its otherwise rather nondescript ideas. The scherzo's favouring of A minor as a point of focus is confirmed in the early stages of the cadenza which links it to the passacaglia. As a dominant preparation, however, this A minor lacks the relative diatonic clarity of the first movement's F major, and is embedded in a context of considerable instability, although there is no shortage of other, local points of emphasis during the scherzo's mercurial progress. What Britten does in the finale is expand the whole range of the argument: the broad tempo and the huge registral gulf between solo violin and trombones at the start is a clear declaration of intent. The passacaglia is the most strongly structured movement, yet, for all its passion, the most restrained. And what is most compelling of all is not the way in which the return to D major is plotted and placed, but the treatment of the re-established D major to fill out the final, most memorable pages of the concerto. Here is the direct and decisive answer to Henry Boys.

In spite of the highly chromatic nature of the passacaglia theme, which is inevitably intensified in contrapuntal combination, Britten places certain pointers to prepare the eventual outcome: most importantly, the dominant/tritone polarity before Fig. 34, where a key signature of one flat returns, leading to a temporary revival of interest in F major at Fig. 35; and also the focus of the harmony on D (though still non-triadic) at Fig. 36. The possibility of a return to F rather than to D is kept open with the move to B flat at Fig. 38, and it is the slow progress from here to the confirmation of D (tempo primo, ten bars after Fig. 42) which provides the movement with its dramatic core. The climax in D at Fig. 43 confirms what is already clear, and the stepwise motion of the bass now prepares the only firm motion from A to D, at Fig. 44 (Ex. 10a): this is the nearest the concerto has come to a conventional perfect cadence in the tonic since Fig. 8 of the first movement.

The movement's long coda, Lento e solenne, is an inspired way of deepening the expressive power of the music while expanding the true tonic harmony. The lamentations with which the soloist decorates the brass chorale may seem a little gypsy-like, but they are not incongruous: their insistence on the major–minor third alternation brings a haunting appositeness and sincerity to what is already as much an argument about large-scale tonal stability as it is the distillation of particular emotions. (The analogy with the ending of Walton's Viola Concerto of ten years earlier is of interest, but if Britten was conscious of the precedent he was clearly not aiming to reproduce Walton's less overtly dramatic manner.) The point, tonally, is that either major or minor will 'do', since D and A are now asserted as the prime elements of the tonic harmony: and although the notation of the last two bars may seem to imply a clear 'victory' for the minor, the very special flavour of the ending is due to the retention of a degree of doubt in the listener's ear after the music itself has stopped (Ex. 10b).

Like the Bridge Variations, the Violin Concerto may seem to some to

Ex. 10a Britten, Violin Concerto, Passacaglia (third movement – finale)

Ex. 10b Britten, Violin Concerto, Passacaglia (third movement – finale)

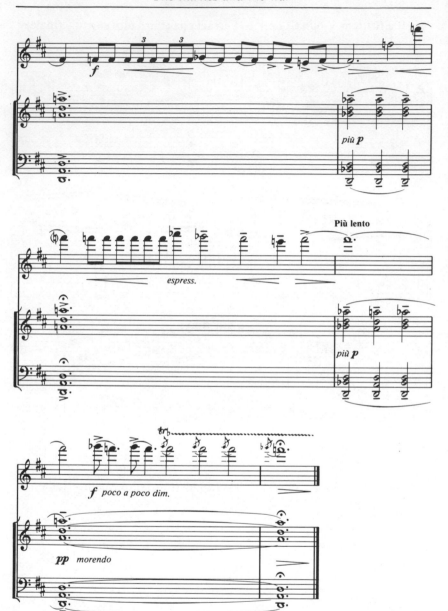

represent a distinct retreat from the concentrated formal integration and pervasive motivic working of the Sinfonietta and other early works. Certainly, in his search for a broader design and a style in which lyric flow could play a more prominent part, Britten had moved away from some of the most rewarding aspects of those early pieces. Yet the enshrining of an ambiguous tonal argument in material of great lyric intensity marks so vital a stage in his development when viewed as a whole that some loss of sheer technical concentration seems a fair price to pay. The Violin Concerto, though flawed, amply redeems itself in the finale; and it is the finale, of all Britten's instrumental movements from the 1930s, which now seems most like the work of a budding opera composer. There is the unmistakable sense of a consistent central character, whose outpourings are controlled and shaped by the composer's sure sense of formal proportion. The character is self-dramatizing to a degree, and vividly mercurial in temperament, with a flamboyance which is the essence of the conventionally operatic. And yet the composer's innate restraint ensures the establishment of the varied psychological perspectives which the convincing realization of such a character demands. In more obvious ways, the vocal cadenzas of *Our Hunting Fathers,* and various moments in the theatre and film music, may also point the way forwards to opera. But simply because opera is about more than vocal display or efficient musical mimesis, the concerto seems to represent an essential preliminary in the broadest, and deepest, musical sense.

4 Tippett in 1939: The Concerto for Double String Orchestra

Britten finished his Violin Concerto in Canada on 20 September 1939, his first work to be completed after his departure from England. With its questing, irresolute ending, the concerto may well appear particularly redolent of the time of its composition, the late months of appeasement, when it became inescapably clear that war was, after all, inevitable. By contrast, Tippett's Concerto for Double String Orchestra, composed during 1938 and 1939, unfolds with such exuberance and certainty that it can only be a faithful transcription of an instinctive confidence and optimism. There is no cerebral calculation here, but an intuitive controlling and directing of what would otherwise be an unstoppable, shapeless flux. It is therefore scarcely possible for anyone – even, in all likelihood, the composer – to draw up a balance sheet of the accidental and the intentional. The music is positive and personal in a very special way, and it is understandable that commentators often prefer to instance its allusions of texture and style rather than discuss its structure, since such a discussion implies a sober self-distancing from the eager emotional embrace of the music. Of course, the analyst can assert that only when

51

what is old about the piece is established can its individual qualities be properly defined and appreciated. But the novelty is so crucially a matter of adaptation of old or existing principles that the two tendencies – to conserve and to innovate – demand to be discussed together. If the concerto sounds like a masterpiece, not because of any technical virtuosity in the handling of contrapuntal texture but because of its exhilaratingly coherent panorama of rich colours and memorably direct statements, the analyst will find one issue intriguing above all: how is this coherence actually created? No doubt the first answer will be 'instinctively'. So the issue must be pursued. What were the means whereby Tippett instinctively shaped the materials of this work into their final, satisfying wholeness?

Like all good concertos of post-classical times, this one is very symphonic: analogies with the textures of Renaissance polyphony, of the baroque concerto grosso, and the ideas about jazz of which Tippett read in Winthrop Sargent's *Jazz: Hot and Hybrid* (1938) do no more than confirm that, to some degree, many great modern works engage most if not all earlier periods of musical history. Tippett's most fruitful formal source is the tonal symphonic structure as broadened by Beethoven to include such features as new development-section themes, highly organized contrapuntal processes and lengthy codas. But his response to that formal source is coloured by a great diversity of stylistic and technical enthusiasms, among which the extension of tonality itself – the suppression of fundamental diatonic relationships and the displacement of triadic harmony from its central position – is particularly crucial.

It seems particularly misleading to stress one component of harmonic character – for example, the role of the Mixolydian mode in the concerto's first movement – when the synthesis represented by the whole, though difficult to define, is so rich. Tippett's first great moment came when he sensed how he could be guided by certain restraints, without merely using them as things to react against: a case, in fact, of 'bless braces, damn relaxes'. The real power of this concerto lies in the way in which the constraints progressively increase, and fulfilment is achieved in part through an advance into more traditional processes. It is not that the late-Romantic journey from darkness to light is paralleled by a motion from radical to traditional. But Tippett's abiding concern with the emergence of true self-knowledge as the high-point of human existence is evident in the way the finale seems to clarify what is latent in the first movement, perhaps as a result of the meditative intensity of the central Adagio cantabile.

In an article written between the composition of the Piano Sonata No. 1 and the Concerto for Double String Orchestra, Tippett posed the question:

Would someone explain the tenacious emotional satisfaction of the tonal system? Here is the answer. The artistic use of the tonal system is based on the fact that music whose tonal centres are rising in the scale of fifths produces an effect of ascent (struggle, illumination) while tonal centres descending the scale of fifths produce an effect of descent (resignation, despair). Beethoven was the great master of these effects . . . What has happened is that since the nineteenth century composers have ceased to produce the sort of themes that demanded Beethoven's clarity of tonal structure . . . This is the difficulty. The tonal system related to sonata form is a highly polarized system. Modern people are not polarized, they are split. It may be true . . . that we are entering on a period of greater certainty, because of a new integration of our split selves, and it may be that the re-appearance of the tonal forms in modern music is a complementary expression. I am not sure. 'Living in sin' with the tonal system is no better than doing the same with atonality; Mahler, Bruckner, Strauss and the rest are a severe warning against this. The integration of the conflicting parts must be an actual experience, and the musical intuitions must begin to correspond to the collective symbols that have sooner or later to be described and painted and sounded for the mass of humanity who have come at their redemption in this way.[1]

The use of tonal relations to create a sense of illumination is indeed central to the Concerto, *The Midsummer Marriage,* and other works, though 'the scale of fifths', or even the structurally significant interval of the fifth, need not be literally so central. As for sonata form, this provides the clearest formal precedent for both the outer movements of the Double Concerto. Since the first movement is the freer in form, the temptation to talk of spontaneous contrapuntal generation is greatest here. There is more immediate evidence of evolutionary continuity than of strong internal contrasts, but the procedural link with the finale of the String Quartet No. 1 is by no means as great as it would be if there were more evidence of conventional fugal by-play. In the concerto the contrasts enable the continuity to evolve towards a goal rather than merely float free of time and space. The evasion of clear cadential punc-tuation, as in the quartet, continues to create harmonic tension and ambiguity, and chordal progression itself is less apparently functional than the rich dubieties which arise when the modal characteristics of scales and the tonal potentialities of modes are allowed to interact.

If the music of the first movement up to Fig. 4 is seen as an exposition, this has its own ternary shape: the first sub-section extends to four bars after Fig. 1, the second, with the most explicit thematic contrast (a scherzando motive) as far as Fig. 2, and the third and largest to Fig. 4; this last sub-section begins to develop the material of the first and com-pletes a shift of tonal emphasis away from A to G. It would be futile to chart in words the various tonal changes and thematic connections which pervade this vigorous music. But it would be still more futile to ignore the determining function of two factors in this exposition: the absence of fully developed thematic contrast, and the avoidance of firmly established tonal centrality. These factors are so positively exploited here that it seems improbable that they should ever have created problems for Tippett the symphonic composer, and led him to question the very close identity between 'form' and 'continuity' which functions so naturally in this concerto. It seems appropriate, in music of such energy, where the bar-line is not the inevitable point of strongest rhythmic emphasis, that the tonality should 'float'. But it does not float in a vacuum, and the overall motion of the exposition from A to G is the most essential controlling factor.

A is recalled in the early stages of the recapitulatory third section of the movement, and the conventional dominant–tonic cadence is hinted at (Fig. 8) in a manner which shows how sensitive Tippett was to the capacity of such devices for meaningful modification (Ex. 11). Most crucial, however, is the retention of an A centre for the third sub-section of this recapitulation (from three bars before Fig. 10) and the preparation, in the coda, of what could be an even stronger clarification of the chord, if not the key, of A major. Yet the final resolution on to A, with only its fifth, E, in support, is made more dramatic (and far less conventional) by the late diversion of the harmony back towards G. This could represent a use of the modal power of the lowered seventh degree to undermine the 'true' tonality, and its effectiveness here is certainly evidence of Tippett's debt to the English 'folk-song' school. It does not prevent the final resolution on to A, or make A seem an arbitrary goal, but it does give it an appropriately provisional tonal status. A minor is of course a close relative of the C major in which the whole work ends but, in tonal terms, G major, as dominant, is still closer to C. Meanwhile it is on G's own dominant, D, that the central Adagio is founded.

Mention has been made above of the English folk-song school; the expansive main theme of the Adagio is the nearest thing in the concerto to the poised, pastoral quality of much twentieth-century British music. Tippett, with his consistent dislike of aimless rhapsody, eventually sought to question what Boris Pasternak, through his character Dr Zhivago, called the 'pseudo artlessness' of pastoral simplicity in art. In *Songs for Dov* (1970), Tippett would quote Zhivago's affirmation, 'the living language of our time is urban', and his later music would be still more directly concerned to explore that language. Nevertheless, not all pastoral dialects are either aimless or artless, and there are several ways in which the second movement of this concerto avoids lapsing into the ruminative placidity which is the worst aspect of the style. First, the supporting harmonies – one may just use the term, though there are few root-position chords, and apart from the bass the inner parts are imitatively active – are distinctly astringent, especially in the seventh bar of the theme. Second, the central section of the movement, while still fairly

54

Ex. 11 Tippett, Concerto for Double String Orchestra, first movement

gentle in mood, is severely fugal in texture (complete with inversions) and vagrant in tonal character. Third, the highpoint of the movement occurs, five bars after Fig. 18, when Tippett achieves a splendid dovetailing between the end of the fugal episode (though this is briefly recalled in the final section) and the return of the main theme. This passage is a fine example of the art of transition. The texture also has room for a 'rocking' figure which is to feature accompanimentally in the finale, and recalls the principal theme of the first movement: see the first orchestra's viola part at Fig. 18.

All the cadences on to the central D major triad of the Adagio occur via the triad on the lowered seventh (C major). Without proposing a devious argument in connection with the ultimate primacy of C in the finale, it is enough to note that this emphasis is the result of the avoidance of harmonic focus on the diatonic dominant A, and indeed of all close diatonic relatives; the only other clearly stressed triad in this harmonization is that of E major (which has the same relation to D as D has to C). The Adagio may be more 'harmonic' in texture than the Allegro con brio, and it is certainly more explicit as to its tonal centrality; but instability, within the richly extended D major, is consistently and poetically employed.

The finale of the concerto is an extraordinary achievement for a composer who, a mere two years before, in the first piano sonata, had still been feeling his way towards full maturity of style and structure. Its formal outlines are sharp where those of the first movement are blurred, and, if it is less ambitiously unconventional than the finale of the first quartet, its propulsive energy is a good deal more fully focused, its material a great deal more memorable. It has an even more infectiously lively thrust than the first movement, and an equally ingenious texture. To fit with the more obvious contrasts of the form, the tonal relationships, too, are more clear-cut, but they also owe little enough to classical precedent, and show that the movement is far from a proclamation of all the old virtues after the earlier questionings. As a tonal structure, indeed, the finale is less 'closed', more progressive, than either of the previous movements. But it also has a wider range of reference and, it might almost seem, less inhibition about certain more traditional chordal constructions.

The exposition runs to seven bars before Fig. 28. After starting with an emphasis on A, still reflecting its slow-movement role as dominant of D, the tonality of G major is clarified for the main thematic statement (from four bars after Fig. 22) in which both orchestras play as one. But the marvellously lyrical subsidiary theme, following another fine transition in which the rocking figure found in both previous movements is heard, is in A flat major. Texture, mood and general shape also suggest considerable contrast, with a much greater degree of relaxation than was permitted in the first movement; but there is a motivic connection with the opening material of the finale, and the ease with which Tippett contrives a return to the opening music at the start of the central section is a measure of his new technical confidence and control. This music is a whole tone higher than previously, so the statement of the main theme is now in A major, the main key of the developmental middle section. The development also includes a scherzando theme (starting three bars before Fig. 30) which is not totally new: it has certain features in common with the second subject.

There is a sense, then, in which the movement is progressing, tonally, by ascending semitone steps: G, A flat, A. But the finale intensifies its impetus by contradicting this scheme, and, as development merges into recapitulation, the key centre veers away to F sharp major, a semitone below the first main point of emphasis and a tritone away from the ultimate goal. The final journey will be the farthest.

Once more the function of transition is crucial, for when the second subject reappears (five bars after Fig. 36) it is in B flat major: the ascent by semitones has apparently been resumed. A further, final step could lead to an ending in B major. But other reasons – the overall relationships within the work as a whole, or even the nature of stringed instruments – give C a prior claim.

Harmonically, the coda is the most stable section of the whole concerto. With its tripartite form, it mirrors the principal formal pattern of the piece; and its theme, though apparently new, moves off from the initial motive of the slow movement's melody. The central episode, as well as being developmental, introduces chromatic colouring. But the outer sections are radiantly diatonic, and even if the prolongation of the tonic triad determines the course of events, with the bass fulfilling a contrapuntal function rather than providing a succession of roots, the central point of relative repose on the dominant triad helps to create that extra degree of finality and certainty to complete the work both structurally and emotionally.

5 Britten in America: 1939–42

Between November 1938 and the spring of 1941 Tippett was occupied with one major work, *A Child of Our Time*. This period was a particularly productive one for Britten: apart from the Violin Concerto, *Les Illuminations,* the *Sinfonia da Requiem,* the *Diversions* for piano and orchestra, the *Seven Sonnets of Michelangelo, Paul Bunyan* and the String Quartet No. 1 were all completed during his years in America. It is a remarkable list, not least because the composer was ill for much of 1940.

In the published catalogue of his works,[1] the Violin Concerto op. 15 (completed 20 September 1939) is followed by *Les Illuminations* op. 18 (completed 25 October 1939). The two missing opuses were a short 'fanfare', *Young Apollo* for piano, string quartet and string orchestra op. 16, which had a performance in Toronto in August 1939 and was resurrected at the 1979 Aldeburgh Festival, and some settings of Hopkins for chorus op. 17.

From Hopkins to Rimbaud is possibly not as large a leap as their names initially suggest, if only because neither exactly favoured a plain and simple style. Britten said in later years that both the Rimbaud and Michelangelo cycles 'were necessary for me in order to shed the bad influences of the Royal College'.[2] They may also have been gestures of independence from the English language in general and Auden in particular, with whom Britten was closely associated at this time. Rimbaud's exotic fantasies are hardly typical of the kind of verse which Britten most commonly chose, and they are very different from the French poems of Verlaine and Hugo which he had set as a schoolboy in 1928. With such a proliferation of extravagant imagery it would be idle to expect the kind of precise delineation of detail from which Britten's most characteristic musical landscapes are built. Yet the very absence of the familiar, the local, can focus the mind – and the technique – in a significant way, and the music of *Les Illuminations* provides a particularly clear realization of certain fundamental tonal procedures which Britten retained, refined and varied over the years, but rarely used again in such an apparently systematic fashion. In *Les Illuminations* he tames Rimbaud's savagery with an imagination which has enough of urgency and deep feeling to put moments of elegance and glitter into appropriate perspective. The wealth of words in several of the poems must be shaped by a strong musical design, and Britten's skill shows itself most impressively in the fact that the design itself is allusive, not naive: even if it was arrived at instinctively, rather than consciously plotted, it is confidently progressive, not anxiously circumscribed.

In the broadest sense, the tonal scheme of *Les Illuminations* is based on both a reinforcement and a contradiction of the traditional structural principle in which tonic and dominant are treated as the closest relatives: one progression from dominant (B flat) to tonic (E flat) encloses another at the distance of a tritone (E to A). In itself, such a scheme has obvious attractions for a composer who is seeking to extend rather than abandon basic tonal connections. Yet to use such a scheme in its simplest form is to risk a rather crude, exclusive kind of stratification. The more a composer depends on ultimate tonal explicitness, using a triadic language in which the bass continues to play the principal structural role, the more he may need to consider ways of distancing foreground from background, of achieving a positive interaction between structural elements whose most powerful property is their mutual exclusiveness. Of course, in the tonal system 'mutual exclusiveness' is a myth, for while the triads of B flat major and E major may have no common pitches, the scales of B flat major and E major do at least have the pitch-class A in common and, allowing for enharmonic alteration, E flat/D sharp. The 'opposing' tritones in Britten's design are therefore richly ambiguous in their reactions to each other.

In *Les Illuminations* Britten shows great resource in elaborating quite simple triadic alternations and progressions against an equally simple background. But in order to increase the harmonic richness of his material he adds a further component to the scheme, intensifying the relationship, rather than the opposition, between B flat and E. The most familiar chord to contain both pitches is the dominant seventh of F major: this chord can neutralize the opposition of the two notes, but it can only 'resolve' that opposition fully if it moves on to the tonic triad of F major. Such a positive, traditional process would be inappropriate for emphasis in *Les Illuminations*, so Britten takes the C major triad which is the most stable component of that seventh chord and uses it as his third main point of tonal focus. It provides an invaluable source for structural elaboration as the work proceeds.

The sequence of events in *Les Illuminations* is very dramatically arranged. The first stage, if preludial, is the most tense and ambiguous, from the very start when the 'Fanfare' bases alternations of B flat major and E major triads on an E/F trill (Ex. 12). It is perhaps not labouring the point excessively to note in passing just how different from Tippett's delight in the ambivalence of elaborate foregrounds this forceful exposure of a fundamental background relationship is. The entry of the voice immediately provokes the most direct opposition of the two ele-

Ex. 12 Britten, *Les Illuminations*, I Fanfare

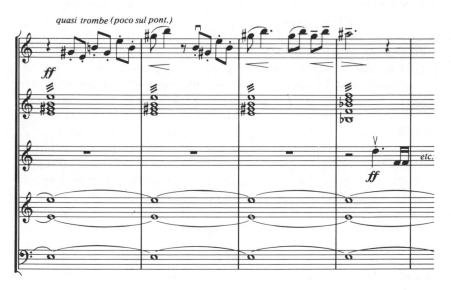

ments (with E the superior, logically, since this is the pitch chosen for the singer's declamation), then the neutralization on to the seventh chord on C, from which a B flat emerges as the sole survivor. The next two movements, 'Villes' and 'Phrase', maintain a high level of ambiguity: the highest in the cycle as a whole. 'Villes' seems to contain within itself two cycles of progression, one centring on B flat major, the other on B minor, which interact, and in which the tendency for B flat to occur as a dissonance against the B minor harmony is notable. 'Phrase' encapsulates in its eight bars a motion from B to B flat, and the latter, a tentative 6/4 triad, is immediately reinforced by root positions in movement IIIb, 'Antique'. The first stage of the cycle, then, has worked out the implications of the initial, neutralized equilibrium, and allowed B flat to emerge as the principal point of focus, not least by representing E as a key only through its dominant B. The interactions in 'Villes' are particularly subtle, since they are not merely between isolated chords, but between two progressions. The tonal 'vagrancy' here is crucial, and the label 'bitonality' will scarcely suffice for a process in which it is evolutionary progress, not static superimposition, which is fundamental.

'Antique' is firmly in B flat, 'Royauté' in E, 'Marine' in A. At the second stage, therefore, the conflict is both more explicit and, ultimately, oriented more decisively away from B flat. Certainly the treatment of B flat major in 'Antique', the thematic shape a sublimated fanfare, has all the simplicity of a final statement. The tonic chord is firmly fixed in the first twelve bars, then the harmony begins to ascend by whole tones: C major (seven bars), D major (eight bars), E major (five bars, where the midpoint is reached), then on to F major, the climax, for a six-bar phrase in which the harmony descends again to B flat, in part by balancing whole-tone motion, for the final fifteen bars.

'Royauté' is distinctly different, not merely in character, but in internal organization. The form is more ternary than binary, which could allow scope for still greater exploitation of tritonal conflict. Nevertheless, it would have been naive merely to turn the basic structure of the previous song inside out: B flats do occur in the chromatic motion of the bass line, but the main alternative points of focus are B and G sharp, E's diatonic relatives. Thus the foundation is laid for the progression from E to its tonic A in 'Marine', and with 'Marine' the second, central section of the cycle is completed.

'Marine' is the most vehement, flamboyant movement in *Les Illuminations*. Britten treats the text strophically, with three 'stanzas', the second a compressed variant of the first, and the third an expanded variant. The turbulence of the text is matched not merely by the rhythmic force of the writing, but by the placement of harmonic intrusions into the determining A major. These intruders are never triads but aggregates of perfect fifths or tritones: that in the first stanza is based on E flat (with B flat, F, C and G), and that in the second stanza on B flat (with F, C and G). The third stanza is more elaborate, since the basic A major is extended through a cadence on C, then reinforced by means of an enhanced dominant preparation. The final tonic flourish has a D sharp embedded in it, but this is scarcely disruptive in context, merely an effect of colour.

The second part of the cycle has moved from the serenely expanded B flat major of 'Antique' to the hectically enhanced A major of 'Marine', through the relatively stable E major of 'Royauté'. The disruptions of 'Marine' have allowed the B flat/E flat connection to retain a toe-hold on the argument, and the diversion on to C in the final stanza has also recalled the mediating role of that chord. In the third part of the work that chord will become a key, and the focus will move from the relationship of E to A to the relationship of B flat to E flat.

The third and final section of *Les Illuminations* is by far the longest, and it begins with a retreat into ambiguity. The material of the 'Interlude', descending, stepwise twining figures which combine with each other and with reminiscences of 'Marine', is very different from that of the 'Fanfare' which opened the whole cycle, but the conclusion is similar. The voice (now quietly) sings 'J'ai seul la clef de cette parade sauvage' against a background of alternating B flat major and E major triads, and the same neutralizing motion on to C major with superimposed B flat occurs. This time, however, it is the C major chord, without the B flat, which both ends the 'Interlude' and forms the tonic for the next movement, 'Being Beauteous'. The harmonic richness of this elaborate yet reposeful setting is such that the C major triad is lost sight of for much of the time, but it remains the only fundamental centre, supported by its dominant (bar 9) and by a recapitulatory section whose harmonic expansion to embrace an E major triad is the only substantial reminder of the main harmonic argument of the work. In these terms, 'Being Beauteous' may seem a mere extension of the 'Interlude' which prepares it. The structural argument is deepened considerably by having the tonal process removed from the stage of conflict to that of mediation. Yet the 'logic' of the cycle of fifths insists that C is actually closer to B flat than to E. The work continues, therefore, with the transformation of C major into C minor and a move from B flat to E flat, matching the earlier progression from E to A but countering the aggressive mood in which that progression was expressed. Britten does not actually use B flat again as a key, so the motion to E flat can more clearly be sensed as taking place over the span of the work as a whole.

The transition from C major to C minor is made all the more dramatic in 'Parade' – the movement based on the March from the unfinished suite for string quartet of 1933 – by the greater emphasis on the dominant, and the increasingly chromatic procession from which at times any tonal outcome seems possible. The crux is after Fig. 10, when the refrain, with its E/B flat alternations, is heard for the last time. Now the process of neutralization is triumphant rather than conciliatory. It is again C major, not C minor, but the plentiful chromatics (with avoidance of the diatonic dominant) help to create a sufficient sense of incompletion. The final song, 'Départ', is not an anti-climax, however. Its restraint is the more impressive for the extent of the contrast, and there is a significant final departure, not from the harmonic stability of E flat as such, but from the simple clarity of the tonic major triad. As the bass descends by minor thirds from E flat to C to A an expansion takes place which the return to more diatonic regions two bars before Fig. 3 is not sufficient to exorcise completely. Six bars from the end, B flat and E sound together for the last time, and the slight shiver of conflict remains unresolved through the single E flats with which the music dies away.

Les Illuminations is a major achievement: but most of Britten's time during 1940–1 was spent on instrumental music. *Diversions* for piano (left hand) and orchestra is a set of variations on a theme whose emphasis on perfect fifths, as many writers have recognized, foreshadows the principal idea of the opera *The Turn of the Screw*. *Diversions* employs a mixture of dance-like movements, including a Tarantella, and other genre pieces: March, Romance, Chant, Nocturne. But the *Sinfonia da Requiem*, which precedes *Diversions*, and the String Quartet No. 1, which follows it, are a good deal more interesting from the structural standpoint: and the fact that they both have the same principal tonic, D, as the Violin Concerto helps to reinforce some of the common concerns of all three pieces. The string quartet will therefore be discussed immediately after the *Sinfonia*, although both the *Michelangelo Sonnets* and *Paul Bunyan* came between them.

The *Sinfonia da Requiem* almost seems to start where the Violin Concerto finishes, with its solemn tonic reiterations. In formal outline, too, the *Sinfonia* echoes the Concerto: its movements are slow ('Lacrymosa'), fast ('Dies irae'), slow ('Requiem aeternam'). This time, however, we are really dealing, as in the Sinfonietta, with a work in which three 'separate' movements are strongly bound together. In its concentration and finely shaped thematic content, the *Sinfonia* is a still more distinguished achievement than the Concerto. Each movement, however artificially subdivisible, is structured as a single span in which stepwise bass motion (which is more likely to use the tritonal counterpole as a subsidiary point of rest than the dominant) may effectively be interrupted by passages of less explicitly directed harmonic activity: but the stepwise motion, when restored, ensures the convincing completion of the design. In the 'Lacrymosa' the tonic can only be decisively reasserted (at Fig. 16) when the bass has progressed from A flat, the tritone, to A, the dominant, then on through B flat and C against a dominant pedal in the inner parts. At this climax the major–minor third alternation strongly recalls the end of the Violin Concerto.

The 'Dies irae' is a *Totentanz* rather than a scherzo, but it retains the characteristic scherzo role, using a rapid tempo and appropriately simple thematic figuration to suspend the tonal argument, or at least to submerge it in a welter of semitonal clashes – a parallel to this climax might be the end of the 'Seconda Parte' of Bartók's String Quartet No. 3. Momentary emphases can, naturally, be observed, but where the harmony does solidify (as at Fig. 26) the addition of an E flat to a first inversion D major triad keeps strong assertion of the work's central tonality effectively at bay. Some apparent dominant preparation at Fig. 29 is deflected and D is only strongly reaffirmed (a minor triad with an added second) at Fig. 34. This D is then the foundation for the long transition through to the 'Requiem aeternam' – a simple three-part form handled with effortless assurance.

Though centred around D major throughout,the tonal extension in the 'Requiem aeternam' is considerable, and finely controlled. For example, in the central section (Figs. 40–3), the bass descends twice by step from D to D, the first descent broken between G and F sharp, the second, more rapid descent omitting the G altogether: both descents omit A. The final section, which, like the first, floats on bass arpeggiations that democratically spread the responsibility for harmonic determination through the entire texture, nevertheless contains a discreetly prolonged motion from dominant to tonic. The technical processes of this movement are a particularly fine match for the oft-described 'troubled serenity' which the music expresses. The unifying processes at work, and their hierarchic distribution, are experienced as unmistakably as the textural variety evident on the music's surface. As a symphonic structure, the work draws positive strength from concentrated forms which, even if not allowing for an orthodox amount of contrast and elaboration within themselves, generate a progressive, coherent structure which deals with the most fundamental symphonic issues as effectively as any comparable work of this period.

The String Quartet No. 1 of 1941 is at once more traditional in formal outline and, in at least some crucial respects, more exploratory in its tonal treatment than the *Sinfonia da Requiem*. The fact that it is also on the whole less successful may be one of the reasons why, from this point on, Britten was to give far greater attention to vocal and dramatic music. Certainly the charms of manipulating the traditional formal schemes of symphonic music came to interest him less than the possibilities for exploiting dramatic conflicts and relationships within the extended tonal system itself. Yet it is precisely because this quartet does not passively accept the received formal and tonal principles that it is of no small significance in Britten's development. In it Britten seems to confront more directly even than in the *Sinfonia da Requiem* the central question facing all modern composers of tonal symphonic works: how tonal should they be? How far are traditional diatonic relations possible, especially when employing forms which came to full maturity through the positive exploitation of such relationships? Britten's answer was to let the strong assertion and elaborate prolongation of the tonic itself justify – indeed, make inevitable – the non-diatonic motions which remain subordinate to that asserted tonic: but the dominant, so crucial as an independent element in earlier tonal music, comes to function most essentially as the agent of extension within the orbit of the tonic itself. When the two processes are associated with different groups of material, as they are in the first movement of the String Quartet No. 1, a particularly satisfying drama of opposition results, though here, as in the finale, it is of opposition, and not of interaction, that one is most conscious. The greater and more orthodox employment of internal contrast in these movements points up the dilemma of the modern 'symphonist' whose instinct is not to give greatest weight to the developmental interaction of motives, but rather to stress tonal and textural polarities which, however symmetrically proportioned, do not knit together into a truly unified form. Tippett was also to confront the problem of integration in the absence of tonal forces strong enough to bind a complete structure into a unity. Where Britten was particularly skilful at this stage of his development was in carrying the tonal discourse across the thematic boundaries. So, in the first movement of the quartet, the C natural which disturbs the diatonic assurance of the D major Allegro material prepares the F major which increasingly dominates its continuation and ensures that the return of the initial Andante material shall itself be centred on F. In the finale, there is a less far-reaching contrast between the two main thematic elements, and transition between them is therefore more natural, especially when, as between bars 570 and 590, it is made the occasion for development. The thematic contrast in the finale is nevertheless most effective as a means of reinforcing the opposition between D and F which was so important in the first movement: as, for example, in the final move on to the tonic between bars 650 and 658. The 'flat-side' undermining of D major is still more evident in the two middle movements. The scherzo is in F, for all its coyness about lingering on a root-position tonic triad. The Andante calmo is in B flat, and here the very directness with which root-position tonic control is accepted makes internal diversion and conflict essential. The most striking diversion is the arrival of D at bar 400, with a prominent added supertonic recalling the very start of the first movement. But B flat is eventually restored through the strength of its own dominant, in bar 431. The opening of the finale is a good example of Britten's ability to use counterpoint as a means of establishing a diatonic emphasis without elaborate metrical variations of the basic motives. Yet in spite of the fact that the Violin

Concerto, *Sinfonia da Requiem* and the Quartet No. 1 have greater thematic distinctiveness than the earlier instrumental works, it was becoming increasingly clear – and, with hindsight, it was inescapable – that he could give a more natural melodic articulation to his instincts about harmonic structure when setting words. To move from a poem, with a sonnet the ultimate in discipline and concentration, to an opera libretto nevertheless represents an enormous change of perspective and scope: it would also be the ultimate test of a musical language whose blend of clarity and ambiguity had flourished so impressively up to this time on a relatively small scale.

In order to consider the first quartet alongside the *Sinfonia da Requiem* we have broken temporarily with chronology: but one of the reasons why the quartet seems less imaginative, even less coherent than the *Sinfonia* could be because of the unsettling experience of writing *Paul Bunyan*, which immediately preceded it. And while *Bunyan* itself is scarcely a composition in which the achievements of all the later operas can be embryonically detected, it in turn was preceded by the *Seven Sonnets of Michelangelo* op. 22 (1940), a song cycle with piano which in its lyric intensity and stylistic focus over a wide range of moods and textures represents a statement of great potential as well as of finished achievement. It is the use of tonality which, in the song cycles, offers the most powerful insights into Britten's technique. There is a relatively narrow range of forms, rarely moving far from the principle of statement, departure or elaboration, and varied restatement (simple strophic form is as unlikely as elaborate through-composition); yet the tonal handling is acutely sensitive to the diverse ways of employing a single, monotonal scheme. The individual songs sharpen the focus on fundamental harmonic procedures which, in symphonic music, will be spread out on a considerably larger scale: the cycles may therefore be less obviously 'unified', but their individual 'events' have a special richness and clarity.

The first of the *Seven Sonnets of Michelangelo* is in A major, with a central section growing ambiguous after an initial emphasis on C. Here, as if to compensate for non-triadic harmony, the accompanimental figuration reiterates temporary tonics and dominants in plenty, but these seem insufficient to clarify a key, and the subtly changing relationship between them and the fourth chords which sometimes contain the same notes, and are sometimes completely different, is a powerful transmitter of restless energy. Technically, the cycle ranges from wholly or predominantly non-triadic numbers – 1, 5, and 6 – to a movement like No. 3, which, appropriately to its serene mood, makes much of triadic consonance (after the example of 'Antique' in *Les Illuminations*). But it avoids the clear root-position dominant, expanding instead into the symmetrically disposed regions of flat-submediant major and mediant major.

The second sonnet offers a particularly concentrated demonstration of a structure rooted in a subtly consistent manipulation of the connection between a tonic and a dominant, even when the context is far from purely diatonic. The unconventional nature of Britten's tonal structure here is indicated by the fact that, once more, the most essential, generative motion takes place within the tonic triad, rather than between tonic and dominant triads. The modal alternation of major and minor thirds is a particularly familiar Britten characteristic, and its deployment as a feature permeating all levels of structure and all types of relationship can lead naturally to an integration of all the chromatic degrees into a structure centred on a single triad. There is a process of evolution and elaboration at work here which is very far from the random avoidance of an implied diatonicism which those most hostile to Britten's music might wish to demonstrate. From its fundamental alternation of major and minor thirds within the tonic triad, the music of the second sonnet expands through consistent linear prolongations of these and similar alternations.

It is nevertheless the final movement of the cycle, in Britten's favoured D major, which is both the most exalted in expression and wide-ranging in technical procedure. The form is determined by the four statements of the piano's ritornello. The first of these prolongs the D major triad through an upward registral shift of several octaves and extends the D major tonality with particular concern for the various modal implications of C natural. The structural significance of changes of octave position as a prolonging device in music which lacks the strong tonic–dominant polarity of 'unextended' tonality is richly demonstrated in this cycle. The initial F sharp of the upper line is transferred to the lower line and taken over by the singer, whose arioso (virtually the same length as the ritornello) refers in its central bars to the ascending motion of the ritornello, but in the larger context of a *descending* D major triad.

The second ritornello uses a strong B flat emphasis to turn the prolonged triad from D major to minor, and the answering arioso completes a downward shift to C in which the apparent D major subdominant of bar 27 behaves ambivalently as a dominant to C. The third ritornello is again seven bars and one quaver long, but it now enshrines a progression from C minor back to a Lydian D, the major third of the tonic triad being used as a passing note to the G sharp, until the voice restores its structural weight. The voice is used throughout the third ritornello section to anticipate the tonal direction of the piano part, and this non-alignment creates enormous tension. The polarity between the outer voices of the texture, and the melodic character of the bass, exemplify a decisive development whereby the lower voice becomes not merely the agent of tonal prolongation but also of more complex tonal extension.

The Serenade op. 31 – especially the final song – will demonstrate the further development of this process, to which the relative flexibility of Britten's mature arioso style is a vital contributory factor. The final Michelangelo sonnet closes with a vocal phrase which outlines the D major triad from F sharp *ascending* to F sharp: and the piano's final ritornello completes the resolution. The only chromatic element is the Lydian G sharp, but again the technique is one of prolongation rather than progression (Ex. 13).

Historians wishing to contrast the 'escapist' Britten of the American years with the 'committed' Tippett will point to the evident differences of subject and style between *Paul Bunyan* and *A Child of Our Time*: they might even comment on the sense in which Britten appeared to have 'rejected' a follow-up to the subject-matter of *Our Hunting Fathers*, whose basic concerns are comparable to those found in Tippett's

Ex. 13 Britten, *Seven Sonnets of Michelangelo*, No. 7, Sonnetto XXIV

oratorio. The long suppression of Britten's two-act operetta inevitably contributed to the suspicion that the composer was not merely dissatisfied with it, but positively ashamed of it. Yet its eventual revision in 1974 and revival in 1976 – it was given the op. no. of 17 left vacant by the rejected Hopkins setting of 1939 – did more than confirm that the composer's feelings about it were characteristically ambivalent. It revealed that the work was something more than a mere 'quasi-musical'; indeed, its mythic overtones and dramatic stylizations, together with the element of nature mysticism which is one of the work's strongest features, would seem to lead more naturally to *The Midsummer Marriage* than to *Peter Grimes*. Given that a composer's large-scale works are more likely to capitalize on innovations first introduced in smaller pieces than to break completely new ground, it is not surprising to find that the music of *Paul Bunyan* grows more obviously from Britten's film and theatre scores of the 1930s than from his concert works. Indeed, once the presence of spoken dialogue is taken into account, the difference between *Bunyan* and the later operas is more one of style and mood than of structure. The later operas may include nothing quite like the straightforward patter of the Lumberjacks' Chorus or the swinging Western Union Boy's Song.

But the Prologue to Act I is, for all its clearly defined sections, an extended piece of through-composition, and there are certain repetitions of material across the structure to give some broader musical cohesion. When text and plot allow a more reflective manner, the idiom deepens into something closer to Britten's 'serious' style: for example, Ink-slinger's Song (No. 14), whose extended B flat major tonality recalls *Les Illuminations.* Chromaticism even reaches the heights of a melody including all twelve semitones just before Tiny's entrance (No. 14a).

It is natural to search *Paul Bunyan* not merely for evidence of a flair for opera, but for hints of how concentration on opera might affect the development of Britten's style. The most obvious point – already touched on – is also perhaps the most important. There is no sign of any inclination to move away from the less actively polyphonic textures of the earlier works involving solo voice, still less to attempt any grand expansion of the rich thematic workings and anti-triadic tendencies of some of his earlier instrumental scores. During the later 1940s Britten was to confirm that his 'flair' for opera was also a 'flair' for tonality, and to this extent his relationship with both operatic and tonal traditions was to become deeper and more complex as the decade passed.

The time when *Paul Bunyan* was written, performed, and in the composer's view 'unmercifully' criticized, was traumatic for Britten, and it is tempting to assert that it was his decision to return to England in 1942 which did most to solve both compositional and personal problems. But what the music shows, unmistakably, is that Britten was continuing to develop. The works of the American years are impressive enough, but the compositions produced between 1943 and 1945 show a deepening expressive power and an expanding technical mastery. The old accusations of cleverness and superficiality would continue to be made by certain critics; but they could not prevent Britten from achieving remarkable success as he entered the most productive period of his creative life.

6 Tippett: An oratorio, a string quartet and a cantata (1939–43)

After *Paul Bunyan*, Britten never again set a text with Auden's ironic, knowing, idiosyncratic tone: like most opera composers, he was happiest and most successful with librettos that did not in themselves aspire to the condition of Art. But Britten continued to believe in the necessity for direct, simple musical statements, and he would use 'popular' elements, Mahler-fashion, when these were dramatically relevant, as they are in many of the operas. Tippett, in his very different way, has also explored the contact between certain popular idioms and his more 'serious' personal style. For both composers these elements have offered a means of intensifying expression through contrast: but the extent to which 'collective' musical statements can be incorporated organically into individual works of art is inevitably limited.

It has already been suggested that, in contrast to Britten's Violin Concerto, Tippett's Concerto for Double String Orchestra is not self-evidently a work with any direct or necessary relationship to events or attitudes of the time of its composition. If anything, in its effortless gaiety and optimism, it seems more like a deliberate counter to the uncertainties and agonizing dilemmas of the late 1930s. Yet throughout the decade Tippett had been acutely aware of the 'stark realities of life for so many people and accepted the overwhelming need for compassion with regard to such things'. He had also felt certain that 'music could have a direct relation . . . to the compassion that was so deep in my own heart'.[1] As a result, his next composition was connected with actual events in a very direct and purposeful way.

It was in November 1938 that a young Polish Jew shot a German diplomat in Paris, and between that date and September 1939 Tippett produced a draft of what was to form the text for the first large-scale dramatic composition of his maturity, *A Child of Our Time*. The story of Tippett's approach to T. S. Eliot for help with the text, and of Eliot's view that the composer, in his draft, 'had virtually completed the job himself' is now well known;[2] but the origins of the work are more complex than the idea of a sudden, spontaneous reaction to the Paris shooting might suggest. Tippett wished to write a dramatic work with the essential theme of 'man's inhumanity to man', and had initially considered an opera on the Easter Rising in Dublin: did he perhaps know the play called *Easter 1916* by Montagu Slater, for which Britten had written incidental music in 1935? But the Irish problem naturally seemed less immediate, less menacing in the late 1930s than the Jewish problem. As Tippett has written:

Although the artist appears to be locked away, doing his particular thing, one could not, at that time, but be aware of what was going on. I was drawn by something of my own entrails into what was happening, particularly in Germany. The Jews were the particular scapegoats of everything, for every kind of standing outcast, whether in Russia or America or even in England. For these people I knew somehow I had to sing songs. Suddenly, in fact the day after war broke out, the whole thing welled up in me in a way which I can remember exactly. I simply had to go and begin to write *A Child of Our Time*. I felt I had to express collective feelings and that could only be done by collective tunes such as Negro spirituals, for these tunes contain a deposit of generations of common experience.[3]

The composition of the music was begun on 5 September 1939, and completed a year and a half later. (Tippett's only other work from this time is the short *Fantasia on a Theme of Handel* for piano and orchestra.) The title was borrowed from a story published in 1938 by the Austrian writer Ödön von Horváth, and the composer's first draft of the text provides a fascinating indication of how certain ideas and concepts derived from the psychology of Jung had been brought alongside the poetic imagery of Wilfred Owen: in his notes for No. 22 Tippett quotes some lines from Owen's 'Strange Meeting', to be set so memorably by Britten in the *War Requiem* twenty years later.[4] But although such basic associations as those between 'war' and 'winter' occur in Owen's poem 'The Seed', Tippett was more concerned to draw a psychological rather than a political message from his material. Peace, as his notes for the oratorio make clear, is not an end in itself: 'the irrational elements in ourselves have got to be reckoned with, even integrated into some new synthesis, if a way through is to be found. "Peace" is the symbol of this new synthesis, as "armed peace" or "War" is the symbol for the effort to solve the problem by neurosis and the tension of the opposites.'[5] To an extent which is hardly surprising considering the pressures present at the time the work was created, it is 'the tension of the opposites' rather than the nature of the new synthesis which *A Child of Our Time* seems to reflect most directly.

The oratorio recalls its immediate predecessor, the Concerto for Double String Orchestra, in the sheer compulsiveness of its impact. But the concerto effortlessly expresses that integrated wholeness which is the highest spiritual and aesthetic goal of creator and receiver, while the oratorio, through striving to embrace extreme diversities, presents a more fragmented form to the world. The contemporary subject, for all its generalized presentation, and the time-honoured form, with its succession of recitatives, arias, contrapuntal choruses and chorale-substitutes, do not make particularly natural partners. The original subject-matter seems more suited to *Wozzeck*-like operatic treatment than to transmutation through the rituals of the post-baroque oratorio: and it could be that Tippett's later sensitivity to the power of opera to carry mythic, and even spiritual, truths stems from his sense of genres in confusion here. But Tippett himself believes that 'while the traditional forms of oratorio do lie behind *A Child of Our Time* they are somehow turned and twisted to carry the charge of our contemporary anxiety'. And he was quite clear, after the idea of an opera about the Easter Rising had lost its appeal, that 'I wanted to present the matter contemplatively rather than dramatically.'[6]

Tippett has written at length about how he came to choose Negro spirituals to replace 'the special Protestant constituent of the congregational hymn' in a work which, because it is 'destined for the concert hall, not the church, cannot merely use the metaphorical language of liturgical Christianity',[7] but the value of this device must still be questioned. Although it is true that 'the listeners in the concert hall' cannot be equated with a 'congregation of the faithful', the spirituals, as collective expression, seem to cry out, like the 'borrowed' hymns in Britten's *Saint Nicolas* and *Noye's Fludde,* for collective performance. But a note in the score of *A Child of Our Time* declares that 'the spirituals should not be thought of as congregational hymns, but as integral parts of the oratorio'. That is perhaps the problem: they are not integral enough, and for all Tippett's acknowledgement of the need for 'allowing the popular words and music to affect the *general* style, within which the "sophisticated" parts of the oratorio had to be written', the distance between individual and collective seems too great. Unlike those later works in which Tippett quotes and incorporates elements from earlier or popular music, the oratorio detaches its expressions of collective feeling and places them on a pedestal. As a result, the listener, the majority in the concert hall, might well feel exploited as well as moved. But Tippett, referring to 'those criticisms pointed at my using negro spirituals within such an apparently sophisticated score', has argued that 'the passage of time has uncovered the connections . . . The transitions from composed music to the settings of the spirituals are accepted now as one of the achievements of the piece.'[8] It is certainly the case that reservations about *A Child of Our Time* are now likely to centre less on the question of such incompatibilities and more on the general loss of stylistic certainty and structural clarity which seems ultimately the result of the desire to write a large-scale work, not excessively difficult to perform, which remains related to the tradition of English oratorio.

The very opening of the work, with its disconcerting shift from chromatic to diatonic and back again, is symptomatic: and the composer's attempt to write in a style which does not make virtuoso demands on choral singers leads to an atypical stodginess of rhythm in which the bar-line once more reigns supreme. In passages like 'We are as seed before the wind' (in No. 3) the idiom is sturdily neo-classical, and in general the use of word-repetition results in much more mundane imitation and sequential writing than Tippett was ever to employ again. The choral textures of *The Midsummer Marriage* are much freer.

Even in places where the instrumental writing quite clearly recalls the Concerto for Double String Orchestra, a more solid metrical accentuation is evident: in, for example, the introduction to No. 6, the tenor solo 'I have no money for my bread'. This movement, with its tango-style accompaniment, is the first obvious attempt to create a stylistic bridge between the more conventional oratorio style of what has

preceded it and the first spiritual (No. 8). In fact this is the only number
in the work to be so radically simplified: the second tenor solo, No. 22 in
Part II, 'The Boy Sings in his Prison', is in the much less clearly directed
chromatic manner which prevails elsewhere.

Yet even when Tippett lacks complete sureness of touch, and the
evolutionary vitality of his most powerful structures is broken by the succession of short, separate forms, he can still create memorable music.
From No. 27 of Part III ('The soul of man') through to the entry of the
final spiritual, there is music which is positively transitional between the
splendour of the Double Concerto and the marvels of *The Midsummer
Marriage*. No. 27 itself has a compelling urgency, a purposeful
harmonic-contrapuntal flow, and an ease of vocal elaboration, while the
orchestral and choral episodes of No. 28 follow on from the powerful
peaks of No. 26 in foreshadowing the music of Madame Sososostris's
unveiling in the opera. Equally pregnant is the wordless, ecstatic greeting of spring with which the soloists preface the final spiritual (Ex. 14).

Ex. 14 Tippett, *A Child of Our Time*, Part III, No. 29

In Peter Evans's tactful words, 'a last spiritual is required by the symmetrical patterning of the work, yet it is possible to feel that, if we have entered into Tippett's own glowing vision of a renewed earth, we have no need to return to the homelier vision of "Deep River"'.[9] Tippett was never again to attempt such a stark progression into collective simplicity as ends *A Child of Our Time*; like his American near-contemporary, Elliott Carter, whose music underwent a considerable transformation during the late 1940s, he was soon to learn that he had to be himself, in all his complexity. He had to shape and control proliferating ideas rather than top and tail them to make them fit predetermined patterns and schemes. *A Child of Our Time* is undoubtedly typical of him in seeking to deal with a live issue at least partly in its own terms. But the dramatic theme of an outcast in conflict with an established order was to receive its finest wartime treatment, not in a contemporary, contemplative, quasi-documentary form but in the transformed operatic traditions employed by Britten in *Peter Grimes*.

A Child of Our Time was not performed until March 1944, three years after its completion, but Tippett's next pair of major works, the String

Quartet No. 2 (1941-2) and the cantata *Boyhood's End* (1943), were both heard during 1943. The quartet is similar to the Double Concerto to the extent that the finales of both serve to clarify the formal outlines of the first movements by means of more explicit tonal and thematic contrasts. As Tippett himself has put it, in the first movement of the second quartet 'the basic sonata form is deliberately loosened to keep the lyricism above the dramatics', whereas the finale represents 'a deliberate attempt to shift the dramatics from first movement to last – as opposed to lightening everything at the end with some kind of Rondo'.[10] Like the finale of the concerto, that of the quartet displays thematic connections with earlier movements, but, as befits the more restrained nature of a chamber work, it lacks the powerful extended coda which, in the concerto, lifts both thematic process and tonal progress on to a new plane.

Since the fourth movement of the quartet ends in the F sharp with which the whole work began, and with a modal form of cadence similar to that which ends the first movement (as well as the middle movement of the concerto), the closed, goal-directed nature of the work's extended tonal scheme is evident. Overall, nevertheless, there is far less precision of tonal perspective than in the concerto. Even in the finale, the quartet seems poised to embrace a consistent kind of 'tonality without progression', concerned primarily with local relationships between degrees of consonance and dissonance, and articulated by linear motions which depend less and less on being projected between points of tonal structural emphasis. The general absence of traditional types of cadence and of root-position harmonies confirms this 'floating' textural treatment. Yet the result is not an intense chromaticism verging on atonality, as might have been the case had Tippett at this time been closer to the expressionist tradition. Here, perhaps more clearly than in any other of his major works, we sense a conflict between form and style, not because textures are too contrapuntal, but because, while the forms still cling to the proportions of the tonally based sonata scheme, the music seems to aspire to the relative structural freedom of madrigal or fantasy, where the hierarchies of fully developed tonal forms have no place. Only in the second movement, Andante, which uses the most tonally sophisticated contrapuntal form – fugue – is there no sense of strain, no tension between the needs of the form and the 'instincts' of the texture. Tippett's later reliance on fugue, notably in the String Quartet No. 3, as well as his eventual espousal of a degree of atonality in more dramatic formal schemes, can both be traced back to the issues raised by, and confronted in, the second quartet. The work is no failure: the control exercised over the proportions of the individual movements ensures that the pervasive flow never disperses into featureless meandering, and it is far better to focus the ear on thematic elaboration and textural interplay than to rely on the sort of crude juxtapositions of tonal poles and counterpoles employed by so many modern tonal composers.

Ultimately, however, as Tippett himself had noted in his 1938 article quoted on p. 53, the classical tonal structures depended on sharply defined contrasts and relationships which are all the more explicit when the relationships are close ones. But during the early 1940s Tippett appears to have been particularly suspicious of non-vocal 'dramatics', and his main technical problem was how best to shape and control his abundant lyric impulse. In the second quartet he seems to concentrate on local rhythmic issues, making sure that the music never gets metrically bogged down: he tends, lyrically, to diversify the flow rather than, dramatically, to interrupt it. In the Double Concerto the sheer textural diversity of the medium determined the presence of contrasts between degrees of homophony and polyphony. In the quartet, homophony is principally the means of slowing-up the music and, eventually, of stopping it. There is less sense of it resolving a genuinely symphonic tonal-thematic 'debate', and Tippett was never again (even in the Symphony No. 2) to attempt so close an approach to the restricted tonal schemes of the past. After all, this is the only one of his mature works (apart from the Suite in D) to proclaim a key in its title.

In *Boyhood's End* one is more conscious of the use of root-position triads as 'prime movers' of a structure which is notably purposeful, though scarcely monotonal. This cantata, written for Peter Pears and Benjamin Britten and first performed by them at Morley College in June 1943, deals with an old man's 'recollected emotions of his fifteenth birthday, when he first became afraid that he might lose his peculiar contact with nature'.[11] W. H. Hudson's prose text depicts an ecstatic oneness with nature, or the illusion of such oneness. And Tippett responds with music rich in tonal allusions, but highly ambivalent about tonality as a force capable of controlling and unifying a complete, complex form. In this, perhaps, the work reveals an affinity with its models, for Tippett has said that the urge to write a vocal cantata (as opposed to a song cycle) came 'out of the study of Purcell and Monteverdi'.[12]

Boyhood's End nevertheless displays the central techniques of Tippett's early period with unsurpassed richness and clarity. Associations are inevitably set up between its harmonic vocabulary, concerned with the tensions, contrasts and relationships between degrees of consonance and dissonance, and that of more conventional tonal music. Since the principal terms of the harmonic vocabulary are concordant, it is possible to identify broad tonal connections through specific triads and, further, to relate non-triadic elements to the basic triads. The work ends on a D major triad, but this is not the tonic of a monotonal structure which emphasizes this area of tonal activity at an early stage: it is rather the logical outcome of processes which prepare the goal so unobtrusively that, while it may not seem inevitable from the outset, it does seem right when it occurs. Preparation is perhaps most evident in the degree to which the work as a whole attaches special weight to the tones of the D major triad, and builds a dynamic structure of prolongation, contradiction and confirmation around them. Thus the cadential emphasis on an A major triad at the end of the opening Recitative and Arioso sections (bars 35–6, p. 3) confirms the structural significance of the motion from F sharp to A in bars 1 and 2. But the second, Allegro section immediately contradicts A major with a shift on to its chromatic neighbour B flat, and a strong assertion of the dominant of B flat in its final stages (bar 107, the last bar of p. 9) provides a springboard for the further chromatic motion which leads to a rapid and decisive conclusion on neither B flat nor A, but F sharp (bar 122, p. 11).

The slow section of the work moves away from F sharp's dominant, but a cadence on A major is soon reached (bar 136, p. 12), and this cadence is reinforced at the end of the section as the C sharp to A motion is recapitulated (bars 179–89, pp. 14–15). Tippett nevertheless declines the invitation to provide a direct progression from A as dominant to D as tonic. The scherzo section initially uses G major as its tonic, and it is only in the first phrase of the final section (bars 224–30, p. 19) that the music moves with significant decisiveness on to D major, by means of a descent from a passing perfect cadence on G through F and E flat (Ex. 15). This progression is at once repeated with extension (bars 231–9), and the music embarks on a richly chromatic unfolding which admits some by-play between A and F sharp (bars 276–80, p. 22), reminders of the diverting power of B flat (bars 288–90, p. 23) and hints of dominant preparation (bars 294, 302, pp. 23–4). The D major of the very last bar is nevertheless approached from F major rather than G, in a reminiscence of the basic progression which launched the final section of the work.

The tonal allusions of *Boyhood's End*, as of *The Midsummer Marriage* and of all Tippett's lyric-ecstatic earlier music, are supremely appropriate for the moods he seeks to create, and for his most characteristic, personal material, which needs to arch freely but purposefully around a few firm points of focus. Hence the importance, if the effect is not to be self-defeatingly tense and congested, of elaborate ornamental prolongation to enrich a relatively slow rate of harmonic progress. Tippett builds his forms in *Boyhood's End* by means of varied repetitions within sections, and the whole is both flexible and organic. In style, it may well be that it was *Boyhood's End* which, more than any other work, made *The Midsummer Marriage* musically possible. But the clarity

Ex. 15 Tippett, *Boyhood's End*

and diversity of its structure was also something which the opera would explore and extend with consummate skill. The really substantial structural organization of the opera could only be achieved when Tippett was able to give the essentially decorative, ornamental character of his melodic flow a sufficiently strong foundation in long-range harmonic relationships which, while not making exclusive use of traditional, monotonal, unifying elements, were consistently integrated and projected.

7 Britten's return: 1942-3

Britten's experiences with *Paul Bunyan* could have left him with highly ambivalent feelings towards opera: and yet it seems almost as if those respects in which *Bunyan* was *not* truly operatic left him with the desire to attempt the real thing. But Britten did not completely abandon in- strumental music between *Bunyan* and *Grimes,* as we have seen: after the String Quartet No. 1 and the *Scottish Ballad,* his second offering for the piano duo of Ethel Bartlett and Rae Robertson, he produced one of his finest short occasional pieces, the Prelude and Fugue for 18-part string orchestra. This was a tenth-birthday present for the Boyd Neel Orches- tra, which had given the successful Salzburg première of the *Frank Bridge Variations* in 1937.

It would be difficult to regard any of the vocal works of 1942 and 1943 as studies for *Peter Grimes,* whether in style or subject-matter. The elegantly symmetrical rondo-form of the *Hymn to St Cecilia* for un- accompanied chorus, written on the voyage back to England in April 1942, retains some of the simple radiance and textural resource of *Paul Bunyan,* while the neatly framed sequence of the *Ceremony of Carols* for treble voices and harp, and the more diverse but still strongly unified structure of the cantata *Rejoice in the Lamb*, are both characteristic but small-scale conceptions which lack the textural and formal ambitiousness of *A Boy Was Born* and *Our Hunting Fathers*, as well as the emotional depth and range of *Les Illuminations* or the *Michelangelo Sonnets.* Later in 1943, however, Britten completed another song cycle, the Serenade for tenor, horn and strings, which marked a new high point of achievement.

The Serenade, like the *Ceremony of Carols,* has a framing Prologue and Epilogue – the titles in the *Ceremony* are 'Procession' and 'Reces- sion' – for a solo instrument. Otherwise the balance in the Serenade is not dissimilar to that of the *Michelangelo Sonnets* in that only two movements, 'Elegy' and 'Hymn', can be said to focus at all strongly on root-position triads, though each movement closes with confirmation of its tonal starting-point. Moreover, it is only the 'Hymn', the lightest, least complex movement in the work, which gives any structural emphasis to the diatonic dominant chord: the more involved 'Elegy' employs a tritonal counterpole. Naturally, these are also the movements in which the bass most clearly fulfils its classical function of controlling events vertically (as well as participating in them horizontally). But in the other four vocal movements, the avoidance of root-position chords is often as important as the avoidance of diatonic structural relationships. Tonality is enhanced by extension.

The exquisite 'Pastoral' is cast in a four-stanza strophic form, each stanza a variation of the others. The setting is, rhythmically, one of Britten's most subtle. A 3/8 time-signature predominates, but more as a background against which the music moves freely, the strings in a lilting 6/16, the voice in a smooth 4/8. Such a floating calm makes the suspension of strongly rooted harmonies poetically apt, and even when, near the end of the third stanza, the horn establishes a tonic pedal of D flat, and sustains it almost to the end of the whole movement, it seems distant, remote, stopping just at the point where the strings are ready to accord it the function of a root.

The 'Nocturne', which follows, may be more diatonic to its basic E flat, but only in the third and last stanza is there an initial and then a climactic use of a root-position tonic; and in the absence of a strong dominant or subdominant, the kind of fourth-chord aggregate which combines all three principal diatonic pitches (plus the supertonic or mediant) is employed. Even when the dominant is actually the bass note, as from Fig. 8, it functions more as a means of prolonging the elements of the previously asserted tonic triad. It is a means of maintaining tension without inappropriate simplification of the harmonic vocabulary.

In the 'Dirge' Britten adopts an unusual solution to the problem of a text with many verses. Here, for once, the vocal part is strophic in the simplest sense, with only the slightest rhythmic variations in its nine repetitions of the same six-bar plaint. The mode on G which the vocal line employs includes a D which the shape of the line stresses: in fact, the line outlines a descending G minor triad. But the orchestral fugue which proceeds simultaneously with the plaint is centred on E flat, and achieves its most dramatic climax with the recall of the previous movement's central harmonic element at Fig. 17. The fugue subject itself is modally inflected, with a strongly stressed dominant, lowered seventh and mediant, but from the start a G flat clashes irreconcilably with the voice's central G natural. Compatibility is probably closest after the fourth entry of the subject in the bars before Fig. 16, but this movement is one of Britten's most radical conceptions in its use of superimposition to strain extended tonal relations to their limits. The fugue is the active, programmatically spine-chilling core of the movement, while the vocal incantation is disturbingly detached, mindlessly self-absorbed, and seemingly unaffected by the *Totentanz* around it.

As already suggested, the 'Hymn to Diana' is the most straightforward number in the Serenade, providing much-needed relaxation for all except the performers, who have to negotiate its demands with no apparent effort, or the effect is spoiled. It is a delightful essay in Britten's favoured vein of the dance-like scherzo, genuinely fast music which is never merely motoric or predictable. But the setting of Keats's sonnet 'O soft embalmer of the still midnight', which forms the final vocal movement of the work, is, quite simply, Britten's finest achievement up to that date. A great poem is so translated into music that no note seems redundant. The vocal line has more of arioso than of song about it, yet its subtle self-recollections (for example, bars 1 and 2 relate to bars 26 and 27, bars 11 and 12 to bar 31) and wholly natural use of word-painting (a similar rocking figure for 'lulling' and 'burrowing') display a perfect blend of art and spontaneity. Tonally, the music is in a D major extended to favour F major as the main alternative point of focus: the only diatonic relative which impinges (G major in bar 25) has a major seventh prominently attached. The music is through-composed, but evolves through four distinct sections, the first three of which begin with references to the chordal string phrase from which the harmonic process grows, and the last section is entirely concerned with that phrase. As a chordal progression it outlines a motion on to a root position D major triad from its second inversion, and in itself it may seem of no great inspiration: there is an echo of the beginning of Vaughan Williams's Tallis Fantasia about it. In the first section (bars 1 to 8) the D major triad is already prolonged and intensified as the outer voices move in contrary motion by step, the cellos descending the octave from D to D, but without establishing another triad at the end. In the second section (bars 9 to 20) the progression is first compressed in duration, then transposed and expanded to arrive on an F major chord (bar 14) which is exquisitely prolonged through to the end of the section. The third section (bars 20 to 30) has a bass which outlines the augmented triad E flat, G, B; and the B is underpinned by its root E natural. The bass line of the original presentation is developed in this section after an initial reference to the chords, which move from F to E flat, and the final stage of this process produces the pitches E, G sharp, D, which in bar 30 lead into the final section. This is a seven-bar coda in which sustained Ds in the upper line are the background for the outlined triad in the vocal part, and the repetitions of the chordal pattern which resolve, as at the start, from C major on to D. In one of Britten's most effective yet simple uses of registral·change, these repetitions ascend through a span which initially embraces both the first and second presentations of the pattern (bar 1 and Fig. 29) but ends with a root position chord of D an octave higher still. The tenor's repeated D is that with which he began the movement, and so his final note is no less than two octaves below the 'bass' of the string chord (Ex. 16).

During the twelve years from 1931 to 1943 Britten had developed from the gifted but still impersonal and indisciplined D major String Quartet to the superbly imaginative music-poetry of the Serenade. But it should be abundantly clear by now that Britten was not a composer who progressed steadily to mastery through distinct and easily definable stages. He achieved complete mastery of quite subtly different aspects of his language very early, after which the quality of inspiration tended to vary more than the degree of mastery. In 1943 Britten was 30, and it was natural that his later works should tend to show less brilliance and more depth, less surface tension and more intense expressiveness than some of his earlier ones. But the brilliance and the tension could certainly be summoned up when needed – the Cello Symphony – and as with all great composers the qualities of the individual works are likely to elude and invalidate the more unwieldy categories of analysis.

Ex. 16 Britten, Serenade, No. 7, Sonnet (Keats)

8 Tippett and symphonic form (1944–6)

Britten's Serenade was first performed in London on 15 October 1943. In January 1944 he began to compose the music for *Peter Grimes,* finishing it in February 1945: the première was on 7 June. As for Tippett, the predominantly structural concerns of his earlier instrumental works remained to be further explored in two extraordinarily rich and ambitious scores, the Symphony No. 1 and the String Quartet No. 3, before he began his first opera in 1946.

Tippett's Symphony No. 1, first performed in Liverpool in November 1945, has obvious weaknesses, which might make it seem to represent a falling-off from the control and sheer consistency of the Concerto for Double String Orchestra. In particular, the arbitrary and aimless ornamentation of the second movement's passacaglia theme seems as unsure in style as parts of the String Quartet No. 1 and *A Child of Our Time*. Yet the first and fourth movements are so powerful and purposeful that whatever miscalculations of detail may be identified, these movements remain remarkably uncompromising and absorbing in their approach to the problem of the large-scale polyphonic structure, as at once a relative of and alternative to the 'Beethoven Allegro' model. One commentator has observed of the first movement that 'Tippett is using counterpoint dramatically and therefore – *in potentia* – symphonically. Thus, although the movement doesn't function like a Beethoven allegro as an interrelation of motifs and keys, the multiplicity of counterpoints does generate tension and therefore drama.'[1] Another view is that 'the nature of his material is such that the dramatic contrasts of sonata form are irrelevant to him. His middle sections are more like extended episodes: his elaborate material necessarily excludes anything like the processes of classical and romantic developments.'[2] Clearly, like the Double Concerto, this is music which both challenges and engages traditional concepts of what is symphonic, and it does so in an entirely positive, exciting way.

Tippett's gift for launching a confident flow of sharply characterized, contrapuntally combined ideas is never more obvious than at the start of the first symphony, and paragraph leads on to paragraph in such a way that it is the tension of enhanced continuity which is the most prominent expressive and structural feature. The first fourteen bars are scarcely introductory in the conventional sense, since they provide a preliminary statement of material which is immediately amplified in the next 23 bars.

Moreover, before that 23-bar paragraph is complete, a second series of ideas has been launched. Not all of these derive obviously from the first, but they retain the textural complexity, rhythmic energy and general tonal orientation (towards an extended A major) of the first group. In a structure where evolving continuity is of the essence, the principal points of punctuation are those places where significant *dis*continuities – changes of texture and new stages of thematic derivation – most clearly coincide. So a third stage of this huge developing exposition seems to begin with the imitative treatment of another idea based on ascending perfect fourths (Figs. 8 and 9), and the traditionally symphonic kind of contrast appears only after Fig. 12, with a rather perfunctory theme in the strings which arrests the flow, and briefly shifts the tonal emphasis away from the elusive but pervasive A on to B major. This new theme is more in the nature of a codetta, the strongest point of punctuation before the resumption of polyphonic evolution, which occurs (three bars after Fig. 13) even before a double bar formally signifies a move from 'exposition' to 'development'.

This development may not display a directed tonal progress on classical models, but the tonal argument is intensified by the shifts of perspective consequent on its B-flattish start. So, too, the thematic argument enters a new stage, with greater elaboration of material which has already been extensively explored in the exposition. If Tippett's thinking had been more under the influence of basic harmonic polarities and tensions, he could have set up a scheme of oppositions between flat and sharp tendencies and worked out a gradual return to the tonic as a resolution of these oppositions. As it is, the density of the thematic working itself generates ample energy, and certain local effects like the timpani reminders of A (before Fig. 16), the quasi-dominant chord before Fig. 17, and the focus on A around Fig. 18, indicate that this central section of the movement is not primarily concerned with avoiding tonic references nor with establishing a 'logical' means of recovering that tonic. The build-up of thematic polyphony nevertheless has the effect of widening the harmonic perspective to the point where no simple succession of points of focus can be plotted, and the use of a dominant preparation on E to provide a climax to the development and a link to the recapitulation is the most perfunctory effect in the movement, simply because it can scarcely be regarded as the natural outcome of the anti-tonal accumulation of the development. Instead, it stops the thematic process briefly in its tracks.

The recapitulation, beginning five bars after Fig. 25, reinforces the first movement's sonata-form background in two ways: first, it is a substantially exact review of the thematic contents of the exposition; second, modifications occur which ensure a more consistent focus on the extended A major, a process which is particularly clear if the two codettas are compared. The final tonic chord, though arrived at after a process of textural thinning-out, is the more stable for the presence of its own diatonic dominant. Ultimately, therefore, this movement is more consistently tonal than its prevailing polyphony might lead one to expect, and its principal dramatic conflict is not between contrapuntal and homophonic tendencies, nor between different groups of motivic elements, but between tendencies to tonal explicitness and tonal ambiguity. Tippett's desire to avoid too decisive a peroration in a first movement is understandable (it is remarkable that in a work of such energy all four movements should end quietly), but the final unemphatic resolution is not completely convincing in balance with the rest of the movement, and there is also a tendency to mark time thematically while more basic tonal issues are being worked out. Even so, this movement is a serious attempt to tackle major issues of form and structure at a time when most composers of symphonies were content with less challenging matters.

The second movement does not exactly advance the tonal argument of the work, principally because its eight-bar ground bass is metrically so uniform and harmonically so predictable in the way it descends chromatically from B only to turn round to the dominant F sharp at the end. The theme is stated twelve times, and, although it moves to other pitch-levels and is varied or modified, it remains curiously detached from the often hectically detailed elaboration that surrounds it. Even the build-up to its return on B at Fig. 7 lacks sufficient strength of motivation. For once Tippett seems guilty of 'eye-music', and for once a baroque precedent has let him down.

The scherzo may be less original than the passacaglia but it is a more efficient and successful piece of work. The harmonic–thematic fourths of the first movement return in what at times sounds like a Vaughan Williams country-dance, with points of harmonic focus shifting around A, B and G. The 'trio' section for strings loosens the rhythmic and textural regularities of the rest of the movement, and there is a full repeat of the scherzo. The final focus is therefore on G, the other side of the work's basic A from the slow movement's B.

In 1945 ten years had passed since Tippett had composed the finale to his first quartet, with its subtle references to fugal form and texture; since then his finales had not been fugal. The finale to the symphony is naturally more complex than that of the first quartet, but it is also even more ambitious: not just an attempt to round off this particular work, but an attempt, it seems, to exorcise Beethovenian precedent by standing it on its head and drawing a concluding harmonic–tonal question-mark out of a driving contrapuntal argument. The issue is now nothing less than the extent to which such a work needs to be 'goal-directed' at all. Indeed, the complex concerns of the final movement of the Symphony No. 3, where Beethoven is actually quoted and the issue of climactic resolution is again fundamental, are already evident in embryo here in a structure where freedom and formality are brought into a finely judged confrontation – so finely judged that it almost becomes possible to regard the tentative qualities of the second movement as deliberately contrived to strengthen the 'programme' of the symphony as a whole!

The finale of the Concerto for Double String Orchestra contained more explicit tonal and thematic contrasts than the first movement, while further clarifying their common sonata-form background. In the finale of the symphony there are also greater tonal and thematic contrasts, but the form, if undoubtedly clearer, is also undoubtedly different from that of the first movement: it is a double fugue. The first section presents six entries of the principal subject, a typically aggressive affair, with Beethovenian trills. The entries are on C sharp, F sharp, C sharp, A flat (G sharp), E flat (D sharp) and G sharp; as in the first movement, polyphonic density precludes explicit tonal progression, but when the section reaches its climax and conclusion on E naturals reiterated in a rhythm recalling the finale of Beethoven's Symphony No. 7, this is a moment of genuine illumination, not an arbitrary interruption. The second fugue begins at Fig. 5 with a more lyric subject, centred on F, and only when this new theme is well established does Tippett bring the original subject into combination and conflict with it (at four bars before Fig. 9). The sense of achievement which is felt here anticipates the orchestral jubilations of *The Midsummer Marriage*. Yet, if the composer merely allowed the flow of the music to determine the points and pitches of subject entries, the result could be dangerously random: so too could forcing entries to fit a predetermined tonal scheme when the rest of the work had not made any basic use of such schemes. Tippett achieves a satisfactory compromise at four bars after Fig. 12 by locating his most crucial combination of the themes (the first on D, the second on B flat) after a pedal F (the pitch favouring the second theme) which leads to the strongest pedal of all, on C (three bars before Fig. 14). Tonally, this tends to neutralize the argument, but purely textural intensity increases. The pedal disappears, and a new stage in the argument begins after Fig. 15, when the second theme on B flat is combined with the first on A (Ex. 17). Because the second theme is more flexible, it is able to conform to a new emphasis on A major, and this is the move which, after Fig. 16, proves necessary to prepare the coda in which E becomes the focus, not just for all the various thematic elements, but for the quite rapid slowing-down of polyphonic activity. Evolution is countered by truncation, continuity by fragmentation, goal-directed counterpoint by a non-resolving

Ex. 17 Tippett, Symphony No. 1, fourth movement (finale)

dominant focus. The whole gesture is strong enough and original enough to seem positive, not negative. Indeed, the ending of the slow movement, where a prolonged dominant does resolve on to a curiously redundant tonic, is the more negative of the two. In the finale, Tippett has devised an argument whose ambiguities and testing of implications succeed in calling the very nature of tonal composition as a goal-directed process into question: and he does it in a dramatically exciting manner, without writing a merely 'neo-classical' fugue. The String Quartet No. 3 reaped the benefits of the hard-fought structural battles evident in the symphony, but not in the sense of drawing any 'ultimate' conclusions from the finale's denial of full tonal resolution: those consequences would not emerge until more than fifteen years later. Instead, the quartet achieved a clearer marriage of tonal and textural considerations, if at the cost of a less powerfully dramatic form-scheme.

Conventional historical wisdom has it that classical composers – Beethoven above all – called on fugue to solve their 'finale problems'; to ensure that the finale was a work's crowning glory, its true goal, and the most intense and elaborate structure, when a 'relaxing rondo' or another sonata scheme might seem anti-climactic. As a texture, fugue is thematically hyperactive, even when it is not actually monothematic; but it is also tonally coherent, confirming the structural relationships between a tonic triad and its satellites as decisively as any other tonal structure, whether essentially 'harmonic' or 'contrapuntal'.

Another branch of conventional historical wisdom observes that the atonal composer who wishes to employ contrapuntal textures is under none of the constraints concerning large-scale pitch relationships or local laws of consonance and dissonance treatment which made polyphony an 'art' in the past. Indeed, apart from wishing to avoid continuations which suggest traditional relationships the atonal composer is apparently free of all rules and restrictions. An atonal fugue is certainly a rare phenomenon, while freer imitative or non-imitative polyphonic textures which can be organized in other ways abound.

The composer using extended tonality is therefore in a 'borderline' position. To the extent that he is able to retain invariant pitch relationships which contain sufficient diatonic properties for a tonic note or triad to be perceived, the idea of fugue remains a possibility. But there is the danger that an ill-defined attitude to local questions of 'consonance' and 'dissonance' may lead to a large area of structural ambiguity surrounding that central tonic assertion. The most common, and satisfactory, solution to the problem of subsidiary structural relationships in extended tonality is the Bartókian one of strong symmetrical polarities which provide a sufficiently far-reaching framework for the issue of consonance and dissonance as distinct entities to be deflected: both are emancipated. Coherence is ensured not by a particular type of chord having prominence but by a clearly defined structure radiating axially, if not symmetrically, out from a central sonority which may be a single pitch, a single interval or a much more complex aggregate.

Such schemes enable the total chromatic to be deployed in order that strong internal contrasts, oppositions, substitutions or complementations can be given positive structural significance. But, as the ending of the Symphony No. 1 shows, Tippett had developed mixed feelings about the nature and function of tonics. He was certainly not seeking techniques whereby the significance of their essential, asserted, recurrent function could be increased. Instead, he seemed to be approaching a kind of tonality without tonics, and the ending of the symphony was the latest example of what we might call tonal relativism. In the Concerto for Double String Orchestra, the concluding tonic is 'logically' prepared, but it does not function as a controlling element throughout the piece. In the symphony, the tonic is absent at the end, but the prevailing tonality survives. In the String Quartet No. 2, by contrast, a more conventional tonal role is assigned to F sharp. With all these different procedures, it is scarcely possible to argue that Tippett was on course for one particular solution, that progress in one direction alone was inevitable. One might assume that whatever happened next would be in the nature of a clarification of issues, if not a resolution of them. Yet the String Quartet No. 3, ambitious and impressive though it is, carried the quest a stage further without providing the decisive clarification. Indeed, it seems to increase the force of the argument against the need for a single, symphonic resolution.

The quartet is symmetrical in form, perhaps reflecting Tippett's awareness of the fourth and fifth quartets of Bartók; three fast fugues alternate with two slow movements. The tonal scheme retains strong diatonic characteristics, however, since both the outer movements end on C and the middle movement favours G. As for the slow movements, the first progresses without decisive commitment to a final chord of E minor, and the second, equally adept at the evasion of unambiguous tonic assertions, 'introduces' the finale by arriving on a chord of fifths (F, C, G, D) of which the bass note is C. These tonics may be held to define structure retrospectively, if they are regarded as goals: but there can be degrees of clarity in the long-term sighting of a goal, and the clue to Tippett's dramatic harmonic procedures could well lie here.

The finale of the third quartet may seem curiously mild in character; it has little of the *Grosse Fuge* about it compared with the finale of the first symphony or, of course, with the non-fugal references to that masterpiece in the fourth quartet. 'Gentle' is the composer's word for it.[3] Yet it is a good deal more purposeful, more bass-dependent, than the first movement, whose introduction, though arresting in character, provides few hints as to how a long-term harmonic process may be set in motion. The fugue subject of the first movement has enough chromatic alternation built into its considerable length to make the traditional pattern of entries (F sharp, C sharp, F sharp, C sharp) seem no more than a tribute to tradition: it is less a case of a specific tonal region being defined, or even hinted at, than of a demonstration that such local definition is in itself of limited value. Particular points of focus, like the A flat one bar after Fig. 7 where introductory material returns, have a dramatic function, but this is scarcely a significant point of large-scale tonal structure. More powerful is the balancing effect when the fugue material returns in a sharper area (from two bars after Fig. 8) in what amounts to the middle section of a substantial three-part scheme. But because the fugue material eventually returns at its original pitch-level for a final, much-concentrated section (from five bars after Fig. 14), chromaticism cannot be exorcised without the subject itself being transformed. What Tippett does is highlight smaller segments of it, allowing a residual opposition between its initial F sharp and later F natural to survive into a final cadence, which nevertheless has a distinctly temporary, unstable sound to it.

The central double fugue has impressive energy and economy: it is also less evasive about its own ultimate tonic of G, and these factors enable it to create a more satisfying vertical–horizontal equation. Here, at least, the basic points of vertical combination seem to relate beyond their own immediate context to the process of the movement as a whole. Economy also intensifies the sheer contrapuntal bravura, and the unforced wit of the non-polyphonic passages in octaves is also splendidly judged.

The finale is far less conventionally fugal than its predecessors, combining some of their thematic concentration with the polyphonic elaboration but greater textural variety of the slow movements. It is thus a remarkable synthesis as well as a tonal resolution, fluently yet eloquently approaching its final C major as a *tierce de picardie* from the flat side of the C minor in which it opens (Ex. 18). Tippett has said that its gentle 9/8 subject is 'emotionally subordinate to a 3/4 motto embedded in the texture'.[4] This motto helps to give the movement the air of a chorale prelude rather than of a strict fugue: a hint, perhaps, of the device used so much more grandly in the final stages of *The Midsummer Marriage.* Yet it is mainly in its more relaxed, freer range of textures and techniques that the finale functions so well as a crown to the work. It is far from the kind of reworking of the first movement material which Bartók favoured in his symmetrically designed quartets, but it has the greater virtue of continuing the process of clarification begun in the

Ex. 18 Tippett, String Quartet No. 3, fifth movement (finale)

céntral fugue. Nevertheless, in spite of the tonal centre of the first movement, it is difficult to feel that a single process, a 'String Quartet in C' has been concluded: it is more that a harmonious balance between various possibilities has been achieved. The quartet is as ambivalent about traditional forms as it is about traditional harmony, and in this ambivalence Tippett was to find a rich stimulus for future developments, and a future relationship with more radical tendencies.

The String Quartet No. 3 was first performed in October 1946 at the Wigmore Hall in London, and the very next month the same hall was the location for another Tippett première: that of the *Little Music* for strings, written for the tenth anniversary of the Jacques Orchestra.

Little Music offers a few hints of the early stages of *The Midsummer Marriage*, with the B flat tonality of the Prelude and Finale, and a G major Fugue whose prominent fifths anticipate Mark's 'Summer Song' from Act I of the opera. The fifths become fourths in the Finale, an exuberant yet fairly intense Vivace whose central stages expand the basic B flat major to such purpose that the bass line contains a complete, unbroken twelve-note cycle of fourths at one point (from the C two bars after Fig. 21 to the G at Fig. 22).

There was a second Tippett première in November 1946, in the shape of the brief *Preludio al Vespro di Monteverdi* for organ, which prefaced a performance of the Vespers of 1610 in the Central Hall, Westminster. But that brought the flurry of new pieces to an end. In his early forties, Tippett was about to embark on that most chancy and challenging of enterprises, a first opera in which he would serve as both librettist and composer. Moreover, he did so while still under the impact of excitement about 'an opera whose professionalism, whose quality, in the best sense of the word, was something which had not been seen in England since the single completed opera, *Dido and Aeneas*, of Henry Purcell, centuries before'.[5] Of course *Peter Grimes* was in no sense a direct influence on *The Midsummer Marriage*. But the remarkable sense of freedom and fantasy in that work could have been strengthened by the knowledge that British opera had already been reborn. In *The Midsummer Marriage* Tippett was responding to a challenge as well as to an example.

9 Britten: *Peter Grimes* (1944–5)

Britten claimed that, in *Peter Grimes*, one of his chief aims was 'to try and restore to the musical setting of the English language a brilliance, freedom and vitality that have been curiously rare since Purcell'.[1] But that oft-quoted remark was preceded by a rather more definite statement of his musical purposes, helping to explain why, despite the 'unmerciful' criticism of *Paul Bunyan*, he actually wanted to write more works for the stage. 'I am especially interested in the general architectural and formal problems of opera, and decided to reject the Wagnerian theory of "permanent melody" for the classical practice of separate numbers that crystallize and hold the emotion of a dramatic situation at chosen moments.'

There is little point in embarking here on a discussion of whether or not all sense of 'separate numbers' is lost in Wagner, and whether or not 'permanent melody' can 'crystallize and hold' emotions. Commentators on Britten have long seen the virtue of pointing out his alignment with Verdi rather than Wagner in respect of form in opera; and it clearly mattered very much to him that strong contrasts of formal and textural character should be positively exploited as the musico-dramatic action unfolded. He may well have approved of, and agreed with the kind of comparisons between Verdi and Wagner which Tippett later presented in his 'Birth of an opera' essay,[2] but he is unlikely to have seen any of his own works, as Tippett did, fusing aspects of Romantic music drama and classical opera buffa. Hans Keller, having described Wagner and Britten as 'the two opposites', points out that 'Britten, following his classical tendencies, has found undreamt-of riches in the cadential phrase.'[3]

These 'classical tendencies' also made it possible for Britten to conceive of something called 'good recitative'. This

should transform the natural intonations and rhythms of everyday speech into memorable musical phrases (as with Purcell), but in more stylized music, the composer should not deliberately avoid unnatural stresses if the prosody of the poem and the emotional situation demand them, nor be afraid of a high-handed treatment of words, which may need prolongation far beyond their common speech-length, or a speed of delivery that would be impossible in conversation.[4]

The distinction between tendencies to 'recitative' and tendencies to 'more stylized music' remains an essential formal principle in Britten's operas, alongside the tendency for certain passages to aspire to the status of 'separate numbers'. In this respect, it is significant that the composer permitted the publication of separate numbers from several of the earlier operas.

For Britten, the absence of a continuous tradition of British opera since Purcell was justification enough for his own task. From the lofty perspectives of history, it might seem ironic that someone should have attempted to create a 'living' British opera just as the entire genre was about to be condemned as moribund by post-war progressives. Certainly it was difficult to conceive after 1945 that opera could ever again become the medium for such radical innovations and new developments as it had been at various times between Monteverdi and Wagner. But this situation could have made the challenge to a 'renovating' composer the more attractive. His concern was not to find the best way in which to be novel, but to discover the form best suited to dealing with the themes which mattered most to him, and offering the greatest scope for the deployment of his preferred techniques. If opera had been relieved of the burden of advancing the development of the musical language, so much the better.

Just as Britten's views on the problems facing an opera composer were practical rather than philosophical – 'the scarcity of modern British operas is due to the limited opportunities that are offered for their performance'[5] – so his choice of subject-matter was determined less by what he felt to be the burning issues of the day than by the nature of his own most intense experiences.

For most of my life I have lived closely in touch with the sea. My parents' house in Lowestoft directly faced the sea, and my life as a child was coloured by the fierce storms that sometimes drove ships on to our coast and ate away whole stretches of the neighbouring cliffs. In writing *Peter Grimes*, I wanted to express my awareness of the perpetual struggle of men and women whose livelihood depends on the sea – difficult though it is to treat such a universal subject in theatrical form.[6]

Britten must soon have come to believe that, in such a symbol-conscious age, 'universals' could virtually be left to take care of themselves. More vital, to him, was the need to establish the right specifics for his various subjects: in particular, the social environment without which the subject itself could scarcely be brought to life. This was a need which Britten shared with the two greatest masters of progressive twentieth-century opera, Berg and Janáček, and, while their music obviously has an expressionist quality which is foreign to Britten, his operas are among the few which can confidently be regarded as worthy successors to those two definitive modern dramas of social conscience, *Wozzeck* (1914–22) and *From the House of the Dead* (1927–8).

Of the eleven stage works which Britten composed between January

1944, when *Peter Grimes* was begun, and April 1960, when *A Midsummer Night's Dream* was completed, two deal with small village communities, and centre on the contrasts between the collective activities or conventional ideas of the majority and the loneliness and misery of discontented individuals. In *Peter Grimes* and *Albert Herring* the collective life of the quay, the inn, the church, and the shop provide the background against which the idiosyncrasies of the principal character stand out. Collective activity is also important in *A Midsummer Night's Dream*, though here the dramatic tension is not so much between a single misfit and the rest as between various groups and individuals: fairies and mortals, the two pairs of lovers, fairy king and fairy queen. In *Gloriana*, by contrast, it is the isolation of the aging monarch from the whole nation which is depicted. And in *The Turn of the Screw* there is little sense of either community or nation; only a small, isolated group – not even a family – and the ghosts which haunt it.

All these operas are 'peacetime' works. But *The Rape of Lucretia* and *Billy Budd* take place as war rages in the background, and the conflicts between duty and conscience which they present are the more intense in view of the implicit assumption that war itself is the ultimate immorality, the outer, explicit expression of violence which makes individual peace of mind within a community affected by war impossible to attain. Such concerns could account for Britten's lack of interest, after *Paul Bunyan*, in a subject such as Tippett chose for *The Midsummer Marriage*, in which the everyday and the marvellous interact. Not until *The Turn of the Screw* did Britten again admit the supernatural, and then as an entirely destructive force. After that, as a complete contrast and an immediate response to the world tour which Britten made in 1955–6, come the exoticisms of the ballet *The Prince of the Pagodas*, with its reflections of the sound of Gamelan music. And the next full-length opera, following on from the miracle-theme of *Noye's Fludde*, was his only exercise in the comedy of the supernatural, *A Midsummer Night's Dream*. Here, of course, the supernatural is, if occasionally sinister, hardly of profound spiritual significance. Britten would always retain the distinction between the sinister, secular associations of the supernatural, and the spiritual power of the miraculous.

It may well be true that Britten's instinctive sympathies and predispositions led him to subjects which involved these various features. It is also true that by the mid-1940s his musical language had developed to a point where it could best fulfil itself through the extended treatment of such themes. In this respect, Britten's transition to opera, like Tippett's, was stylistically motivated. There was no question of needing to develop a new style to suit the new form.

Britten's fluency as a music-dramatist depended on the flexible

97

application of a very simple formal principle, or scale of procedures, in which the successive stages of the action are unified and related by exact or varied recurrences of material. Indeed, his development as an opera composer may best be described in terms of the testing and elaboration of some more far-reaching unifying principle for each work than is provided by recurring motives alone. But, in the four full-length operas of the period 1944 to 1951, the build-up of individual scenes, and the similarity of technique underlying the diverse and inspired response to the greatest variety of dramatic situations, provide the real key to the structure of the whole, and to the success of each individual work.

Naturally, therefore, everything depends on the appropriateness, memorability and malleability of the recurrent elements, and *Peter Grimes* is exemplary in the immediacy with which the technique is demonstrated. The Prologue has as its determining ritornello the first four-bar orchestral statement, which characterizes the pompous lawyer–coroner Swallow and, more generally, the rigid, unsympathetic Borough society. The theme itself is not initially unstable, nor does it focus on a non-diatonic tritone, like other more important motives in the work. But its motion from B flat to A (Ex. 19a) outlines one type of instability, the tension between notes a semitone apart, which actually spans the entire opera – a feature shared with *The Midsummer Marriage.*

The recurrences of this initial phrase and its offshoots are frequent enough to bind the scene together in simple formal terms: its first completely diatonic statement is at Fig. 2 (Ex. 19b). Thereafter the semiquaver figure depicting rumour and gossip becomes its most important derivative (it is taken from the setting of Swallow's words 'Why did you do this?') until all the material is welded into a paragraph which fixes B flat as a central tonality. Contrasting material in the Prologue is provided by Grimes's arioso-like phrases with their sparse chordal accompaniments: only the three-note bass figure at Figs. 1 and 6 seems to promise something more melodic in character. Clearly, Grimes is oppressed and repressed: not until his first exchanges with Ellen Orford, which provide a transition to Act I, does a lyric line emerge, and in a context of extreme tonal tension, only gradually moving on to E, the dominant of A.

There are of course important respects in which Britten's operas amplify the formal procedures of his smaller-scale works. Certainly the technique of 'frames and repetitions' is fundamental to *Peter Grimes,* since the music which begins Act I Scene 1 returns in the final scene of Act III. In Act I Scene 1 the chorus has five stanzas, in Act III Scene 2 three stanzas. Two other elements complete the form-schemes of these scenes: the ritornello-like recurrences in the orchestra which continue the 'First Sea Interlude' material, and the distinctive interjections of the

Ex. 19a Britten, *Peter Grimes*, Prologue

Ex. 19b Britten, *Peter Grimes*, Prologue

various Borough residents, of whom Auntie is the first to be heard in Act I and the last in Act III. But *Peter Grimes* works so well as the unfolding of a dramatic tale because of the way a progressive accumulation of tension is projected across the small-scale frame and refrain forms, a progressiveness particularly evident when material from one section is carried over into others. The Dawn music of Act I does not merely underpin the first choral scene but returns, after the episode of the capstan, to permeate the discussion between Keene and Hobson (Fig. 23). As for Hobson's own straightforward single stanza, this is not merely taken up – a minor ninth – by Ellen Orford (Fig. 27), but forms the bass for the ensuing choral reproach of Ellen. Such economical extension of material is always dramatically appropriate as well as musically illuminating. Perhaps the most striking example of it comes in the 'lynch' chorus of Act III (Fig. 41), where the mob transforms the banal *Ländler* dance-tune which has been heard earlier off-stage. Such thematic interconnections, like the recurrences of the principal motives themselves, reveal the dynamic fusion of music and drama in the simplest possible way. And it could be argued that the dramatic climax of the work is its simplest and most concentrated episode; the first part of Act III Scene 2. Apart from having the most persistent internal recurrences, this episode takes most of its material from earlier in the opera. Its form is controlled by the repeated fog-horn E flat, which is at once a 'tonic' to the huge choral build-up of the previous scene, and the tritonal opposite of the troubled A major of the opera's framing chorus. Together with the E flat there is also the repeated 'dominant seventh' chord (which has characterized Grimes in the Prologue), and the off-stage cries of Grimes's name, which take a variety of forms, including one (the dolce E flat triad) which is 'out of character' for the vengeful chorus, but which evokes the tenderness of Ellen, whom Grimes is remembering at this point (Ex. 19c). The scene is a concentrated compendium of earlier material, a free fantasia held together by the accompanying repetitions. The threads are drawn together in an understated manner which is most moving, even if the abandonment of music for speech at the end of the scene always seems false.

The recurrent fog-horn pedal can even be seen as the most concentrated representation of a principle of repetition which is evident in the passacaglia bass and in strophic songs. The Interlude between the scenes of Act II is of course a proper passacaglia, and other sections of the work – the Act I Round, the Act II Hymn and Canticle, and the Act III dance music – employ forms built up from small-scale repetitions. The clearest use of strophic form can be found in the Nieces' duet (Act I, Fig. 67) with its sequence of similar statements separated into two main parts by Balstrode's interjections. Auntie's ensuing song (Fig. 68) also

Ex. 19c Britten, *Peter Grimes*, Act III Scene 2

takes the form of two verses with a refrain: a third verse is cut off after its first two notes (Fig. 69). But these, and other similar episodes – one of the most beautiful is Ellen's two-stanza song after Fig. 10 of Act II – can only function within a much larger form-scheme, by virtue of their very clear-cut internal organization. The inn scene, Act I Scene 2, is exemplary here. Scene 1 has been most crucially underpinned by the change from the calm Dawn music to the stormy figuration which first explodes in the fugal ensemble (Fig. 31). But Scene 2 is wholly controlled by the brief recurrences of the storm music which has developed from Scene 1 through the second Interlude. These recurrences may be the merest punctuation, coinciding with the opening and closing of the door, but there are five of them before the climactic outburst at the end of the Round (Fig. 83) which is carried over to the end of the scene, and they determine the character of the music, as well as defining the stages of the form.

Much of what is most impressive in *Peter Grimes* derives from the diversity of formal schemes and dramatic situations. For example, the simplest collective expressions, like the opening and closing choral scenes, which contain only brief comments from individuals, are not simply stanzaic in form, but rooted in mixed A major–minor harmony which focuses on the prevailing harmonic tensions of the work. At the opposite extreme from stanzaic or framed forms is the evolving solo scene, like most of Act II Scene 2, where Grimes moves through a wide range of moods, and recurrent elements are much more localized, though the unity of the work is reinforced by references to music from Act I and Act II Scene 1. The plot enabled the composer to employ large-scale numbers (especially ensembles with chorus) but there is usually one character to provide an element of contrast: the exceptions are the 'storm' fugue of Act I and the 'lynch' chorus of Act III.

The connection between subject and structure which analysts of *Peter Grimes* have most commonly noted is the way in which Grimes's irreconcilable conflicts – primarily between his desire to find security and respectability and his instinct to preserve his isolation by acts of cruelty and irrationality – find reflection in the exploitation of tritonal and semitonal opposition, both within themes and between larger areas of tonal emphasis. Britten is able to engage the central character in music so effectively simply because Grimes is more than a negative anti-hero. He is too impulsive to be consistent in his behaviour, and the opera hinges on his capacity for being cruel to children while idealizing women. Britten's musical response to this is remarkable, for while both the sadism and the sentimentality are admitted, and are brought into memorable conjunction in both scenes of Act II, they are treated with a sympathy which eliminates any distasteful or mawkish overtones. One critic has even argued that the power of the music in *Grimes* is so remarkable that 'we accept the self-contradictory figure of Peter, and imagine him to be an entity corresponding to the musical organisation which we encounter' – the 'self-contradiction' having arisen from the librettist's attempt to whitewash the Peter of Crabbe's poem 'to gain him sympathy', and then being 'forced back . . . into something nearer Crabbe's original conception . . . Crabbe's Peter is struggling with

Slater's Peter'.[7] The Britten–Slater Grimes is certainly a figure of contradictions, but his impulsiveness and irrationality are made plausible, rather than ennobling or logical, by the musical ideas and the way in which they are organized. The character is certainly different from, and perhaps less straightforward than Crabbe's: but Britten found the musical means to bring that character convincingly to life.

Discussion of *Peter Grimes* still tends to centre on its novelty, the phenomenon of the long-delayed rebirth of British opera being launched by a composer whose instinctive sense of the lyrical and dramatic was expressed in so direct and approachable a manner that to look for sources and influences seemed irrelevant. But even early commentators were intrigued by the closeness of the 'We strained into the wind' theme to a prominent idea from Mahler's Symphony No. 5, and more recently other pertinent associations have been noted. Eric Walter White has shrewdly observed the influence of radio drama in the rapid shifts and interplay of the inn scene;[8] while Bayan Northcott has made the still more striking suggestion that 'Peter Grimes is audibly steeped in *Porgy and Bess'.*[9] Such ideas indicate that there is still much to be learned about a work which, although it may not surpass certain earlier compositions of Britten's simply 'as music', exercised the greatest influence on his own further development.

10 Britten: The *Donne Sonnets* and the String Quartet No. 2 (1945)

During the ten years from 1944 to 1954 Britten composed no fewer than six full-length operas and a considerable number of other vocal works. The only substantial instrumental composition of the period is the String Quartet No. 2, completed on 14 October 1945 and with the same dedicatee – Mrs J. L. Behrend – as Tippett's Quartet No. 3 (1946). In 1946 Britten wrote two shorter works on themes by other composers: the *Young Person's Guide to the Orchestra* and the Prelude and Fugue for organ on a theme of Vittoria. Four years then elapsed before the composition of a third such work, the *Lachrymae, Reflections on a Song of John Dowland*, dated April 1950. The brief *Six Metamorphoses after Ovid* for oboe solo followed in the spring of 1951; but the emphasis on vocal music is as striking during this period as the sheer fertility which enabled Britten to produce a stream of such memorable works at a time when he was closely involved in the setting up of the Aldeburgh Festival, and in increasing demand as a concert performer.

The Holy Sonnets of John Donne op. 35 were completed in August

1945, six months after *Peter Grimes*. This is Britten's only cycle, apart from *A Charm of Lullabies* op. 41 (December 1947), between the Serenade of 1943 and *Winter Words* of 1953. Its use of the sonnet form naturally recalls the Michelangelo cycle. Here, however, the subject-matter is neither pastoral nor passionately romantic, but firmly fixed on sickness, death and loss. In the Keats sonnet which ends the Serenade, sleep seals the 'hushéd casket' of the soul in an image of tenderness and peace: but the soul invoked in Donne's first line is a black soul, summoned by sickness, 'death's herald and champion'. An immediate cause of this deepening and darkening of Britten's chosen imagery can easily be found in the fact that the cycle was composed when he was ill and under the impact of revelations about the concentration camps immediately after the end of the war. But although the opening of the cycle is Britten's grimmest and most uncompromising yet, the work ends positively, with the note of Christian hope which is so significantly absent from *Peter Grimes,* and which was to be rather uncomfortably grafted on to *The Rape of Lucretia.*

Belief and doubt, the 'health' of innocence and the 'sickness' of experience, are the familiar themes of Britten's chosen texts. But one enthusiasm of Britten's – an enthusiasm he shared with Tippett – had a directly musical significance, and that was his devotion to the English music of the later seventeenth and eighteenth centuries. True, there had been earlier evidence of a neo-classicizing interest in baroque 'gestures', most obviously in the first song of *On This Island.* But after *Peter Grimes* Britten seemed to have gained a greater confidence, not merely in his own true heritage, but also in his own position as a positive continuer of that heritage: hence the Purcell arrangements, and the adaptation of *The Beggars' Opera.* Yet Britten managed to avoid any kind of confrontation between overtly neo-classical tendencies and a language rooted in non-British, late-Romantic extensions and questioning of eighteenth-century tonal structures. After all, the greatest neo-classical composers, Bartók and Stravinsky, had both moved a good deal farther away from late-Romantic roots than Britten would ever do, and it remained true that Mahler was a greater influence on Britten's style than Purcell. Purcell's influence was technical in the sense of encouraging economy, a paring-down with no loss of expressivity: but Britten was never in any danger of attempting to outdo the late-Romantic Mahler in emotional extravagance, and Purcell was just one exemplar – Mozart and Stravinsky were others – to confirm his overriding belief that 'control' was the one essential element of good compositional technique. Britten was also able to synthesize 'folk' and 'art' elements with unique effect in his folk-song arrangements. And all this was possible because, by the mid-1940s, he was sufficiently assured and in control of his still evolving style and still developing technique to ensure that any new components were effortlessly absorbed. The evidence of the music seems to suggest that Britten would never admit a new technical feature until it could be safely accommodated, and this may be the reason why so long a period elapsed before he found it possible to incorporate a serial element into his music.

The *Donne Sonnets* show Britten's characteristic balance between the linear, stepwise harmonic motions, which convey chromatic tension most directly, and the overriding structural prolongations and progressions which ensure a firm foundation. Appropriately, the most remarkable balance between the simple and complex, the ornamental and funda- mental, can be perceived in the ninth and last sonnet, which was also the last to be composed. The chaconne bass, though of great rhythmic subtlety, outlines the B major triad in such a way that the D sharp and F sharp seem more prominent than the B itself. The first five statements of the theme do not substantially modify its 'floating stability', but the sixth to ninth statements bring forward the lowest note, the D sharp, as a temporary point of focus, and provoke a conflict between this and the D naturals which arise from a neighbour-note motion concordantly harmonizing the F sharp as a first inversion triad of D major (Ex. 20). The third section of the movement, comprising the final three statements of the bass (the twelfth and last extended to provide the root position B major ending), confidently dismisses this chromatic tension; but a more basic tension is sustained through the sheer strength of the linear motion, and the way it ultimately clarifies its most essential elements. The final sonnet is, in a sense, an enormous expansion of the B major triad which has been built up gradually (and then virtually lost) in the first sonnet. There, too, the broadly spaced stepwise motions and persistent chromatic colouring of a more conventional chordal kind also make

Ex. 20 Britten, *The Holy Sonnets of John Donne*, No. 9, 'Death, be not proud'

sense primarily as a long-term projection of a single process: F sharp
yielding to G, then returning as a component of the chord of B major or
minor. This powerful setting contains two principal processes: thirty out
of a total of forty-two bars comprise the prolongation of the dominant
note, which approaches the auxiliary G of bar 23 with a process of
increasing complexity. The prolongation of the tonic triad begins at the
point where the vocal line recapitulates the melody originally harmonized

by the dominant note in octaves. Once again the bass moves by step on to G before a B major triad is established, and this survives for the final four bars of the song, though it loses its third in the last two and a half bars. Although the harmonic goal of this song may be regarded as the B major triad, it is certainly not a framing tonic sonority to the extent that, for example, the C minor triad of the second Michelangelo sonnet is such a sonority. The tension between the claims of major and minor third, so evident in the vocal line throughout, is therefore given much-needed perspective by the strongly asserted dominant–tonic relation of the accompaniment; and the process of completion is also a process of re-establishing the initial octave position of the upper F sharp.

The particularly crucial ambiguity of the enharmonic alternation of D sharp and E flat which can be observed in the notation of the vocal line in the first phrase of the first sonnet, and at the climax of the last, at 'why swell'st thou then?', can also be seen as an indication of a large-scale tonal process, since five of the settings are centred on B and its diatonic relatives (E, F sharp, D) and four on C minor and its relatives G minor and E flat (major and minor). In particular, after Nos. 6 and 7 have stressed the opposition between the two tonal 'directions' — No. 6 in E flat, No. 7 in D — the last two sonnets integrate them. No. 8 is in E flat minor, but at the end Britten makes audible the fact that its tonic chord has two notes in common with the B major of No. 9. It would naturally be gratifying to discover that the composer himself had seen the whole cycle as a working-out of the initial incompatibility of B minor and C minor as presented in the first two sonnets. Because such conflicts between centres a semitone apart are so frequently found in other works, it seems unlikely, to say the least, to have been wholly accidental.

The String Quartet No. 2 was completed less than two months after the *Donne Sonnets,* on 14 October 1945. As Britten's last non-vocal sonata-type work for fifteen years (the next was the Cello Sonata of 1961, also in C major), it has occasionally been scanned by those who hope to find conclusive evidence of some fundamental incompatibility between the composer and purely instrumental forms which only became fully apparent after the composition of his first successful opera. If the quartet is flawed, however, it is not because of any lack of imagination or inspiration. Its flaws are rather the result of an ambitious attempt to advance beyond previous achievements and not the consequence of some inherent clumsiness which overtook the composer when he sought once more to do without a text.

In outline the quartet most closely resembles the *Sinfonia da Requiem*, with two slower movements enclosing a single fast one. In the quartet, however, the central movement functions more as an 'entr'acte' between the massive but very different structures of the outer movements. In their official timings the quartet, at 31 minutes, is half as long again as the 20-minute *Sinfonia*, and there is much less sense of a symmetrical single span in the quartet; there are no 'attaccas' here.

The main flaw of the quartet lies in the first movement, which has the most memorable and appealing material, but the least convincing structure. The idea of a sonata-form scheme in which three facets of an extended lyric theme are exposed successively, then, at the climax, superimposed in a compressed recapitulation, might sound novel and attractive in theory, but in practice it produces a movement of peculiar proportions and uncertain direction. In the 148-bar exposition, the problem is principally one of contrast, or the inappropriate placing of it, and this problem is not solved by regarding the exposition as a double one on the lines of those in classical concertos. The first paragraph presents the three related melodic statements focused on C, G and D respectively, and followed by a developmental transition centring on a complex chord which has G as its bass note. The new material in this transition is the main agent of the more lively mood which ensues in the 'animato' (from Letter B), but which offers only a rather routine contrapuntal exercise around this new material. The note C is reasserted as principal focus, and some development of one of the main ideas follows over a pedal C (from Letter C). If this were the first stage of concentrated working-out, leading to tonal as well as thematic argument, the scheme might well succeed, but it turns out that both these paragraphs, between Letters B and D (still, of course, basically in the tonic), comprise a bridge passage to a second group which is itself an expansion of the second 'clause' of the first paragraph, just as the third clause is subsequently expanded into a long codetta. The problem, then, is that the lyric mood and material are reinforced at Letter D, just when really strong contrast is needed. There is certainly tonal contrast here, and a sense that the material is continuing to evolve, but the loss of formal control is unmistakable, and increases as the bridge material is brought back at Letter G to protract the exposition still further. Although the development proper does build up tonal and thematic tension as far as Letter K, this too is dissipated in a central episode before the effective preparation of the compressed recapitulation (Letters L to M). It is not so much that the exposition fails to balance the remainder of the movement (development plus recapitulation), but that the exposition itself lacks the necessary momentum. The lyric and dramatic aspects make uneasy partners, and the basic tonality of C is not as effectively challenged as the immediately established tonic of such a vast structure needs to be: only in the last bars of the development does a truly tonal drama spring into focus. It might be that a more strongly contrasted theme at Letter D (in shape if not in mood) would have served better, and less transitional padding would also have been desirable. In this, as in other matters, the more concentrated first movement of the String Quartet No. 1 is more successful, its evident diversities engaged in an attractively paced argument. The first movement of the second quartet attempts three things at once: to be more economical in material, more expansive in design, and more explicitly unified in spirit. Maybe Britten was trying to integrate his responses to both Mozart and Mahler, and for once one even feels that some kind of progressive tonality would have served the composer's purpose better: but whatever lies behind the music, and whatever its weaknesses, it is certainly very much Britten's own.

The ternary second movement, in which each of the three parts is tripartite in turn, is simpler, shorter and, as tonal drama, more successful. The first part only establishes the central C as the root of minor triads at Letter A, the start of its middle section, and then retains this focus for the recapitulation. The focus shifts to F for a 'Trio', which has neat thematic links with the main scherzo material, and the episode ends with an apparent dominant preparation. The scherzo returns, but skilfully varied, and with the bass stressing C sharp, not C natural, until, after cleverly controlled stepwise motions and some subtle anticipations, a C major triad is achieved, just before the coda turns back to minor arpeggiations. The prominent B flat here is important in that the finale's chaconne theme progresses chromatically from B flat to C, and it is in the harmonic tension between these two pitches that the movement's structure is founded. In *Les Illuminations* Britten had given prominence to a C major triad with B flat, enshrining in an ambiguous chord the major second which was such a stimulus to his imagination. In the Quartet No. 2 the chaconne theme is more a homage to Purcell than an anticipation of the 12-note variation theme used in *The Turn of the Screw*. And even if the mass of rather repetitive figuration makes the movement seem overlong, and the cadenzas diffuse the structure still further, it retains a powerful grip through tonal planning alone: more precisely, through the presentation of various solutions to the problem of how such a chromatic theme can be harmonized at all.

In the first of the finale's four main parts (the theme and the first six variations) the process of conflict is initiated. For three variations, C is the principal focus (indeed, it is a pedal in the third) but the superstructure grows increasingly neutral in order to accommodate the B flat, which itself assumes the role of a pedal bass (Fig. 5): it is then the turn of the C to sound extraneous in the upper parts. The combinations and alternations of the two pitches are elaborately projected, but perhaps the most important event of all is the setting aside of both in the early stages of the third part, after Fig. 14, and the long process of approach to

109

resolution which begins with the alternations of G and C in the bass at Fig. 16. In a movement which has remarkably few pure triads, the C major clarification at the end of the third part (nine bars after Fig. 19) is especially important, and in the final part, although the opposition is if anything intensified, it is on the basis of B flat and E flat clashing with, but failing to contradict, the increasingly strong and stable C (Ex. 21).

Ex. 21 Britten, String Quartet No. 2, III Chacony (finale)

111

11 Britten: *The Rape of Lucretia* and *Albert Herring* (1946-7)

Peter Grimes was an immediate and substantial success. But the prepara-tions for the first production were anything but happy, and appear to have been the kind of experience which could have permanently deterred a musician less familiar than Britten with the stresses, strains, prejudices and tantrums of life in the theatre. *Peter Grimes* reveals a natural flair for the traditional kind of opera, involving pit and proscenium: indeed, it was hailed by many precisely because it demonstrated that a British composer could succeed in the medium of Mozart, Verdi, Wagner and Strauss. To the opera-going public, understandably, innovation mattered less than the convincing use of well-tried procedures.

Britten soon answered the practical question of how to follow up his own success, and exploit his own ability, while minimizing the problems inherent in relying on a production company to which he did not really belong and which had little sympathy for him. *The Rape of Lucretia* was first performed at the post-war re-opening of Glyndebourne on 12 July 1946, and could therefore have used larger forces than it actually did. It was the possibilities for chamber opera which that work pioneered which acted as a further stimulus to the establishment of the English Opera Group, guaranteeing the composer at least a degree of independence of the larger London opera houses.

To describe *Lucretia* as a 'pioneering' work might seem misleading, since British opera contained the fine precedents of *Dido* and *Sāvitri*; nor had *Paul Bunyan* required large orchestral forces. But *Lucretia* was nevertheless a new venture for Britten. The dawning of 'the age of austerity' might have suggested to him that a new approach to stage presentation could be adopted which, if it did not get music drama out of the theatre, would at least make it independent of conventionally designed opera houses. The possibilities which Stravinsky had explored during the First World War in *Renard* and *The Soldier's Tale* remained to be followed up, and in Britain the best-known piece of 'music theatre' was a superior cabaret entertainment, the Walton–Sitwell *Façade*, which had not been followed up either. 'Grand Opera' would still be possible when the subject-matter demanded it, but meanwhile more intimate themes could be exploited more intensely if fewer singers and players were involved. Not until the Church Parables of the 1960s, with a prelude in the form of *Noye's Fludde* (1957), would Britten escape from both pit and proscenium. But the more intimate scale of the chamber operas fitted in well with his avowed desire 'to tear all the waste away'. One may in fact regret that after *Peter Grimes* he seldom seems to have attempted to 'achieve perfect clarity of expression' through enrichment as well as intensification. But, in stating that 'music for me is clarification',[1] and in contrasting himself with Schoenberg, Britten revealed that anything smacking of an expansively grand manner would always be achieved against the grain: and so the overwhelming climaxes of *Billy Budd*, *Gloriana*, and the *War Requiem* may be savoured all the more for their relative rarity.

It was Eric Crozier, the producer of *Peter Grimes*, who suggested the subject of *The Rape of Lucretia* to Britten; but apart from their climactic suicides, the subject-matter of the two works is as different as the literary style of the texts. *Lucretia*, with its obvious analogies to the story of *Dido and Aeneas*, is the only operatic theme of Britten's, apart from the biblical episodes of the Church Parables, to retreat past Shakespeare into antiquity; and much of the special character of the work stems from the sense in which the ancient characters are made contemporary, in speech if not behaviour. The one great modern precedent for the musico-theatrical treatment of a classical subject (much more 'ancient', of course, than *Lucretia*) is the Stravinsky–Cocteau *Oedipus Rex*, a work which Britten described in a diary entry for 12 February 1936 as 'one of the peaks of Stravinsky's output'.[2] Even so, he was not completely convinced by it. 'Another hard nut to crack is the typical later-Stravinsky method of the drama. The combination of set, stylized sections in the music, the Latin words, the masks worn by most of the actors, give the impression of an impersonal comment on Sophocles rather than a re-enaction of the drama.'[3] Of course, Britten would find a use for masks himself in later years. But in 1946 he was still so opposed to 'impersonal comment' that in *Lucretia* he accepted the need for narrators who, while nominally outside the action, react very directly to it. At all costs the 'old' story and the ancient characters must be given contemporary relevance and not merely, as in *Oedipus Rex*, a contemporary framework; and this must be done not only by their mode of expression, but by the introduction – at the composer's insistence – of Christian sentiments and interpretation.

Britten's early reaction to *Oedipus Rex* is of great interest, though he may well have thought differently about the work ten years later, and grown able to accept that its cumulative impact is far from impersonal or detached. What *Oedipus* 'lacks', if that is the right word – and in spite of its hints of Italian operatic style – is any vestige of the naturalistic or realistic traditions of nineteenth-century opera. The emotions could not be more real, but the action is highly stylized. By contrast, *The Rape of Lucretia* attempts a blend of naturalism and stylization in its presentation which, to some extent at least, matches the blend of pagan and Christian imagery in its treatment. *Oedipus Rex* is an overwhelming study of the consequences of guilt. But *Lucretia* is less about innocence, in the sense in which this quality normally occurs in Britten, than about virtue. It is made abundantly clear that Lucretia is a woman of experience, but of experience 'within the law'. It is the loss of virtue, not the loss of innocence, which destroys her, and she swings between restraint and passion as disconcertingly as the drama swings between the formalized and the naturalistic.

The 'tone' of Ronald Duncan's libretto has aroused strong feelings, both for and against. Its verbal flights, expressed in such concentrated form, must have presented the composer with considerable problems, and its erotic imagery is closer in spirit to the heterosexual ecstasies of *The Midsummer Marriage* than to anything else in Britten. The hysterical build-ups to the rape and Lucretia's suicide offer both Duncan and Britten at their least plausible. But the treatment of the rape itself has a stark power which ensures that its pivotal role in the drama is neither shirked nor laboured.

Seekers for similarities between *Grimes* and *Lucretia* will note that Britten uses interludes to ensure musical continuity during changes of scene in both works, though in *Lucretia* the interludes can be vocal, since the narrators are outside the action. The narrators 'frame' the action of *Lucretia* much in the way that, after the Prologue, the chorus frames the action of *Grimes*, and the tonal organization corresponds in the two works to the extent that both end where they begin – once again excluding the Prologue to *Grimes*, and accepting that in *Lucretia* the Prologue as far as letter G is preludial to the main structure. Though *Lucretia* is in only two acts, it also retains the formal principle of dividing each act into two large scenes, each subdivisible and linked by an interlude. As in *Grimes*, again, the subdivision of each scene may be compared to the extent that each approaches a strophic or simple rondo form – unified by recurrences of distinguishable musical material. Such recurrences may be basically harmonic, as with the punctuating chords of the first scene's introductory recitative, or as melodic as the passacaglia theme of the final scene. There is a particularly striking set of strophic variations in the chorale-like central interlude of Act II, while extreme, alternating contrasts occur in the first main scene of Act I (from Fig. 8) between the male chorus's musings and the drinking repartee of the Roman generals (Ex. 22).

Peter Evans's analysis of the opera has demonstrated the extent to

Ex. 22 Britten, *Rape of Lucretia*, Act I Scene 1

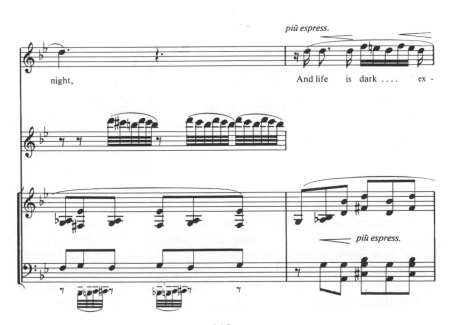

cept where wine sheds light......................

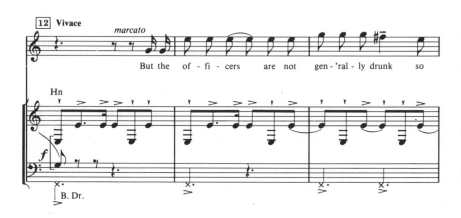

12 Vivace

marcato

But the of - fi - cers are not gen - 'ral - ly drunk so

Hn

B. Dr.

which unifying controls over thematic and tonal–harmonic aspects of the music have been exercised by Britten.[4] Yet the work scarcely makes a wholly unified, or even coherent, impression, simply because of the sheer range of dramatic characteristics which it possesses. The most startling, in the prevailingly serious, even sanctimonious context of the dénouement itself, is the ending of Act I. In Act III of *Peter Grimes*, the little 'Goodnight' ensemble provides a moment of effectively placed lightness before the tragedy enters its final phase. But even in *Grimes* the treat-

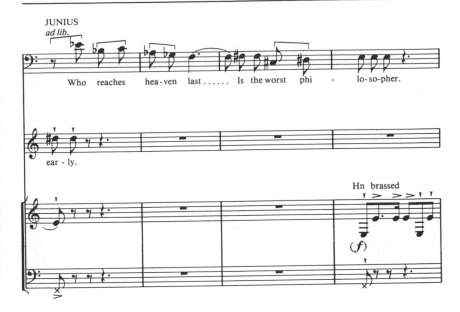

ment of Mrs Sedley, with her 'murder most foul it is', is set apart from the honest hypocrisies of most of the other Borough worthies and given an element of caricature which might seem dangerously at odds with the prevailingly serious tone were it not for the effectiveness of its distancing irony. All the more remarkable, in *Lucretia*, is the ironic effect when 'all, with due formality, wish each other a final good night'. The formality is vital, of course, since Tarquinius's violation of established social convention is an essential element in the drama. After the crude onomatopoeia of the ride to Rome, the ensemble provides a superbly 'down-beat' conclusion to the Act. The trouble is that nothing in the rest of the work, save for the moment of common sense when Lucretia's old nurse Bianca tries to stop the messenger fetching Collatinus, rings so true. And it would have been far more effective to end with the anger of Collatinus, and retribution for Tarquinius, than with consolation for those who have observed Lucretia's unnecessary death. The cold-war relevance of lines like

> All tyrants fall though tyranny persists,
> Though crowds disperse the mob is never less.
> For violence is the fear within us all,
> And tragedy the measurement of man

still seems a good deal more memorable than the male chorus's final 'sermon', however. Perhaps the opera should have concerned itself more with the consequences of violence, and risked a more explicit treatment of the analogy between war and rape.

In the Epilogue's attempt to disperse the stark horror of unnecessary suffering and death, there is a preview of the much more ambiguous but not wholly dissimilar attempt at the end of *Billy Budd* to suggest that Budd did not die in vain. It may be that Britten himself never decided whether there was any solid ground between the rejection or acceptance of all the tenets of Christianity. But his music remained consistently more successful at expressing doubt than certainty, despair rather than hope. 'Is it all?' Maybe – or maybe not.

Lucretia is an ambitious, uneasy work, untypical of Britten; indeed, its verse-drama orientation and attempt to place feminine psychology at the centre of the action tell us more about librettist than composer. But the music never sounds weakly disengaged from its subject, and the liberating effect of writing for a large chamber ensemble may well have compensated Britten as he wrestled with the complexities of the text and the motivations of the characters. Once more, the consequences of this sense of freedom were to take a long time – almost twenty years – to be fully realized: in the conductorless, much more freely notated textures of the church operas. But although *Lucretia*'s immediate companion piece was to have a very different subject (or at least a very different kind of text and location) the orchestra required for *Albert Herring* is identical, with the minor difference that the oboist is not required to double on English horn. In particular, alto flute and bass clarinet are as important to the tone colour of *Herring* as they are to *Lucretia*.

The Rape of Lucretia and *Albert Herring* share one other common feature: both are derived from French originals – *Lucretia* from a play by André Obey, *Herring* from a story by de Maupassant. But while *Lucretia* could hardly be transposed from Rome, de Maupassant's tale suffers not at all by being transported to a Suffolk community of rather different character, if not wholly dissimilar content, from that of Grimes's Borough. *Herring* is, of course, a comic opera, and comedy, as something more 'down to earth' than tragedy, is often more naturalistic, more true to life. In comic opera, where the humour must be more the result of character and situation than of purely verbal wit, the establishment of character often means the employment of caricature, though perhaps more often in the way parts are performed than in the way they are written.

If it is difficult to discover a clear precedent for *Herring*, that is no doubt because there are so few even moderately successful twentieth-century comic operas. Indeed, it is surely the case that no purely comic opera of major significance has been composed since Verdi's *Falstaff*. Apart from Strauss's 'comédies sentimentales' – most notably *Der*

118

Rosenkavalier and *Capriccio* – and anti-romantic farces like Prokofiev's *The Love of Three Oranges*, comedy has not found favour, though Tippett has argued that *The Midsummer Marriage* is, above all else, a transcendental comedy in its concern with love and marriage. *Albert Herring* is, clearly, neither a Savoy frolic nor an Aldwych farce; nor does it achieve the Mozartian comic ideal of illuminating character in depth through a series of misunderstandings and confusions. Perhaps for the closest precedent we should look to the cinema, and to the appealing Chaplinesque persona of the put-upon little man who wins through in the end; or to such fictional characters as H. G. Wells's Mr Polly. Albert undeniably matures during the course of the opera, if only so far – he does not, after all, get the girl – but he at least ceases to be the butt of all and sundry, and turns the tables on his fiercest critic, his mother. There is certainly more than a touch of the 'fool who becomes wise' about him.

Britten's music conveys Albert's essential timidity very skilfully, and the best scene, which can create a genuine shock in a good performance, is that in which his 'break-out' is provoked by his involuntary witnessing of Sid and Nancy's embrace. There is true pathos in Albert's sense of frustration and inadequacy, and the shallowness of most of the other characters seems the greater in comparison. Indeed, in the way a kind of voyeurism leads to a deep illumination, the scene looks forward in atmosphere a quarter of a century of *Death in Venice*.

In *Peter Grimes* most of the local worthies are motivated by delight in power, on however small a scale, and turn naturally to persecution of any whose faces fail to fit. Herring's Loxford is rather less sinister a place than the Borough, but even here the pressures and claustrophobia of convention can be strongly sensed. One thing which prevents the characters from being mere caricatures is the precise depiction of the environment in which they are placed, and this skill, so closely allied to Britten's feeling for pointed musical economy, was to remain evident throughout his career. Even without the precise natural framework of sun, sea and storm which is so powerfully evoked in *Peter Grimes*, the social hierarchy of Loxford is neatly sketched in. As in *Grimes*, moreover, that hierarchy is most effective and menacing when it acts with maximum unanimity – as it does when Albert reappears after his night on the tiles and everyone realizes that he is not dead after all.

It is in Act III of *Albert Herring* that the possibility of an element of *Grimes*-parody occurs to the attentive listener: not only does Mum's 'all that I did' have a similar chromatic dolefulness to Mrs Sedley's 'murder most foul it is', but the rapid cross-questioning of Albert recalls the inquest in the *Grimes* Prologue: both scenes include the words 'the whole truth and nothing but the truth'. There are certainly more associations between the manner and method of *Herring* and *Grimes* than

119

between *Herring* and *Lucretia*, even if the issue of 'virtue' so crucial to *Lucretia* is touched on: 'Is Albert virtuous?' Nevertheless, not only is the music of *Herring* more expansive than that of *Lucretia*, but in spite of its formal emphasis on various ensemble groupings it restores the soliloquy to a position of importance. Alongside *Lucretia*, *The Turn of the Screw* or *Owen Wingrave* it may seem less obviously or strictly organized and unified. But such explicit unity is hardly essential in operas where development and transformation of character are more of the essence than obsessive recurrences and inescapable conflicts. *Herring* may be appropriately looser than either *Grimes* or *Lucretia* in its musical structure, but there is nothing random about the choice of keys or harmonic characteristics. It is simply that textural or timbral appropriateness is the determining factor rather than some grandly symphonic harmonic scheme.

Britten's skill in large-scale organization which builds its progress from a blend of evolving recurrences and new material is particularly evident in Act II Scene 2 of *Herring*, the scene in which Albert returns to the shop after his 'coronation' and decides to 'burn his boats' and do 'what must be done by everyone'. This scene is framed by the D flat major 'night-music' for alto flute and bass clarinet, whose first appearance (from Fig. 60) encloses as subsidiary idea the 'May King' horn-call theme which had begun Act II (Ex. 23). Before the first recurrence of the night-music (at Fig. 67), Albert's music is made up essentially of tipsy

Ex. 23 Britten, *Albert Herring*, Act II (Interlude)

references to earlier material – the anthem 'Albert the Good', the vicar's slightly pompous refrain from the coronation scene, and Mum's characteristically busy music in compound time. The first return of the D flat night-music accompanies the gas-lighting routine, and some expansion of the horn-call idea (from Fig. 71) leads into the main body of the scene. To further development of the anthem tune Albert recalls the food and drink he has consumed. He also recalls, in a brief lyric arietta, the attractions of Nancy. However, Nancy 'belongs to Sid, not me', and from Fig. 76 the music of their Act I duet is recalled to prepare for their actual appearance. The assignation is conducted mainly in rapid recitative, though the horn-call theme is subtly woven in as Nancy refers to the exploitation of Albert. The main duet for the lovers (from Fig. 80) uses an accompaniment figure which was anticipated at Fig. 78, just before their

121

entrance. As the lovers depart, Albert's solo of self-realization begins. The main reminiscence here is again of the anthem, further distorted at Fig. 91. At the moment when Albert actually leaves the shop the music associated with Sid's 'audacity and tenacity' is heard (Fig. 97). Then the night-music returns as coda.

Apart from Albert himself, the most fully developed characters are Sid and Nancy. They are probably Britten's most successful attempt at a conventional romantic couple; the sense in which they represent a threat to Albert's none-too-reluctantly cultivated innocence about 'adult' relationships is very well suggested in this scene, and they have none of the simpering, sentimental attributes which often accrue to such couples in opera. Largely because of Sid and Nancy, Albert emerges as a figure with much of the genuine pathos of the traditional clown, but a pathos which dissolves naturally into the sane common sense with which he reacts to his own presumably quite ordinary experiences – exaggerated to 'pay off' the hypocritical citizenry. Albert has learned from his experiences, but we never learn exactly what those experiences were, nor where, if anywhere, they will lead him. For once, in a Britten opera, the ending, dramatically, is on a question mark – though the music is quite unambiguous. Albert seems almost smugly content.

12 Britten: From *Albert Herring* to *Billy Budd* (1947–51)

When *Albert Herring* was first performed at Glyndebourne in June 1947 Britten had completed the remarkable feat of composing three full-length operas in three and a half years. No fewer than eleven opus numbers separate *Herring* from the next large-scale opera, *Billy Budd*, begun in February 1950, a graphic indication of the alacrity with which Britten responded to the almost infinite variety of commissions and opportunities which now came his way. Nor was the stage entirely neglected. *Albert Herring* was the first opera which Britten composed specifically for the English Opera Group, though it was first heard in Sussex, not Suffolk. His practical involvement with the new company was also the prime motivation for his realization of *The Beggar's Opera* op. 43, first mounted at the Arts Theatre Cambridge in May 1948. It was not until the following year that a Britten stage work was given its first performance in Aldeburgh itself. *Let's Make an Opera*, incorporating *The Little Sweep*, was premièred at the Jubilee Hall on 14 June 1949, during the second Aldeburgh Festival.

In November 1947 Pears and Britten gave the first performance of

Canticle I Op. 40, *My Beloved is Mine*, at a Memorial Concert for Dick Sheppard, the founder of the Peace Pledge Union. Just as Tippett had owed an element of the inspiration for one of his most individual works, the cantata *Boyhood's End*, to the vocal works of Purcell, so Britten spoke of his Canticle as 'a new invention in a sense although . . . modelled on the Purcell *Divine Hymns*'.[1] It is a particularly concentrated and concise piece, the balance between evolution and unification perfectly struck, since the total structure reflects the smaller-scale procedures of the first section. In this, the piano ritornello is developed, in alternation and combination with the vocal line, the last statement being closest to the first. The second section, a recitative, is structured around varied recurrences in the piano of a figure which evolves from the ritornello which ends the first section. So the principal contrast comes at the start of the third section – 'Nor time, nor place, nor chance, nor death'. This is harmonically ambiguous, though ultimately stressing the dominant of G, the work's principal tonality. Thematically this section is highly unified in its imitative emphasis, but it is nonetheless evolutionary in its formal procedures. So too is the final section, of whose three related but distinct parts only the first shows its own small-scale frame-form: it is no less unified in content than the other two, but it is slightly larger. The third part is also framed to the extent that the piano ends it with a reference to the voice's first phrase.

The closely integrated evolutionary procedures of this Canticle provide a reminder of the techniques of Britten's early single-movement works – techniques which he would further transform in later years. But in the late 1940s and early 1950s most of his works are multi-movement in design. The song cycle for mezzo-soprano and piano *A Charm of Lullabies* op. 41 and the *Five Flower Songs* for unaccompanied chorus op. 47 might be called 'slight' were this term not to carry with it the implication of a lack of personality: they are certainly unpretentious, but sharply focused and vividly characterized. Such qualities were also required for Britten's most ambitious venture to date into the sphere of occasional music for (partly) amateur performance. *Saint Nicolas* op. 42, was commissioned for the centenary celebrations of Lancing College, Sussex, though its first performance actually took place during the first Aldeburgh Festival in June 1948. It might seem eccentric to suggest that this necessarily episodic cantata has very much if anything in common with the work which followed it, the *Spring Symphony* op. 44 – beyond a tenor soloist and a boys' choir. But the form of the symphony is much closer to the cantata principle than to such approximations to the hallowed classical scheme that the most important choral symphonies had hitherto attempted. There is a unity created by the prevailing formal procedures which matches the common themes of the text, but it is not carried through into significantly recurrent motivic elements, or into any traditionally integrated tonal design. Like *Saint Nicolas*, the *Spring Symphony* is a determinedly evolutionary work: the entire mood and material, as well as the tonality, are different at the end from those of the beginning. It may therefore be preferable to regard the symphonism of the work as involving an increasing clarification of tonal procedures, not just an overall progression from one key to another, however closely related. The fact that the work moves from F to C is therefore a good deal less important than the fact that the F is ambiguous, the C much more explicit. In their chromatic density and 'anti-triadic' character, the earlier stages of the *Spring Symphony* offer an important precedent for the powerful harmonic arguments of *Billy Budd*, which was begun six months after the symphony was completed.

Before resuming his relationship with grand opera in a work which was not only the result of a commission from the Arts Council for the Festival of Britain but also his first designed specifically for the Royal Opera House, Britten put his flair for inventing simple yet far from featureless music for young performers to a further test in *The Little Sweep*. With most of its eighteen numbers separated by dialogue, this 45-minute opera could be studied simply as a demonstration in varieties of strophic form: strongly contrasting material within the individual numbers is very much the exception. It is perhaps a pity that its Suffolk-orientated subject-matter is not more contemporary – or timeless; it depends very much on cheerfully accepted nineteenth-century social distinctions, and the music, though surprisingly unsuperficial for a score written down in a fortnight, does nevertheless have the blandness of a conception in which entertaining and moralizing get in each other's way. Britten did not repeat the experiment for nine years, and in *Noye's Fludde* skilfully avoided the more patronizing aspects of *The Little Sweep*'s subject-matter by taking a universal myth as theme. It was not for a decade after that, in the *Children's Crusade* of 1968, that he found a genuinely contemporary theme for a children's work. But, much more immediately, the theme of the little boy forced against his will to sweep chimneys was to lead directly into the theme of the young man who, while not an unwilling sailor, was driven beyond endurance by hostile forces.

Billy Budd: the name suggests a harmless, willing fellow, a close relative of Albert Herring. But whereas Herring's strength is latent in his weakness, Budd's weakness and strength are in open conflict. He is not, like Grimes, a visionary sadist, but a down-to-earth seaman with two basic physical attributes – good looks and a stammer. Grimes is a solitary; so, to a degree, is Herring. But Budd, generous and open-hearted, gets on well with his shipmates and is anxious only to help them. It may seem odd that such a straightforward, well-balanced person should suffer from a stammer, unless one argues that he has become what he is precisely because of the impediment. In the opera it first afflicts him when he admits to being 'a foundling', but he appears to suffer no remorse or guilt on this account. It is more as if the stammer, the defect, is the price he must pay for his virtues, his 'beauty, handsomeness, goodness'. When the virtue and the defect conflict, they result in violence, and the whole opera shows the inescapable association between conflict and violence on all levels. The conflict within Billy, the conflict between him and Claggart, the conflict between the English and the French: only the devious Captain Vere avoids such conflicts or, it is possible to feel, uses Billy to fight his battle for him.

The dramatic issues are explicit and all-pervading, but the music does not merely match them: it takes possession of them. In purely musical terms, *Billy Budd* is sometimes said to resolve a persistent conflict between the tonal centres of B and B flat in favour of B flat, which symbolizes the implicit triumph of good over evil. Yet it is more appropriate to speak of emphasis than of resolution, particularly when the 'discovery' of the B flat triad takes place in the context of Vere's precarious feeling of self-justification in the Epilogue. The dramatic and musical essence of the opera is in the conflict, and the whole 'message' of the work is that evil is not vanquished by good, but at best submerged beneath it, often to a depth which makes it difficult – and perhaps even unnecessary – to confront and exorcise. The apparently triumphant chord of B flat certainly suggests that, in Billy, the good is the dominant, conscious element: it may also suggest that Vere has at least a foothold in reality. Yet the possibility of any degree of permanence for that foothold becomes highly questionable as the major chord dies away and the lights fade (Ex. 24). No sooner has Vere finished telling the story and justifying

Ex. 24 Britten, *Billy Budd*, Epilogue

old man now,..... and my mind can go back in peace....

...... to that far-a-way sum-mer of sev-en-teen hundred and nine-ty-seven,...

.... long a-go........ now, years a-go, cen-tu-ries a-

-go, when I, Edward Fair-fax Vere, commanded the *In-dom-it-a-ble.*

SLOW CURTAIN

End of Opera

126

his actions than, like some Ancient Mariner, he must begin again. His life has become a treadmill from which the only escape is provided by those brief moments when he remembers that Billy did not blame him for displaying that awareness of his own dark side which Billy himself was never able to experience.

This interpretation may well have neither occurred to nor appealed to the librettists or the composer. But in an opera as rich in resonances as this – it is surely Britten's richest – the ambiguities inherent in the powerfully unified musical fabric are bound to suggest a variety of interpretations, and project a whole series of alternative views of the drama itself, its content and meaning.

In the original novella, Melville does not condemn Captain Vere for not urging clemency on Billy's judges – Vere's own subordinate officers – and suggests that at the moment of his own death (in the novel, Vere dies in action) the captain feels no remorse. The facts of war have justified his actions; and although, as Melville points out, Vere need not have had Billy tried summarily at all, the possibility of mutiny leaves him no choice. The only real evidence of potentially mutinous discontent among the ship's company has come to Vere from Claggart, of course, but this is sufficient to convince Vere that only a display of violent ruthlessness, the execution of Billy, will restore discipline.

It would be consistent with what is known of Britten's beliefs, and with the atmosphere of many of his other works, for the Vere of the opera to be seen as fundamentally corrupt, and for that interpretation to be expressed more directly than in Melville. Yet it is war itself which the opera implicitly condemns, rather than the tools of war, however gladly Vere and his subordinates clutch at the comforting certainties of its simple morality. Vere, for all his breeding and education, is inevitably forced into practices which are dishonourable – the condoning of press-gangs and the kind of shipboard policing which enables Claggart to terrorize and corrupt. Yet in the opera Vere is not simply a good man driven by the realities of war to compromise with the forces of evil. He is a man who positively welcomes the realities of war as a means of either repressing or resolving the weaknesses and contradictions of his own personality. War has made Vere a ruthless man, and the action of the opera makes clear that the ruthlessness is as real as the war.

In the epilogue to the opera, the aged Vere reflects that he could have saved Budd. This is, arguably, a fantasy, for to have released Billy on a verdict of self-defence would have been to condemn himself for tolerating, or at best not perceiving, Claggart's viciousness. Instead, Vere fails to act on his earlier boast to the absent Claggart: 'The boy whom you would destroy: he is good, you are evil. You have reckoned without me – you shall fail.' To agree with Mr Ratcliffe that 'the boy was provoked' into striking the master-at-arms would not necessarily be to admit prior knowledge of Claggart's evil ways, but in his guilt Vere seems to assume that his own failure to act promptly against Claggart would inevitably become known if Billy were reprieved. Perhaps he prefers the ship's company to assume that 'starry', saintly Vere is ignorant, rather than aware but unwilling to act. Claggart may have been Vere's Argus, a protection against dissension: but Vere might have recognized that Claggart was in danger of provoking that very mutiny which it was his prime duty to prevent. It is surely this vacillation, rather than any hesitancy over the actual condemnation of Billy, which torments Vere in the later life allowed him in the opera. If Vere is to survive it is Claggart, not Billy, who must be treated as the innocent victim: as Melville puts it, 'in the jugglery of circumstances preceding and attending the event on board the *Indomitable*, and in the light of that martial code whereby it was formally to be judged, innocence and guilt personified in Claggart and Budd in effect changed places'.[2]

Vere surely remains the central character of the opera, in spite of the librettists' aim 'to make Billy the hero',[3] and his prologue sets the tone for the whole work with its phrases about the inevitable union of goodness and imperfection. It is with the character of Billy that the emphasis shifts from the specific evils, the inevitable corruption of war, to the more complex but, in this context, no less inevitable corruption of human nature itself, however beautiful and innocent the external appearance. As Vere describes it, Billy's stammer is not merely a defect, but evil. Budd 'possesses' evil, yet behaves guiltlessly: he is ignorant of the war within himself. In the novella the stammer is associated only with those moments when Billy is under real pressure, and it is a weakness in the opera to suggest that it can apparently emerge independently of an inner conflict, of any need to suppress strong aggression. Yet, as noted above, the first onset of stammering in the opera at least establishes that Billy has no guilty feelings about it: he is unaware of the repressed forces within himself, and so fails to suspect evil in others – until the evidence is unmistakable, and he can only react violently.

Billy is not totally innocent, but he acts without premeditation, impulsively. Melville notes that 'sailors are in character a juvenile race',[4] and 'Baby' is not an inappropriate nickname for Billy. Yet even his normal geniality, more memorably portrayed in the opera than in the book, is suppressing aggression, just as his eloquence masks his stammer. When he finds Squeak rifling his kit, he reacts with natural resentment, and the two fight. Billy is no saint, except in Claggart's diseased imagination, which at times seems more appropriate to a late nineteenth-century aesthete than to a ship's master-at-arms in 1797. Melville calls Billy 'a sort of upright barbarian'.[5] Hence, perhaps, his inability to fear death, though he reacts politely to the Christian homilies of a chaplain who, in the novel, is portrayed as the unquestioning servant of a corrupt, war-dominated society.

The most famous and controversial moment in the opera is at the end of Act II Scene 2, when Vere leaves the stage to give Billy the court-martial verdict to the accompaniment of a long sequence of major and minor triads, all of which harmonize the pitches of the chord of F major. These triads may represent the only real moment of direct communication between the two characters: they may therefore represent Billy's strength, his willingness to accept whatever Vere decides. On the other hand, they may represent Vere's strength: the music is totally different from that which depicts his self-indulgently anguished indecision earlier in the act. The triads brusquely sweep aside his previous posturing: 'I am the messenger of death. How can he pardon? How receive me?' Vere knows that Billy will accept the verdict without fuss – angelically – and in the novel the captain's address to the court reveals his confidence in Billy's capacity for understanding that clemency is impossible, because of the war. So the anguish is caused by Vere's guilt, not by fear of how Billy will react to the news of the death sentence.

Billy makes little reference to this encounter with Vere during the final stages of the opera. Having pleaded for mercy and failed to gain it, he expresses no word of resentment. Near the beginning of the novella, Melville writes that 'like the animals, though no philosopher, he was, without knowing it, practically a fatalist',[6] and the librettists have made skilful use of this clue. 'But I had to strike down that Jemmy Legs – it's fate. And Captain Vere had to strike me down – Fate. We're both in sore trouble, him and me, with great need of strength, and my trouble's soon ending, so I can't help him longer with his.' This belief in fate is also convincing because it may encourage the feeling that one cannot be guilty of performing acts to which there are no alternatives. Yet in war necessity itself corrupts, and when the court-martial officers announce 'We've no choice' (to a hint of Beethoven's 'It must be') they are in effect abdicating real responsibility: the war is to blame, not the men who wage it.

As for Billy, he 'stays strong'. He goes to his death with no inkling of the dark side of his own nature. So the true tragedy is not Billy's death: it is the unresolved conflict between good and evil within him. Innocence is ignorance: Billy has never known the need, nor possessed the means, to discover the truth about himself. Like Vere, and Claggart, he too is corrupt: but in a world of comparative peace, rather than protracted war, he would at least have had a fair chance of living out his life in unregenerate, if not blissful, ignorance.

The deep pessimism which lies at the dramatic core of *Billy Budd* could easily have turned the work into a cold-war tract: after all, it was composed under the shadow of the Korean War and Soviet Russia's emergence as a nuclear power. Certainly, the opera would have little impact or distinction were it not for the power and coherence of the musical forces which embody the drama. This does involve extending the symbolic connotations beyond themes into tonal relationships themselves, if only in the generalized sense that any juxtaposed, conventionally unrelated or distant keys, particularly those a semitone or a tritone apart, will represent conflict in the minds of those able to perceive such factors. But the richness of *Billy Budd*'s music has less to do with carefully worked out processes of conflict between tonal centres than with a range of densities in which extremes of dissonance and consonance are employed with a directness that the luminously solid orchestration and rich, all-male vocal textures make powerful and palpable. The great transition in Act I, when the chorus are heard singing a shanty off-stage, and are then brought fully into focus after an orchestral fantasia on the shanty, is as essentially rooted in consonance as is the scene at the start of Act II in which the ship prepares for battle. The ability of concord to expand into regions of pungent discord is never more functionally controlled and exploited in Britten's music than it is in *Billy Budd*. In so resourcefully integrated a score, where the essential tonal relationships generate the themes, there is little room for the more obvious operatic conventions, but there is ample variety, both in the mood of the music and in the manner of vocal characterization. In both reflection and action, the music is vivid and mobile. In its economy and avoidance of formula, it is Britten's most powerful conjunction between two convictions: that only pacifism (not, as in *Lucretia,* Christian belief) can keep the corruption inherent in human relationships at bay; and that only a music which deduces richness of detail from a symbolically apt fundamental conception will be vivid enough to realize the dramatic potential of the subject and communicate it to the whole audience, whether technically 'aware' or not.

Billy Budd can scarcely be said to have brought a clearly defined phase of Britten's development to an end, and not everyone will agree that it is his finest work for the stage. The 1960 revision of the four-act version, with its pruning and compression, is by no means a total improvement on the original. But in both versions the sense of the composer's potential as the advocate of a certain kind of subject, expressed through a certain kind of music coming fully into focus – more fully, dramatically, if not purely musically, than in *Peter Grimes* – is unmistakable. The future would involve both the deepening and the dilution of the passion and breadth evident in *Billy Budd*. Above all, its broader social theme and utterance were never to re-emerge so directly and controversially. Britten was to be both admired and criticized after 1951, but he was rarely to disturb and challenge so compellingly as in *Billy Budd:* the rituals of religion, in the *War Requiem,* or of art, in *Death in Venice,* would make a still powerful impact more bearable.

13 Tippett: *The Midsummer Marriage* (1946–52)

Tippett himself has described a very explicit connection between his first two mature attempts at musico-dramatic composition, *A Child of Our Time* and *The Midsummer Marriage*:

It is clear to me that already as the first performances of *A Child of Our Time* were being given, I was toying with the idea of trying to give dramatic expression to the experiences of knowing the shadow and the light, and of wholeness, not by the method of example and contemplation proper to an oratorio, but by the method of action and consequence proper to an opera.[1]

As noted on p. 71, Tippett had contemplated writing an opera on the 1916 Easter rebellion in Dublin before deciding in favour of a 'contemplative' oratorio; and he would eventually find a tractable war theme for an opera in *King Priam.* Meanwhile, it was the 'light' rather than the 'dark' aspect of the oratorio's subject-matter – not man's inhumanity to man, but man's need and ability to understand himself – which demanded and received operatic treatment.

The plot of *The Midsummer Marriage* nevertheless develops, like that of any drama, as a series of miniature 'wars'. The hero, Mark, is introduced by his launching into an argument with the Ancients, who are the guardians of inherited wisdom and awareness. The central struggle in Act I is between the lovers Mark and Jenifer, a struggle representing their still imperfectly integrated personalities. Even at this preliminary stage, however, they are united in their hostility to Jenifer's possessive father, King Fisher, the most comic of all the characters in the sense that he is a man of great power behaving like a small, spoilt child. The Ritual Dances of Act II present a more Britten-like vision of struggle in the natural world, divided into hunters and hunted – a vision from which humanity, in the shape of the second pair of lovers, Jack and Bella, recoil. The obscenity of predatory pursuit will be contrasted with the all-justifying power of love in the final Act.

In Act III the incompatibility of Mark and Jenifer is resolved, and the central confict is between them (with their mouthpiece Madame Sososistris) and King Fisher, who tries to deny maturity and self-knowledge to his daughter. He is destroyed more by his persistent possessiveness, his own immaturity as a parent, than by lingering hatred of the united lovers. His death establishes no bonds of guilt, but releases exultant joy in the survivors.

Tippett has pointed out that 'the mechanism of hindrance to successful marriage, or to any relationship, is our ignorance or illusion about ourselves',[2] and in view of the fact that he has often been accused of obscurantism in his essays and librettos it is worth stressing just how single-mindedly this idea is followed through in *The Midsummer Marriage*. Man's curiosity about himself is obviously a laudable and serious matter. It is also absurd because, dramatically, it can be discussed only in a relatively clumsy, incomplete manner. When it comes to writing an opera, not around a plot which reflects at several removes the underlying theme of man's search for integration, but which is directly about that search, it is obvious that a whole scheme of symbolic representations must be devised which in themselves will be more or less comic, more or less absurd to the extent that they are relatively crude materializations of complex psychological and spiritual phenomena.

To no small extent the essential comedy of *The Midsummer Marriage* lies in this immense gap between the inner and the outer, between the essential idea and what we actually see on the stage. There is also comedy in the very humourlessness of the central pair of characters, Mark and Jenifer, whose behaviour we tend to observe in a detached manner because Tippett takes care to present them as more sympathetic to each other than to us. Their most human trait is impulsiveness. Thus it is only on her wedding day that Jenifer frigidly decides that 'it isn't love I want, but truth', her assumption that the two are mutually exclusive offering clear evidence of her immaturity. Truth, she believes, is something to be found only in isolation from family and friends, and when she returns in the final scene of Act I she describes her 'heavenly' experiences in terms which reinforce the timid, asexual nature of her vision of reality. Mark's vision, the result of his corresponding visit to 'hell', is sharply different. He finds truth in a celebration of aggressive sensuality, of man's oneness with the self-renewing earth. Separate, still in conflict, these extremes are false. With the real truth as far away as ever, the two lovers change places and resume their search.

Through the medium of Madame Sosostris (Act III Scene 5) we learn that Mark and Jenifer, on this second search, have been brought together to discover their true sexuality, compounded, in each, of a true, Jungian balance between masculine and feminine elements. Their union as a couple mirrors their new-found integration as individuals; they return to 'earth' (reality) with the affirmation that 'truth is assumed in love'. The once separate concepts are fused, and the lovers' ignorance and immaturity are transcended by this discovery.

132

Tippett presents his subject-matter in such a way that it has few religious overtones. King Fisher, a version of the Shavian 'heavy father', delivers conventional moral concepts with a minimum of conviction, and even his faith is in human, not divine power. The second pair of lovers, Jack and Bella, are much more explicit about their desire to undertake a conventional marriage than are Mark and Jenifer, but here too the references are to practical matters like wages, houses and children. The emphasis of the plot is not simply on the apparently all-conquering nature of love, but rather on the fact that true love is impossible without mature self-knowledge. Only when the lovers have understood and guilt-lessly confronted the opposing principles, male and female, spiritual and carnal, within themselves, can they be integrated: there can be no complete marriage except between personalities which are already aware of, and in control of, their contrasted inner impulses.

The rich and positive imagery of *The Midsummer Marriage* makes the opera seem like an optimistic answer to the prevailing cultural pessimism of the earlier twentieth century, established and sustained most memorably by T. S. Eliot's great poem *The Waste Land* (1922). It is the quest for truth, for integration, which in Tippett's hands becomes an exploration of human nature not as something inevitably circumscribed by innate and inescapable evil but as containing within itself the capacity for an adequate degree of self-knowledge and self-fulfilment. Man is contrasted with the elements and animals in the Ritual Dances as much as he is symbolically represented by them, since the elements and animals are truly governed by Fate in unchanging cycles of action and reaction. The only human 'victim' in the opera is King Fisher, and he is a rather straightforward martyr to his own arrogance; rather than trying to understand his own humanity he attempts, unrealistically, to be super-human. But Mark and Jenifer do not triumph for the traditional dramatic reason that they are sympathetic, attractive characters. They have been able to learn that wholeness is achieved, not by futile attempts to eliminate the dark side of man, but by using the light side to understand and define the dark. 'Hell' (the shadow) is as useful, and as necessary, as 'Heaven' (the light). The only real myth is of absolute goodness or absolute evil.

It might by no means follow inevitably from an account of the subject-matter of *The Midsummer Marriage* that it should be a staged rather than a concert work. But not only did Tippett become concerned at an early stage of its long gestation to harness the power of movement itself – of the dance – his first 'illumination' for the opera was a visual one. 'I saw a stage picture (as opposed to hearing a musical sound) of a wooded hilltop with a temple, where a warm and soft young man was being rebuffed by a cold and hard young woman . . . to such a degree that the collective, magical archetypes take charge.'[3] Even so, the opera was not created in successive, separate phases of visual, verbal and musical inspiration. As Tippett goes on to say, 'once I had got as far as this and understood the kind of material presenting itself, and so the kind of opera I had to write, then the nagging question of what kind of music would do all that I wanted became instant'.[4] And it was perfectly possible, once basic situations had been established, for the 'kind of music' to come to mind even before the necessary words had been written:

For example, when I *saw* my *prim'uomo* and *prima donna* returned to the level of the stage all armed with immediate experience of heaven and hell, I *heard* them begin to sing, one against the other, in two arias; the soprano's having coloratura, and the tenor's being rhapsodic; and this long before any words were there. That is, I sensed the musical metaphors before I searched for the verbal.[5]

And even if such musical promptings did not invariably precede the actual formulation of the text, it is clear from a letter which the composer wrote to a friend while working on the opera that 'I'm learning all the time to write text and music almost together, scene by scene.'[6]

Tippett's expression – 'what kind of music' – almost suggests that the compulsion to create a music drama on a 'quest' subject might itself have prompted a quest for a new musical style. But the truth, as he no doubt sensed, was that his musical style, as it had developed by the mid-1940s, needed precisely such a subject to achieve its fullest flowering, and to make further developments possible. He had certainly 'discovered himself' musically before *The Midsummer Marriage* was conceived. But only in this work did he fully realize the potential of what he had discovered. The style as such did not have to be discovered: the structure did.

In his essay, 'The birth of an opera', Tippett argues from the premiss that 'in opera the musical schemes are always dictated by the situations'.[7] In *The Midsummer Marriage* the situations make possible a blend of opera buffa and music drama:

There is nothing in the marriage part of it, the comedy, which is not to be found in the schemes of *opera buffa*: recitative, aria, ensemble, and some Verdi and Puccini techniques. And there is nothing in the midsummer part of it which is not to be found in the schemes of music drama: e.g. orchestral music to a natural phenomenon like a sunrise, considered as part of the drama.[8]

And so an inevitable formal problem resulted which could be solved only by a stylistic instinct, not by structural ingenuity. 'We want to move smoothly from the everyday to the marvellous, without relying on scenic transformation and during an act.' (The 'we' is because Tippett is comparing his needs with those of contemporary verse dramatists.) So the opera composer must find a musical unity of style which will, e.g. let an *opera buffa* chorus of young people of the present time sing themselves into a mantic chorus akin to that of the ancient Greek theatre. In point of fact (as the verse dramatists find), the real difficulty is in the descent to everyday – partly because it brings one dangerously near musical comedy, and generally because unsentimental simplicity is nowadays almost impossible to rescue from the banal.[9]

A Child of our Time had been an ambitious attempt to relate the public and private worlds, in which, as Tippett's notes, already quoted, make clear, 'peace' is not merely a matter of relationships between societies and social systems, but a symbol of a 'new synthesis' in which 'the irrational elements in ourselves' are 'reckoned with, even integrated into some new synthesis'.[10] *The Midsummer Marriage* is an even more ambitious attempt to subsume elements of both tragedy and comedy, ultimately derived from the world of the Greek theatre, and filter them through a Jungian interpretation to underline and demonstrate the workings of such a new synthesis. The difference between oratorio and opera is therefore not merely that between contemplation and action, but between a suggestion of synthesis, and its actual enactment.

In *The Midsummer Marriage* dramatic theme and musical structure come together most significantly in the relation between concepts of renewal and goal-directedness. In an essay on Stravinsky, written when his first opera was still in its relatively early stages, Tippett argued that

Stravinsky had a natural sympathy for both the religious mysticism of the Russian soul, and the sceptical pessimism. In *Petrouchka* the pessimism is at its strongest. *Le Sacre du Printemps,* on the other hand, is a drama of renewal. But it is a renewal only at the cost of sacrificing a virgin girl. Life is only renewed by death . . . *Les Noces* is also a drama of renewal, through marriage and the begetting of children – but where *Le Sacre du Printemps* is deadly serious, *Les Noces* is fundamentally comic (in the high sense), though the same ingredients of religious feeling and sceptical pessimism are in the theatrical mixture.[11]

Tippett himself has not compared his first opera directly with *Les Noces*: he has preferred to make the point that it is 'quite traditionally English in its use of fantasy, while being in the same kind of category as probably Busoni's *Doktor Faust*. An opera where the imaginative and symbolical element is of more consequence than the strictly dramatic, throwing, as that always does, great accent on the magic of the music.'[12] Certainly, to see the work as more dream than ritual might be to justify a sense of inconsequentiality by the standards of the through-composed, post-Wagnerian music drama, where purposeful progress towards goals, and the frustration or attainment of goals, will be the most fundamental structural principle, ensuring a richly diversified unity. But it is not really surprising that the relative absence of 'everyday' realism in the drama should promote rather than undermine purely musical continuities. One senses that Tippett, like Wagner almost a century before, is renewing tonality through expansion, and in a symbolically apposite manner: 'illumination' is indeed a goal to be aimed at and progressed towards. But in attaining it the power and potential of man are renewed, and renewed perpetually as long as illumination remains attainable. The appropriateness of the mandala image when Mark and Jenifer are finally revealed as united is so great simply because the goal which they have achieved as individuals is simultaneously the perpetually rediscoverable state of mankind's highest attainment.

No doubt most operas can be discussed in terms of tonal processes which replace a single, symphonic concept of all-embracing unity by a sequence of distinct yet variously relatable goal-directed processes. But in no opera does this happen with a closer dramatic relevance than *The Midsummer Marriage*. We can now see why, to Tippett, the 'unity of musical style', not the unity of musical structure, was the vital thing. The style brings potentially disruptive contrasts – between the eternal and the everyday – under the control of a continuous musical flow. The structure is the background which allows the style the maximum room for manoeuvre; and the balance of unity and diversity, concentration and expansion, in the treatment of fundamental tonal relationships, seems so rich, and at the same time so spontaneous, that the capacity of tonality to extend and renew itself indefinitely might be posited from this one work alone.

Tippett's remarks on the use of ascending cycles of fifths to produce an effect of 'illumination' have already been quoted. Though they date from 1938, their use of the word 'illumination' is a striking anticipation of the symbology of *The Midsummer Marriage,* and Tippett's reference to one of Vincent d'Indy's textbooks, where the same process of ascent is described as achieving 'l'expansion lumineuse', is even more significant. In the same essay, Tippett noted that the Beethovenian balance ('clarity' is Tippett's term) was soon lost. 'Wagner's use of rising and falling tonal centres is not conditioned by the theme or the form but by the dramatic situation.'[13] As we have already seen, Tippett was later to comment that 'in opera the musical schemes are always dictated by the situations', and although his argument is not fully developed in either place, it seems clear enough that complete operas can scarcely be expected to emulate the unified tonal processes of classical sonata designs.

Tippett's argument that before Wagner operatic tonal structures were determined more by thematic and formal considerations than by 'the dramatic situation' may be open to question, just as in the sonata itself 'the dramatic situation' may actually have had more influence than he allows – at least in Beethoven. But *The Midsummer Marriage* is a magnificent example of a musical structure which uses the fifth relation as both an extending and a prolonging phenomenon. It balances, in a sense, the Beethovenian and the Wagnerian (as Wagner himself had surely done), to the extent that relations between tonics and dominants are the initial and crucial stage in a technical process which tends to favour chromatically extended rather than diatonically prolonging progressions or relations.

The major triad is still the focus of harmonic and structural activity in the opera, and its constituent intervals – perfect fifth, major third, minor third – are therefore charged with particular structural and expressive energy. In the relatively small-scale formal units, tonal extensions can function quite straightforwardly through background progressions from tonic to dominant and back to tonic: the March of the Ancients in Act I is perhaps the most clearly detachable formal unit in the entire opera, and its pure Lydian modality colours but does not destroy such a basic background progression. Even here the presence of B natural in what would otherwise be a pure F major gives some emphasis to the third stage of the cycle of fifths from F – the 'secondary dominant' of G major. But this little March, with its toy-like tone colours, still seems almost comically controlled by its tonic triad (Ex. 25a). Though built as a char-

Ex. 25a Tippett, *The Midsummer Marriage*, Act I Scene 2

137

acteristic Tippett statement and expanded variation form, it lacks dynamism, as signified by the fact that the upper line achieves only an octave transfer downwards of its focal C: there is no descent on to the tonic. A more orthodox extension of a tonic triad may be observed in the E major section of Sosostris's aria in Act III, though the form of the whole is not closed off after the manner of the March (Ex. 25b).

Ex. 25b Tippett, *The Midsummer Marriage*, Act III Scene 5

In both these instances the dominant achieves a degree of independence within the extension of the tonic. But Mark's 'summer
song' (Act I, Figs. 27 to 30) all but reverses this principle, in that the
dominant is more prominent than the 'true' tonic, which tends to be
passed through, rather than stressed, as part of a scheme of progression
by fourths or fifths which reaches outwards on both sharp and flat sides
of G. One might say that, in its evasion of unambiguous centrality, this

music is all aspiration, without true illumination; and the opera as a whole is more concerned with expanding around tonics than with evading, or even underemphasizing them. So it is appropriate that Tippett should reserve his most extended demonstration of this technique for the work's apotheosis. Others have discussed the matter of key symbolism in *The Midsummer Marriage,* and it is in any case quite clear that A major is the main key of the opera: not merely the goal which is revealed at the end of the quest for full illumination, but a key which appears at other, earlier points with sufficient frequency to ensure that its final prolongation is sensed as a confirmation of its pre-eminence, not just a long-delayed clarification of something hitherto in doubt. In Act III the penultimate approach to a full cadence in A major is made at Fig. 451, the first time the words 'Fire in summer' are heard. But the full perfect cadence is postponed until those words are repeated at the end of the final Ritual Dance, at Fig. 476. Then the whole of Scene 9 – about 15 minutes of music – proceeds to the final affirmation of A major by means of a structure which in the simplest terms encloses strong tendencies to C major within the A major prolongation. Thus the clear progression away from A to C, by Fig. 479, sets the precedent for interaction, and this interaction comes into full focus after Fig. 501, as the 'chorale prelude' music in the orchestra establishes the dominant as well as the tonic of C. It is only when the C major dominant before Fig. 521 resolves for the third time on to the A major tonic that the final bars of the opera can confirm A by means of its own dominant, eight bars before the end.

The fact that Tippett ends *The Midsummer Marriage* with a grand re-working of the fundamental tonal relation found in the Concerto for Double String Orchestra naturally helps to confirm one's sense of the later work fulfilling the potential of the former. Yet it can scarcely be doubted that form, as such, is at least as significant as tonal structure in the opera: indeed, the repetitions, variations, and integrated transitions ensure the coherence and inevitable progress of the work rather more than what is, in some ways, a distinctly arbitrary tonal design. The formal categories of repetition, variation, and contrast are undeniably more potent than the formal genres – aria, ensemble, recitative – in which the analogies between Tippett and other composers are obvious. But formal categories cannot seriously be discussed without reference to musical content; and by defining the nature of musical content one moves from description to analysis, from characteristics of style to elements of structure.

In view of the energy and elaboration of Tippett's earlier music it comes as no surprise to hear him confess of *The Midsummer Marriage* that the search for lyric simplicity was . . . for me the hardest thing of all. I did not want to match the strangeness of the story with obscurity in the music. On the contrary: as the moral of *The Midsummer Marriage* is enlightenment, then the music must be lucid. The big moments seemed to take care of themselves. The little moments had to be struggled for.[14]

The work is a triumph because so little of that struggle survives. Whether the big moments really took care of themselves or not, they seem the reverse of random. *The Midsummer Marriage* is indeed lucid: but it is also strongly structured, richly textured, and intensely expressive. To have sustained the exalted tone of the work over the six years of its creation is remarkable enough: but to have refined that tone so that the music communicates so positively and immediately is little short of miraculous.

The contrast between the productivity, and public impact, of Britten and Tippett during the years between 1946 and 1952 scarcely needs stressing. Tippett was so absorbed with the process, and problems, of creating *The Midsummer Marriage* that it seems surprising that he was prepared to turn aside for any other works at all. There were only two: the short *Suite for the Birthday of Prince Charles* (1948) which, among its 'found' material, uses the March of the Ancients from Act I of the opera, and the song cycle *The Heart's Assurance,* which Tippett finished in early April 1951 while working on Act III of the opera. Dedicated to the memory of Francesca Allinson, the close friend to whom Tippett had inscribed the Piano Sonata No. 1 in 1937, this consists of settings of three poems by Alun Lewis and two by Sydney Keyes, both poets who died during the Second World War. Their often rather Lawrentian style may have dated, but the subject-matter touches, however obliquely, on Tippett's abiding concerns – the need for honesty, self-knowledge, and revulsion at man's destructiveness. Tippett has written: 'The unity of mood which entirely joins these poets together is what I have called the experience of "Love under the shadow of death" – I tried to express in the setting of these poems their dominant quality, the threat which death gave to love.'[15] Perhaps because of the problems in scaling down his overriding operatic–orchestral concerns, the music seems to have rather more of rhetoric than true exaltation about it; but its technical processes reveal the full resources of Tippett's tonal language.

In 'Song' the essential image captured by the piano's constant demi-semiquavers is the 'endless belt' whose 'cruel revolutions' separate lovers in wartime. For five bars the music accommodates itself to the two-sharp key signature, but stressing fourths in a modal context: there are no emphasized triads, no leading notes. Chromaticism soon submerges this purity, but the song does not wholly discard all reference to the initial collection; it concludes with a hint of a perfect cadence in A minor (the two-sharp signature has long disappeared) but with a 'tonic chord' which employs the minor thirds above and below A, and excludes the fifth from its final statement.

No. 2, 'The Heart's Assurance', also ends with A as tonic, as a consequence of the extended G major to which the music refers at the start of each stanza. The one-sharp key-signature is much more consistently in evidence, and is actually retained throughout No. 3, 'Compassion'. Once more, the form suggests variations, with six related sections centring tonally on the two fifths E–B–F sharp: an extended E minor which the final cadence confirms by making the F sharp the only survivor after strong movement from B to E in the bass. The fact that there is such prominent use of a dominant triad in this song is unusual, but supports the rather exaggerated rhetorical emphases of the vocal line.

The form of the fourth song, 'The Dancer', involves two initial shifts of pitch-level up a perfect fourth at the start of the second and third stanzas, after which the later part of the final stanza re-establishes the initial pitch-level, and confirms the extended B flat major (encompassing clear suggestions of G minor, among other subsidiary areas). The textural lightness is served by the avoidance of root-position triads, and this makes their repeated use in the finale song, 'Remember your Lovers', seem the more portentous. Here the bugle-call refrain punctuates a structure full of chromatic sidesteps and enharmonic switches which nevertheless evolves steadily towards the clarification of its recurring five-flat key-signature as representing a modal complex around F major. Whether one regards the song as being throughout in an extended B flat minor which happens to close on the dominant, or in an extended F major which tends strongly to its subdominant minor, the concluding cadence, with its Phrygian melodic descent, may seem almost arbitrary in its very finality (Ex. 26). But this is a song whose dramatic postures are offset rather than undermined by the complexity of the harmonic processes. It shows that, as the composer emerged from the experience of creating *The Midsummer Marriage*, a new concentration could quickly lead to increased tensions, and an increasing threat to the relative stability of the triad-centred extended tonality which had served him so far.

Ex. 26 Tippett, *The Heart's Assurance*, No. 5, 'Remember your Lovers'

14 Britten: From Canticle II to *Winter Words* (1952–3)

Canticle II, *Abraham and Isaac* op. 51, was Britten's only composition between his Festival of Britain opera, *Billy Budd*, and his coronation opera, *Gloriana*; he wrote it during January 1952. Canticle II has an exemplary simplicity of manner and suppleness of form. Its dramatic theme is Britten's most familiar archetype, save that here, unusually, the mortal threat to innocence is lifted – though by divine providence rather than human compassion. The work's procedures, balancing evolution and recurrence, are also typical, but they are given special force by a single-movement structure within which recitative and aria sections alternate to create the impression of a compressed cantata. There are no pronounced breaks between sections and, as in all Britten's best works, the musical treatment of the dramatic climax makes a purely structural point as well. The most fundamental tonal shift occurs in Abraham's first recitative, when the sudden assertion of D flat as a substitute for the hitherto unchallenged tonic E flat indicates a tonal process in which close diatonic relatives need not play a significant role. It is the D flat which, in enharmonic transformation as C sharp, prepares the next new tonality of A major for the first main aria-like section (actually a duet). The music has thus travelled its maximum distance, across the tritone, in a very short time, and even this tritone shift has been anticipated by the A naturals in the piano against the tenor's sustained E flat (p. 5, bars 3–4). The work will continue to alternate unstable recitatives with stable quasi-arias, but the fundamental symmetry of its background progress ensures that when E flat is finally regained it is once more through the enharmonic change from D flat to C sharp against which, on p. 21, the tritone G becomes increasingly firm.

This background of symmetry – E flat, D flat, A, D flat, E flat – is countered by two factors. First, the second D flat section is a good deal more stable than the first: aria as opposed to recitative. Second, A major is treated as a dominant, and leads to the agitated D minor section (p. 11), which strongly recalls the D minor aria in *Saint Nicolas*. The basic tonal scheme is therefore E flat, A, D, D flat, E flat: the note a tritone from the true tonic of the piece is able to function as an independent dominant, while the 'true' dominant, B flat, always remains firmly within the orbit of its own tonic. In this way, Britten gave structural force to his chromatically extended tonality.

Britten began work on *Gloriana* in October 1952, and finished the music on 13 March 1953. Eric Walter White has noted that *'Gloriana* is the only through-composed opera of Britten's in which the acts are not unbroken musical entities.'[1] Opinions are likely to be divided as to what constitutes a 'break' in opera, but since the composer himself divided the various scenes into sections with separate titles, the distinctions between operatic genres – recitative, song, ensemble, and so on – are particularly clear. It is moreover a characteristic of these separate sections that they contain internal repetitions. But no suggestion that *Gloriana* is merely an incoherent succession of separate formal units will long survive a study of the score, even though the courtly and choral dances *can* be detached and performed separately, and Britten also made a Symphonic Suite from the opera; the only time he did so. Evolutionary forms are also employed, however, perhaps most notably the Second Duet in Act III Scene 1, whose eight sections involve relatively little repetition or cross-reference. Britten was also careful to ensure that a larger formal control can be sensed in scenes by using his favourite device of framing material: this is particularly clear in Act II Scene 1, and contrasts with an extended evolutionary scene like Act II Scene 3, which is built round a suite of dances. (In the Coranto, the relationship between stage band and pit orchestra recalls Act III Scene 1 of *Peter Grimes*.) Act III Scene 2 is a large-scale rondo, and the final scene of all matches its own internal cross-references with the climactic large-scale reminiscences, first of Essex's second lute song, then of the chorus of homage. This scene, with its punctuating use of spoken dialogue, has in the past been singled out as encapsulating the weaker side of the work, by revealing an uncertainty as to how far to let the grimness of the Queen's decline register in what was, after all, an opera 'dedicated by gracious permission to Her Majesty Queen Elizabeth II, in honour of whose coronation it was composed'. But the entire dramatic presentation, not just the music, ensures sympathy for the Queen, and also brings the public and private, social and individual worlds into poignant juxtaposition. The point is not simply the banal one that 'queens are human too'. It is that they are likely to experience greater, more disorienting conflicts of motives and responsibilities than mere commoners. When Captain Vere, in *Billy Budd*, refers to himself as 'King of this fragment of earth' he is being typically self-indulgent. But the 'message' of *Gloriana* is that any sovereign who can find permanent personal happiness is fortunate indeed. After all, in Britten's world, such happiness is the lot of few enough commoners: it tends to be achieved in dreams rather than in reality.

Because of the facts of history, Gloriana's fate is different from that of Britten's two other female 'principals': she neither kills herself, like Lucretia, nor goes mad and kills herself like Phaedra. She dies of old age; but aging as a theme did not concern Britten greatly until *Death in Venice* – indeed, old people tend to be caricatured, like the Vicar in *Peter Grimes* and the General in *Owen Wingrave*. As already argued, *Gloriana* is much more concerned, like *Billy Budd*, with the anguish of those in authority, and this aspect of the Queen's predicament is stressed throughout Act III, rather than her lack of youth and beauty. This theme of vulnerable authority naturally has links with that of the personality of the outsider, the person unable to 'connect', and it links Vere, Gloriana, and the Governess in *The Turn of the Screw*: all experience agonies of indecision, and act, on the whole, for the worse.

There is one particular bond between Vere and Gloriana: each confirms a death sentence on a favourite. But just as the Epilogue of *Billy Budd* makes good sense if we regard the aged Vere as remembering only what he wants to remember, so any sense of confusion and sentimentality in the Epilogue of *Gloriana* can be lessened if the climactic recurrence of the music of Essex's second lute song is seen as representing, not the man himself, but all that Elizabeth has forgone in personal happiness and fulfilment for the sake of the State – or because of her unique position within the State. Commentators have waxed critical of Essex and his presentation in the opera, but the fact that the Queen can be devoted to such an apparently shallow, deceitful character surely confirms her all-too-human difficulty in forming serious, stable, suitable relationships. Yet the Queen is, in most respects, very different from Britten's other principal characters, and not just because she is a historical figure. To class her with all the other outsiders in his dramatic works still leaves much unsaid, and again the closest parallel is with Vere, the commander uneasy with those he must command. Elizabeth is allowed to express such appropriate sentiments as 'never thought was cherished in my heart that tended not to my people's good', and Britten was remarkably successful in devising grandly regal music with genuine depth: her Soliloquy and Prayer at the end of Act I have a broad rhetorical sweep which is rare in his music, and the switch to minor harmony in the final phrases is a particularly pointed yet simple example of the dramatic use of semitonal conflict in a diatonic context, a telling device employed to make an essential dramatic point (Ex. 27).

For all its modal consistency and triadic solidity the music does in fact enshrine some very intense conflicts between diatonic and chromatic tendencies, and between 'modern' and 'ancient' styles, which powerfully parallel the conflicts of loyalty and emotion in the leading characters. All twelve minor triads occur in the second duet of the Queen and Essex

Ex. 27 Britten, *Gloriana*, Act I Scene 2

in Act III Scene 1, and there are striking and memorable passages throughout where the insistent repetitions and transpositions of small cells push the diatonic basis of the music well into the background and anticipate the pared-down chromatic language of *The Turn of the Screw*. The anguished contours of the string melody at the entrance of the Queen in Act I, and also the music for 'The Queen's Announcement' in Act II (Scene 3, No. 12) have more of the rhetoric of *Budd* than the introversion of the *Screw* about them, however: and the same can be said of Essex's assertive arioso, 'By heaven, my voice', in Act II Scene 2. It is in the thinner textures of, for example, the exchange between the Queen and Cecil (Act I Scene 2, No. 4) that the 'total thematicism' of the later works is foreshadowed, and even when the mood changes drastically in this scene for Essex's first lute song, the apparently straightforward harmony remains uneasy because the sustained bass note, while modally assimilable, casts the shadow of discord over the scene: such an effect returns as late as the final bars of *Death in Venice*. Britten's expressive use of chromaticism always requires some evidence of a traditional, stable background to make its full effect, and in *Gloriana* there are particularly startling effects when that background is the style of Elizabethan dance music: a good example is the Pavane at the start of Act II Scene 3, which Peter Evans analyses in detail.[2] The pure bi-modal clash between major and minor triads is an effect which is more suitable to momentary employment than extended development, but when used as it is at the end of the Act II quartet 'Good Frances do not weep', its role as the encapsulation of a structural device of much wider and deeper significance is enhanced.

The dramatically appropriate exploitation of musical conflict in *Gloriana* is perhaps most explicitly evident at the end of Act II, where the exuberantly diatonic Coranto played by the stage band is steadily undermined by the chromatic assertion of a theme in the main orchestra representing Essex and the dangers he poses. But such a blatant superimposition is only justified by the potent yet transitory dramatic effect which it makes. Structurally, the elements tend to cancel each other out: there is conflict rather than interaction.

It will probably be generally agreed that both *Billy Budd* and *The Turn of the Screw* are finer operas than *Gloriana*, and their more direct treatment of the twin themes of ambivalently exercised authority and corrupted innocence have much to do with this. But *Gloriana* offers a powerful glimpse of one side of Britten which rarely appeared again. In *Billy Budd*, the Epilogue builds to a great climax of illusion, the discovery of the B flat major triad in the final bars, from which the music quickly subsides into silence. In *Gloriana* there is also a grand musical 'apotheosis' whose meaning is ironic and, in the best sense, pathetic.

This occurs with the orchestral version of the second lute song at the start of the Epilogue, and is reasserted with particular force when its major mode phrases are reached. Perhaps the only later work of Britten's to contain a comparable effect is the *War Requiem*, where the great G minor climax of the 'Libera Me' occurs even earlier in the structure, and the 'dying fall' is still more poignantly protracted. (There is no achieved climax in the 'In paradisum', but only the intensification of musical elements which depend for their identity on non-resolution of what, traditionally, would eventually be resolved.)

It is perhaps surprising that there was not a more radical change on Britten's part from public 'commitment' to private self-communing after the cool reception of *Gloriana*. The first work to be completed after the coronation opera, the Thomas Hardy cycle *Winter Words* op. 52 (September 1953), ends with an intensity of pessimism whose directness is new. But Britten continued to devote most of his time to music for the theatre, and even (three years later) composed a full-length ballet, *The Prince of the Pagodas* op. 57, to a scenario which is whole-heartedly escapist and worlds away from his usual subject-matter. *The Prince of the Pagodas* may be exceptional, but its existence reinforces the necessity for accepting that Britten's *essential* subject-matter was his own personal musical language, which continued to evolve, to reveal new possibilities, throughout his life. The literary and dramatic themes are fairly constant too, but even those works with different themes, or the relatively rare non-vocal works, share in the process of stylistic and technical development.

Four of the non-operatic vocal compositions of the period between *Gloriana* and *A Midsummer Night's Dream* (1960) – *Winter Words*, Canticle III, *Nocturne* and *Six Hölderlin Fragments* – are among Britten's finest and most important. It is certainly possible to regard them, and also the *Songs from the Chinese* op. 58, as reflecting increased concern for concentration, explicit formal and thematic unity, such as is demonstrated on the largest scale by *The Turn of the Screw* and, immediately after the Shakespeare opera, by the *War Requiem*. The works of the years 1954 to 1961 therefore adumbrate the special qualities of Britten's final period, which needed only the more consistent abandonment of the triad as the principal unit of harmonic and textural organization to achieve its fully realized form.

The first of these works, *Winter Words*, is 'looser' than most of the others, in the sense that the individual songs are not linked either by transitions or by thematic cross-references. Recurrence of such 'fingerprints' as the sequences of trichords in Nos. 1 and 3 (Ex. 28a) is evidence of stylistic consistency rather than thematic unity, and any sense of tonal

Ex. 28a (i)   Britten, *Winter Words*, No. 1, 'At Day-close in November'
       (ii) Britten, *Winter Words*, No. 3, 'Wagtail and Baby'

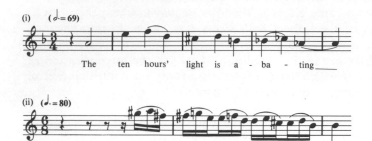

progress through the cycle as a whole is tenuous, beyond the fact that the first and last songs have the same tonic. A more significant unifying element is provided by the way musical form reflects or shapes poetic form. Only one of the eight settings has a strong central contrast: the Vicar's stanza from No. 5, 'The Choirmaster's Burial'. Otherwise, whether the subdivisions are into four, three or two sections, the songs proceed by restatement and variation rather than by contrast: and 'The Choirmaster's Burial' itself is framed by the superbly atmospheric harmonization and variation of the 'Mount Ephraim' tune. Tempting though it may be to argue that all the songs vary the same formal scheme, however, it is the differences, contributing to the brilliantly realized individual worlds of each setting, which most merit discussion.

The first song, 'At Day-close in November', has a tautly controlled irregularity stemming from the nine-bar piano introduction. This is the basis of four related vocal phrases (9, 11, 15 and 10 bars respectively) all of which, except the longest and most developmental third phrase, cadence on the same octave Ds. The third phrase also cadences on D, in bar 45, at the conclusion of a process of transferring the initial gesture of the song up an octave. The long final section, from bars 55 to 88, then prolongs the concluding Ds of the fourth phrase through reference to the tense blur of fused tonic and dominant elements derived from the fourth and fifth bars of the piano introduction. When the lower octave D is reached in bar 69 a pure D major triad is heard, and is prolonged for two bars. But the chordal process moves on from this point to a repeat of the octave Ds under the last note of the vocal part, and the final prolongation of the Ds in the piano's coda opens up a huge six-octave area of superimposed neapolitan fifths and dominant triads before the piece ends on octave Ds which are *not* preceded, as on every other occasion, by a preparatory sequence of chords.

150

'At Day-close in November' has unity and evolution in perfect balance: unity in that strong contrasts are small-scale, evolution in that exact repetitions are avoided. No. 2, 'Midnight on the Great Western', is the only song in the cycle to contain a strophic repetition: the second stanza has only rhythmic differences in the vocal line. The onomatopoeic ostinato may seem unsophisticated, but it is a perfectly judged complement to the tender concern of Hardy's text. The poems invite the regularity and balance of a relatively simple song style, but Britten also finds opportunity for an element of arioso. The narrative aspect of No. 3, 'Wagtail and Baby', shows this at its least obtrusive; the first section of No. 5, 'The Choirmaster's Burial', at its most subtly explicit. It is perhaps appropriate, then, that the least song-like and most tonally ambiguous item should have a particularly interesting structure. In No. 7, 'At the Railway Station, Upway', the tone and context of the story of the little boy with a violin are artless. Britten's treatment, marked 'lightly and like an improvisation', divides the text into three parts (or two with coda) by means of recurring phrases. Yet because the complete variations of the accompanying 'violin' always begin some way into each vocal section, the resulting overlaps add to the 'freedom' to which the text refers so ironically. The effect is appropriately guileless, but the use of variation in the song is extremely subtle, and its economy of formal control and the deft characterization are technically very far from naive.

'Before Life and After', the final song, has the same kind of cumulative inevitability as Britten's arrangement of 'The Ash Grove', where contrapuntal motion against a plain harmonic background leads to extreme discords as the most appropriate representation of emotional disorientation: in Hardy's bitter phrase, 'the disease of feeling'. This song closes the cycle by returning to the tonal centre (though now major) of the first song. But it has its own very special relationships between detail and totality. There are, broadly speaking, four stages to the musical argument, corresponding to the four stanzas of the poem. The first stage moves diatonically from D major to G major, while a free canon between the piano's right hand and the voice generates distinct but not yet disturbing dissonance with the left-hand triads. The second stanza – 'None suffered sickness, love, or loss' – begins to extend the harmonic vocabulary with non-diatonic motions and strengthening dissonance: in particular, the voice's B flat for the word 'hope', against a major ninth on A in bar 12, helps to create such instability that when the chord of D major is reached as a cadential goal three bars later it takes on the more urgent role of leading to the E flat major cadence which ends the stanza (Ex. 28b).

The third stanza, from 'If something ceased', initially prolongs the chord of E flat, then begins to move towards the highly unstable B

Ex. 28b Britten, *Winter Words*, No. 8 'Before Life and After'

major, at 'No sense was stung', the left-hand triads increasingly unrelated to the upper lines. As a result, the fourth stanza is the first in the song which does not move away from a major triad, although the contrary motion in the accompaniment itself does use B major as an initial focus. At the climax, 'nescience' is 'reaffirmed' by stepwise resolution back on to the primal D major, and a framing restatement, varied and extended, of the song's opening bars.

In spirit, *Winter Words* potently anticipates the doom-laden atmosphere of *The Turn of the Screw*, composed during the following year. Hardy's 'Ere nescience shall be reaffirmed, how long?' is the very antithesis of the 'Death, thou shalt die', which ends the Donne cycle on a note of hope. The relationship between despair and hope takes many forms in Britten's works, but nowhere is the ultimately illusory nature of the latter more powerfully presented than in 'Before Life and After'.

15 Tippett: From the *Corelli Fantasia* to the Piano Concerto (1953–5)

Tippett's long and concentrated period of work on *The Midsummer Marriage* could have created the need for strong contrast in the ensuing works, but the *Corelli Fantasia* and the Piano Concerto are touched by the same lyric spirit as the opera, even though the connections are not as literal as with the later works which grew from *King Priam* and *The Knot Garden*. The *Fantasia Concertante on a Theme of Corelli* for string orchestra (1953) has the textural richness and opulent ornamentation which are even more characteristic of the opera than of the Concerto for Double String Orchestra, but its framed, single-movement form is more like something from early Britten than from any of Tippett's own earlier instrumental works. The variation process is certainly a good deal more subtle and complex than in his *Fantasia on a Theme of Handel*, yet the plain character of the original Corelli material, and of the Bach fugue on themes of Corelli quoted during the course of the work, do not have an entirely natural relationship with Tippett's intensifying embellishments and extended tonality. He was obviously aware of such experts in the field of 'baroque-modern' synthesis as Stravinsky and Hindemith, but by 1953 he was assured and original enough to move in a very different direction. The *Fantasia* evolves through some distinctly piquant contrasts into a penultimate section where a transcendent pastoralism, instead of dissolving into a dreaming coda, brusquely resolves into a final, cadential vivace. Such sudden, almost bald simplicity is a bold stroke in a work whose fascination centres on the way Tippett deals with that most essential of all baroque devices, the perfect cadence. In *The Midsummer Marriage* the ultimate harmonic gesture is represented by the way in which the 'chorale' texture progresses from C major to A major, and the hint of baroque style in the chorale aptly symbolizes the certainty and security of the drama's end. In the *Corelli Fantasia*, with less solemnity but equally rich imagination, the world of extended tonality finds room for plenty of dominant chords; but there is surely a touch of irony about the ending (Ex. 29): if only things were that simple!

The *Corelli Fantasia* was followed by the *Divertimento on Sellinger's Round* for chamber orchestra (1953–4), another work incorporating 'found objects'. In the Suite in D these had been folk or hymn tunes, apart from the Ancients' march. In the *Divertimento* they provide a

Ex. 29 Tippett, *Fantasia Concertante on a Theme of Corelli*

rapid survey of British music from Gibbons and Purcell to Arne, Field and Sullivan. Rather incongruously, in view of its distinctly 'national' attributes, the work is dedicated to Paul Sacher, and was first performed by his Collegium Musicum in Zürich.

Tippett has written that his Piano Concerto, composed between 1953 and 1955

proceeds directly out of the world of *The Midsummer Marriage*. The music is rich, linear, lyrical, as in that opera. But it had its precise moment of conception years before when listening to a rehearsal of Beethoven's Fourth Piano Concerto as played by Gieseking on his return to England after the war. I felt moved to create a concerto in which once again the piano may sing. In fact a piano cannot sing except by imitation and trick. The methods of doing this, stemming, shall we say, from Chopin, had become stereotyped and impossible. So the search for viable newer methods was very long. It is also easy to see . . . that it is the sound of the score of *The Midsummer Marriage* (which took six years to write) which is the true originator.[1]

This return to extended symphonic music after the experience of writing an opera makes the Piano Concerto one of Tippett's most intriguing and absorbing compositions. The continuing force of Beethovenian precedents is to be noted, and although the more 'lyric' Beethoven of the Piano Concerto No. 4 is rather different from the dramatic sonata and fugue composer to whom Tippett was more primarily indebted, both the Double Concerto and *The Midsummer Marriage* itself had already proved notably successful in bringing lyric reflection and 'active' counterpoint into a highly purposeful relationship. In the Piano Concerto lyricism keeps drama at a distance; but the purely tonal and harmonic 'argument' is still rich and fascinating, while the formal consequences of the lyric emphasis took Tippett's always complex relationship with the conventions of the classic-romantic tradition forward to a new stage.

Because the first movement of the Concerto is leisurely, and essentially lyrical, it turns the conventions of Beethovenian sonata form inside out. The tendency is for change to take place gradually: ambiguity and the avoidance of the explicit are exploited for their capacity to arouse expectations of coherent continuation. So, in the germinal five-bar phrase with which the movement begins, C (the eventual tonal goal of the finale) is the bass note, rather than the A flat which the melodic and harmonic material treat as central. The stage is set for another working out of third relations.

The first paragraph of the movement unfolds and intensifies steadily over the C pedal, and other notes are progressively added until at the end of the paragraph – one bar before Fig. 7 – a 'cluster' (C, D flat, E flat and B flat) has been built up as a background for ornamentation which increasingly favours the pitches of the A flat major scale. There are six thematic phrases in this first paragraph, all of which vary the same melodic statement. There is, however, a preliminary, preludial air about this 'development', which reaches a climax as the bass shifts to A flat at Fig. 7 for a short transition. At Fig. 8 the first group of derived ideas is heard, but this itself (a tutti) is tonally transitional: the first main shift of tonal centre, on to E – the major third the other side of A flat from C – occurs at Fig. 11, as the tutti continues with ornamental development of the first idea. The soloist returns at Fig. 18 for the final section of the exposition, with further derivations from the thematic generator, and a concluding reminder of the dance-like rhythms of the first transition.

The character of this music is determined, essentially, by two elements. On the one hand, it proceeds steadily by similarity, so that new stages in the thematic process always have clear connections with earlier ones. On the other hand it proceeds, in rather unBeethovenian fashion, by tonal allusion more than by tonal emphasis: a consequence not only of Tippett's by now familiar tendency to build structurally significant chords from fourths rather than thirds, but also of the persistent prominence of chromatic decoration. For all its lyric connectedness, the music is insufficiently diatonic and triadic to encourage reliance on traditional cadential structuring. The technique seems at once open-ended in its capacity to float free of traditional tonal hierarchies, and limited in that it still depends on reference to the formal designs with which those hierarchies are most commonly associated.

The Piano Concerto is perhaps more ambitious than *The Midsummer Marriage* or the *Corelli Fantasia* in seeking less explicit reliance on those agents of conventional tonal resolution, while preserving formal schemes which remain close to tradition, at least in the outer movements. In both first movement and finale, tonality retains the capacity to provide thematic statements with a familiar formal context. For example, in the first movement there is an elaborate recapitulatory return to the main material in its original pitch area (Fig. 42) after a development which begins at Fig. 24 with that material in a strongly contrasted pitch-area (bass note E, tonal centre C) and which avoids the region of A flat throughout; and in the Rondo-finale, which is more concerned with the connections between A flat, C and E flat, such recapitulation is equally necessary. The second movement is more radical and forward-looking, its textural and tonal conflicts embodied in a polyphony which is elaborate even by Tippett's standards, and with a tripartite form which is progressive rather than symmetrically closed. But even here the fundamental B major (which confirms a characteristic concern with different types of third-relation in the work as a whole) acts as a significant point of focus for the extended canonic phrases of the first section and the dramatically contrasted dialogues of the third. The first section (up to Fig. 81) moves towards a clear emphasis on the tonic note, and divides, just before Fig. 78, with emphasis on the dominant. The third section reinforces the dominant as bass note of a punctuating chord, and prepares the way for a final, shy outlining of the B major triad in the piano at the very end (Ex. 30).

Ex. 30 Tippett, Piano Concerto, II, Molto lento e tranquillo

The blurring of tonal focus in the first movement is highly effective, since it seems at one with the reflective character of the music, and the canonic priorities of the slow movement, coupled with the elaborate ornamentation, require only a very basic harmonic framework which can be alluded to without being made to seem merely perfunctory. The finale is less memorable because the new need for exuberance and the continuing need for ambiguity tend to get in each other's way. Another expansive, reflective movement is clearly impossible, but if contrast of mood brings with it a more firmly, even triadically, focused tonal language, the stylistic coherence of the concerto will be threatened. Perhaps the consideration of problems such as these helped to show Tippett that the focus on purely thematic interaction could be much sharper if he no longer attempted to control purely tonal, harmonic relationships with the object either of promoting or obscuring resolutions. He could continue to work with the idea of intervallic invariance as the source of chords or themes: but those chords or themes need no longer be required to act as substitutes for triads with specifically tonal structural functions. What is remarkable in Tippett's development during the late 1950s and early 1960s is the rapidity with which he moved from an extended tonality in which the triad and perfect cadence may be little more than hinted at (though their 'effect' may still seem strong through rhythmic procedures) to a virtual atonality, in which a thematic process assumes the primary structuring role. The extended C in which the Piano Concerto ends has more of minor than major about it, and movement from dominant to tonic can be traced in the lower voices. But the final progression, in which descending minor scales come to rest on a major triad, effectively ends the work on a distinctly unstable note, and so the finale succeeds to the extent that an equilibrium has been good-humouredly maintained. Since it is lighter in mood than its two predecessors, it may seem more superficial, and its material is certainly not particularly memorable or imaginative: but it succeeds in fulfilling the structural implications of the work's evolving argument. After all, music which is structurally ambiguous does not have to be either solemn or visionary in character.

16 Britten: *The Turn of the Screw* to *Noye's Fludde* (1953–7)

The Turn of the Screw is the first opera by Britten whose title does not identify a central character. That, as *Death in Venice* confirms, need not of itself imply the absence of a central character. But Henry James's title is symbolic as well as thematic, and in its presentation of a sequence of inexorably intensified events and emotions it is comparable to a good many of Britten's other operatic subjects. In this particular case, two kinds of interaction are involved: the first between right-thinking, vulnerable, innocent adults and deceitful, single-minded young people; the second between the human reality of honesty and unselfishness and the anti-human menace of ghosts who exist solely to threaten human happiness. Hence it is the events, as a sequence implying an inevitable outcome, that dominate the characters. As usual with Britten, time matters to the extent that it is not the present. But for the first time in his operas there are no significant public resonances or social perspectives: the conflicts are not seen as reflections of tensions within society (though the repressions of Victorian and Edwardian conventions can easily be brought out in a production), or of tensions between a single 'outsider' and the rest. It may be justifiable to offer an interpretation of James's story which concludes that the non-family life of absentee guardians, inexperienced governesses and ineffectual or positively evil servants is decadent: the true villain would therefore be the hierarchic social system. But no such issues are evident in the opera itself. The characters are psychological constructs rather than social beings; they are programmed and confined by their inner needs and natures. All this therefore encourages a view of *The Turn of the Screw* as a decisive retreat from the world of *Gloriana*, and in some respects a more sharply focused return to the issues most salient in *Billy Budd*.

Such a subject demands restriction, concentration, so the unprecedented control which Britten exerts over form and pitch organization as he returns to the medium of the chamber opera is justified. The main consequence of his belief that the music, in metaphorically 'translating' the title, should be strongly unified yet inexorably progressive was his early decision to use a sequence of short scenes separated by, but relating to, instrumental interludes; all of these vary a twelve-note theme – a theme presented initially as three four-note groups or tetrachords – but whose source trichord is 0, 2, 5 (Ex. 31a). The obsessive, though not of course

Ex. 31a Britten, *The Turn of the Screw*

serial, schemes of *Wozzeck* may have been in Britten's mind: certainly *Wozzeck* is the most obvious and important precedent for the use of elaborate structuring to control and concentrate the intense emotional content of a music drama. The narrowing of focus is also reflected in the fact that there is no attempt to use the characters to form a chorus, as in *Lucretia* and *Herring*, in both of which certain broader social perspectives are skilfully sketched in. But at Bly there are no neighbours, no vicar, policeman, shopkeeper, to intrude into the action. Only the Prologue – decided on after the first three scenes had been completed –

provides comment on the action; and the action itself continues, almost uncomfortably, so audiences might feel, to the very end. Part of the function of the Epilogue of *Billy Budd* is to lower the emotional temperature which has reached its height with Billy's execution to a po:nt where the audience may decently be expected to 'come down to earth and applaud. *Grimes* and *Lucretia* have comparable 'codas' – so, less extensively, does *Gloriana*. But it was perhaps only in *Death in Venice* that Britten achieved the ideal concentration of intensity and release in the very last bars of an opera.

Eric Walter White, noting that the composition of Canticle II followed hard on the heels of *Billy Budd*, observed that 'Abraham's dilemma over Isaac is similar to the problem that confronts Captain Vere and Billy Budd'.[1] Yet the sacrifice of a male child, so happily averted in the Chester Miracle Play which provided the text for the second canticle, is part of the price that the Governess in *The Turn of the Screw* has to pay for the repose of Quint's soul: and she may well feel that her own eternal damnation will complete the payment. The contrast of theme is therefore total: it is also very different from the poignant portraits of innocent, hopeful youth which Hardy painted in 'Midnight on the Great Western' and 'At the Railway Station, Upway', set by Britten in 1953. Whereas in *Peter Grimes* the death of the apprentice, however sadistic a sacrifice, can seem almost accidental because his only sounds are a few sobs and a scream, Miles is a fully characterized creation, and so essential to the drama that Britten was prepared to make successful performance of a major work dependent on a rare phenomenon, a boy soprano who can act, and whose voice will carry in a theatre. A similar subject was not to recur for another ten years, but when it did, in *Curlew River*, the Christian context ensures a kind of happy issue – the child's spirit brings his demented mother peace of mind. For the Governess, however, the future surely holds nothing but torment. She is the most powerfully drawn of all Britten's 'ineffectual' women – as destructive as she is ineffectual. Such female destructiveness was later to resurface in the character of Kate Julian in *Owen Wingrave*. But the relationship between adult and child recurs most powerfully in *Death in Venice* and this, in a sense, inverts the situation of the earlier opera. In *Death in Venice*, the youth 'destroys' the adult – not least, it seems, by means of his mysterious silence. Tadzio does not even speak, he dances. And this time there is no third party involved. The Governess fights Quint for Miles, and loses: Aschenbach fights himself, and loses.

Since *The Turn of the Screw* is invariably discussed in terms of its unifying processes it should be noted that these are not so all-embracing as to indicate a desire on Britten's part to use a single structuring device. Naturally, since there are fifteen variations and sixteen scenes, it is not

possible for each variation/scene pair to use the appropriate member of
the sequence of pitch-classes in the twelve-note theme as tonal centre.
Nor does that theme (Ex. 31a) have a second hexachord matching the
first in the relationship I-11, to mirror the relationship between the tonal-
centre sequences of the two Acts (Ex. 31b). This sequence may indeed

Ex. 31b Britten, *The Turn of the Screw*

symbolize the extent to which Act II is a darker reflection of Act I; and
the fact that Act II starts in the tonal area where Act I ends (A flat),
while the opera as a whole – excluding the Prologue – begins and ends in
A, is an important, pivotal relationship, recalling similar fundamental
connections between semitones in *Grimes*, *Lucretia*, and *Budd*. Logically, however, it might be argued that the retreat in Act II from the
supernatural evils of A flat to the starting point of A, albeit by another
route from that traversed in Act I, is more appropriate for a subject
which ends, if not with a positive resolution, then at least with a restora-
tion of the status quo. But the structural scheme of *The Turn of the
Screw* seems right because of its rigour and coherence, not because it in
any literal fashion 'symbolizes' or 'represents' the dramatic material.
Britten followed most opera composers in using thematic material,
rather than tonality, to carry the principal weight of extra-musical
association.

There are other musical parallels with earlier works. For example, the
convenience of semitonal conflicts as a symbol for irresolvable dramatic
tension is, as mentioned above, familiar. In *Billy Budd*, B natural and B
flat confront each other to such effect that the ultimate 'victory' of B flat
seems distinctly hollow, if not utterly sham. In *The Turn of the Screw* the
overall progression from A to A flat and back to A lends special significance to the actual conflict between these centres in the final scene (a

161

conflict which Britten's revisions intensified) and in this case the hollowness of the A major 'victory' is quite unambiguous. This negative resolution is all the more striking since, as has already been noted, the final scene for once contains the climax of the action. The passacaglia no longer provides a meditative interlude, as in *Grimes*, or the basis for reflective, if impassioned, comments, as in *Lucretia* and *Herring*. Because it initially needs to reflect Miles's apparent nonchalance – he 'saunters in' – the smooth, elegant material is a perfect background against which to project the climactic conflicts which are also, in Britten's most effective fashion, the climactic recapitulation of earlier, by now familiar material concerning both Quint and Miles. Maybe the music of the final scene never quite achieves the haunting intensity of the well-nigh all-thematic episode in Act I where Mrs Grose tells the Governess about Quint and Miss Jessel. Here, primes and inversions combine in concentrated allusion to the work's essential structural concept, evil in death as the black opposite of innocence in life. But the coda to the final scene adds a further diversifying element for the sake of dramatic and verbal neatness. Miles's 'Malo' song may start off by filling in the fourths of the 'Screw' theme, but it flowers independently of that theme's actual pitch-sequence. What is appropriate is the sheer intensity of its own motivic coherence, and the specific importance of transposition and inversion as an agent thereof. As introduced in Act I, Scene 6, it contradicts the prevailing F major and, by its final cadence, provides a particularly clear adumbration of Quint's A flat, still two scenes away. (Its first phrase itself spans the B flat to E flat of Quint's own perfect fourth, first heard at Fig. 26 in Scene 4.) It is the fourth which occurs at the first hint of evil: 'Mrs Grose, he's dismissed his school' (Scene 3, Fig. 15). Now, at the end, it overlays the final A major with the kind of chromatic colouring which reinforces the need to view the whole work's much-discussed sequence of tonalities as a background (Ex. 31c). It is not so much that other tonalities occur during scenes where only one has the primary claim, but that the local chromaticisms of this 'Malo' theme, and of Britten's compositional style, transfer the wholly chromatic sequence of principal tonal steps as shown in Ex. 31b from the substructure to the surface. Never exactly, of course, for just as the opera leaves the listener doubting what is 'real', so it leaves us suspecting that comforting coherence is an ideal which modern art can only hint at.

A little more than two months after the Venice première of *The Turn of the Screw*, Britten completed Canticle III at Aldeburgh. The structural and stylistic connections with the opera are obvious. But the text – 'Still falls the Rain – The raids, 1940, Night and Dawn', by Edith Sitwell – show a return to Christian imagery and ideals after the God-less horrors

Ex. 31c Britten, *The Turn of the Screw*, Act II (finale)

of the opera. Once again, therefore, musical resolution expresses faith in the eventual redemption of man: 'still do I love, still shed my innocent light, my Blood, for thee'. The Canticle is in effect a concentrated development of the opera's form-scheme of alternating scenes and variations. But its duration is only some eleven and a half minutes, and so, unlike the opera, there is only one clearly established tonal centre, the all-pervading B flat. Also, all the verses, which alternate with the purely instrumental variations until Variation 6 (which functions as a coda), are marked 'free recitative'. The more formally balanced music therefore tends to be in the more melodic variations, and in the recitatives Britten controls the rather prolix syntax and imagery of the text by keeping the accompaniment close to a very basic focus on B flat and F. The music therefore holds its chromaticism under constant constraint. The initial presentation of the theme uses explicit, complementary inversion in apparently serial fashion, like the tonal centres of the acts of *The Turn of the Screw*, and the piano has a complete twelve-note cycle in its first five bars; but the matching coda purges the chromatic tendencies to a considerable extent, in keeping with the pure piety of the text.

The Turn of the Screw is so concentrated and specific, so disturbing and authentic a treatment of its theme, that it is indeed difficult to imagine it being followed up – at least in the same medium. That its formal and technical procedures were quickly utilized, and further concentrated, is evident from Canticle III, and certain aspects of twelve-note serial procedures were to remain a feature of Britten's technique from this point onwards, in various fruitful 'compromises' with more traditional aspects. But whereas Britten was quite soon to find appropriate material for song cycles after *Winter Words* – in Hölderlin, Blake, and Soutar – the further exploration in the theatre of the eerily tragic vein which *Grimes*, *Lucretia*, *Budd* and the *Screw* display was only to re-emerge more than fifteen years later, in *Owen Wingrave* and *Death in Venice*.

Britten had composed six full-length operas in ten years. It is therefore not altogether surprising that he should, in his early forties, have felt the need for some respite from the sheer hard grind of all aspects of opera composition and production. It could also be that he felt that his drama- ·tic subjects, culminating in *The Turn of the Screw*, were too negative, too despairing, and however suited his musical language and temperament were to such themes he need not, should not, be limited to them. Certainly the dramatic works of the late 1950s – the ballet *The Prince of the Pagodas*, *Noye's Fludde*, and *A Midsummer Night's Dream* – are not simply a retreat from 'negative' realism into escapist fantasy. They recognize the other side of the coin: and the looser the traditional tonal bonds, the stronger the power of new means of construction became to support images of vulnerability – and of survival.

The Prince of the Pagodas is, of course, a fantasy. Britten returned to Covent Garden three years after *Gloriana* with a much happier tale of royalty, which, while it shares *Gloriana*'s relish for ceremonial music, is unique in the composer's output for presenting an unequivocally heroic male character – the Prince himself. It seems unlikely that Britten could ever have centred an opera on a male protagonist so unassailed by the least hint of weakness or vulnerability, and in most respects John Cranko's scenario is a rather thin, conventional affair; one wonders whether Britten ever contemplated a more modern subject, perhaps on the lines of Bliss's *Miracle in the Gorbals*. Even so, Act II of *The Prince of the Pagodas* effectively pursues the archetypal dramatic theme of the quest: a reminder that Cranko had choreographed *The Midsummer Marriage* for its première in January 1955. But although the subject-matter itself never transcends the conventions of traditional ballet, by no means all the musical numbers resort to balletic clichés. The principal themes all have Britten's characteristically surging lyricism, and the strongest echoes, particularly of Prokofiev, occur on the periphery – the music of Belle Épine, for example. The orchestration is dazzlingly resourceful and rich: for once the composer did not need to avoid swamping voices, and the integrated nature of the musical design is suggested by the fact that Britten himself never attempted to draw suites from it: only the 'Pas de Six' was published separately during his lifetime. As is well known, the work reflects interests in non-Western music which long pre-date the composer's world tour of 1956. Those interests were eventually to have a much deeper influence on Britten's later development, principally on the style and form of the Church Parables. By the mid-1960s, the opulence and expansiveness of *The Prince of the Pagodas* were very much a thing of the past for Britten: but it may be simply because it is unique in his output that the ballet has never received its due.

A connection can easily be made between the characteristics of the ballet and the exotic, pantomime element which has an important function in *A Midsummer Night's Dream*, composed four years later. Moreover, in the ballet's immediate successor, the six *Songs from the Chinese* for tenor and guitar op. 58, texts and timbres again ensure a degree of exoticism, which is now allied to the more austere, technically progressive characteristics stemming from the greater chromaticism of *The Turn of the Screw* and Canticle III. Indeed, with their high degree of tonal instability and concentrated motivic integration – No. 5 is the most forward-looking in this respect – the Chinese songs mark a distinct step along the path to the less traditionally harmonic, more totally thematic emphasis of the 1960s and 1970s. These progressive features stand out in part because the actual forms of the individual songs are so simple and straightforward; stanzaic repetitions and variations, ritornello-like recurrences are all that Britten needed as formal foundation for one of his most personal compositions.

Noye's Fludde is, of all Britten's dramatic works, the one most directly concerned with the theme of survival. Of course, its roots are in the hymn-book homilies of *Saint Nicolas* rather than the sceptically viewed, off-stage religious observances of *Peter Grimes*, but in its compression, as well as its subject-matter, it is in effect Britten's first parable for church performance. Like the trilogy of the 1960s, it shows God as ultimately benign and man as ultimately regenerate. Paradise is possible after all, and while life on earth may be more in the mode of hell than heaven, it can be made bearable through the consolations of religion. Any work which involves amateur and child performers to the degree that *Noye's Fludde* involves them could easily degenerate into coyness, but any such danger is effectively offset by the concentration and vigour of the musical fabric. Nowhere are these virtues more apparent than in the episode which relates most obviously to *The Turn of the Screw* – the 'storm' passacaglia whose recurring theme gradually uses up all twelve notes. Even so, this 'completeness' is balanced both by making the theme tonally centred, and by its simply evolving motivic content, hinting at shapes in the very plain hymn-tune for 'Eternal Father', which emerges as the storm subsides. Whether another motivic connection (the passacaglia's initial pattern of descending minor third, ascending minor second, descending minor third exactly inverts Miles's 'Malo' theme from *The Turn of the Screw*) was conscious or not is one of those intriguing questions which provide the analyst who concentrates on motives with ample material for speculation. But Britten's ability to repeat himself on the small scale is more than compensated for by his gift for devising new and appropriate structural contexts. 'Basic shapes' may often be similar, as they are in many great composers: but their treatment, and their relation to the total structure of which they form a part, is richly diverse and inventive.

17 Tippett: Symphony No. 2 (1956–7)

It is often easy to imply, in comparing Britten and Tippett, that the first was the 'realist' and the second the 'visionary': Britten was the practical, versatile man of music, Tippett the 'ivory-tower' composer, who was not too concerned with how, or even if, his music could actually be performed. But this absurd opposition ignores the fact that Tippett was directly involved in teaching and amateur performance from 1924, when he started to conduct a madrigal group, until 1951, when he resigned as Director of Music at Morley College, a post he had held for eleven years; and into his seventies Tippett has remained an authoritative conductor of his own works. The opposition also overlooks the fact that Tippett continued to provide arrangements and occasional pieces throughout the

1950s and 1960s. His editions of early music, principally Purcell, but also including Blow, Handel and Humphrey, were made in collaboration with Walter Bergmann, and reflect with particular clarity his sense of feeling closer to this more distant English music than to more recent varieties. Nor did he allow Britten a monopoly in the field of folk-song arrangements, as two products of 1956 show: the Northumbrian Folksong set for unison voices and recorders, *Bonny at Morn*, and the Four Songs of the British Isles for unaccompanied chorus. As for occasional music, he produced works as diverse as the Sonata for Four Horns (1955), which only virtuosos can hope to tackle, and the cantata *Crown of the Year* (1958), designed for the girls of Badminton School, and including, after the example of the *Suite for the Birthday of Prince Charles*, and the *Divertimento on Sellinger's Round*, several references to folk or popular tunes. Few composers can exist creatively, and still less commercially, on a diet of major works, and it is only since *The Knot Garden* that Tippett has virtually given up all such smaller tasks.

In the closing stages of *The Midsummer Marriage*, Tippett had used C major as the tonality for the affirmative chorale-like material which seems simultaneously to hint at and transcend the baroque-based neo-classicism of so much music from the first half of the twentieth century. With this association in mind, it is striking to recall the composer's account of the conception of the Symphony No. 2, which took place some four years before the composition itself was begun.

About the time I was finishing *The Midsummer Marriage* I was sitting one day in a small studio of Radio Lugano, looking out over the sunlit lake, listening to tapes of Vivaldi. Some pounding cello and bass Cs, as I remember them, suddenly threw me from Vivaldi's world into my own, and marked the exact moment of conception of the 2nd Symphony. Vivaldi's pounding Cs took on a kind of archetypal quality as though to say: here is where we must begin.[1]

The opera's C major 'chorale' may be a less obvious stimulus for the opening of the Symphony than Sosostris's A flat major 'meadow music' was for that of the Piano Concerto, though in view of the particular significance which Tippett appears to attach to repeated Cs, the link may still be a valid one. Whether it is or not, however, the Symphony is usually considered more in the light of its anticipations of future developments than of echoes from the past, and it is true that the problems of form and style which it raises help to explain why the radical rethinking of these elements, which is found in parts of *King Priam* and the Concerto for Orchestra, was so salutary: if only, ultimately, to provide a new perspective and impulse for synthesis.

In one essential respect, certainly, the Symphony No. 2 looks forward, since it has passages where superimpositions of different types of material cease to observe the requirements of conventional polyphony to make collective tonal and harmonic 'sense'. The third section of the finale (Figs. 170 to 181) has a string melody which at first centres strongly on A flat, recalling the tonal contrasts of the first movement, and indicating that relations which result from dividing the octave by major thirds seem especially important – an interesting anticipation of later symmetries in the Piano Sonata No. 3 and String Quartet No. 4. But the ornamental counter-material, while subject to its own process of varied repetition, is far from confirming this tonality of A flat, or providing a clear alternative (Ex. 32). Such suspensions of function, like the strongly contrasted juxtapositions of tone-colours and materials in the second movement,

Ex. 32 Tippett, Symphony No. 2, fourth movement (finale)

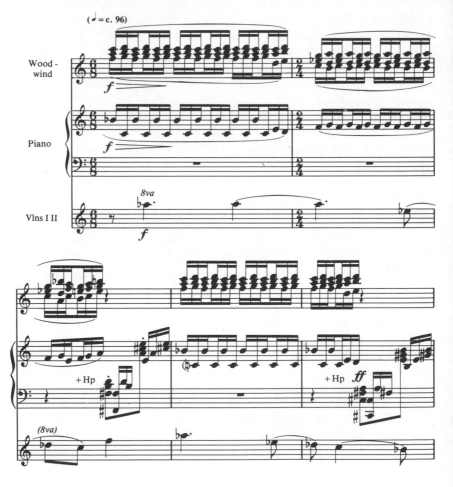

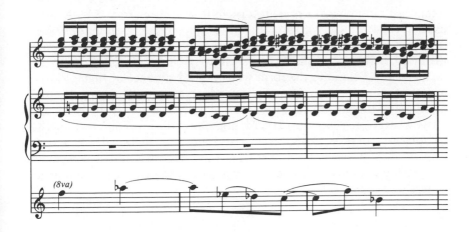

may well stem from the more radical processes of the Piano Concerto's second movement, where even the overall form, though intensely variational, is evolutionary rather than symmetrical. But the first movement of the Symphony No. 2, in contrast to that of the Piano Concerto, follows tradition in subordinating lyric contrast to the energetic main material. However subliminal his baroque, Vivaldian inspiration had become by 1956, Tippett here wrote his most explicitly neoclassical movement, one which is splendidly well made, even to the extent of fitting in a second development between recapitulation and coda, but which, lyric contrasts aside, is so Stravinskian as virtually to identify the need for classicizing order with that composer's middle-period style.

The tonal explicitness of the Allegro is balanced by the ensuing Adagio, which confirms the demonstration in the Piano Concerto's slow movement that Tippett's 'magical' style, with its contrasts between slowly unfolding melodies and elaborate colouristic filigree, can survive extreme stretching of tonal centrality. Nevertheless, the form of the Adagio is uncomplicated. So, too, is that of the scherzo, which, with its brilliantly effective and sustained use of additive rhythm, establishes and ultimately reinforces a tonal centre of D. It is the finale which most determinedly questions the formal logic and apparent 'conservatism' of the first movement. In fact, the finale challenges the premises of the rest of the work, yet progresses towards a coda in which C major, and the generating motive of the first Allegro, are re-established. Order is cyclically restored, but the first two sections of the finale, before extended melody reasserts more familiar stylistic characteristics (at Fig. 170) seem almost eccentrically unformed and disruptive. Tippett described the movement as a fantasia in four unrelated sections, and the first section, 'short and entirely introductory', seems the oddest – abrupt in the extreme, yet embodying a preparatory shift of centre from E to A. The usual formal principle of proceeding by varied restatement *within* sections has not been abandoned, though contrasts are strong even within the first five bars. And the second section, 'a close-knit set of variations on a ground',[2] employs the form which, in the absence of fugue, canon or passacaglia, is the most obvious representative of Tippett's admired pre-classical designs. Even if the four main sections of the finale are unrelated, therefore – and the matter is arguable – the procedures within the sections remain more characteristic, and more conventional. The movement as a whole concludes the symphony as effectively as it challenges its own earlier assumptions, and makes a convincing case for C major as goal as well as generator.

18 Britten: The *Nocturne* to the *War Requiem* (1958–61)

In the *Nocturne* op. 60 for tenor, seven obbligato instruments and string orchestra, composed during the summer of 1958, Britten continued to explore the consequences of formal procedures and pitch processes employed in *The Turn of the Screw*. A sequence of basic tonalities descends from the confrontation between C and D flat in the initial section (Shelley's 'On a poet's lips I slept'), through B flat, A, A flat, F sharp, E and D to the return of the same music, and the same tonal confrontation, at the end. The essential semitone clash is familiar, but the tonal plan itself, if such it is, is on the whole much less explicit than in *The Turn of the Screw*. In the opera there is only one section, before the final twelve-note variation, where the tonal centre is not made unambiguously clear (Variation 12). But in the *Nocturne*, the most obvious structuring feature is not the assertion of centres as such, but thematic; the recurrent 'rocking' music, which often links movements together, and also appears within several of them.

Explicit tonal centrality is nevertheless pronounced in No. 2, Tennyson's 'The Kraken', where the notes of the B flat major triad are used as a kind of ground for most of its length. The tonality is characteristic of the later. Britten: extended, to encompass a strong admixture of chromatic degrees, and avoiding both triads and diatonic progressions. No. 3, the Coleridge setting, is even more firmly rooted by its initial presentation of the complete A major collection as a 'tonic thirteenth' chord. There is much less chromaticism here, but a similar avoidance of progression, and only one conventional cadence: the dominant–tonic motion between the end of the first main section and the beginning of the second, at the words 'The moon was bright'. No. 5 – Wordsworth's 'But that night', from *The Prelude* – sustains octave F sharps during its early stages, and this seems to function, even in the absence of diatonic triadic procedures, as a dominant to the eventual B (Fig. 19). But No. 4, Middleton's 'Midnight's Bell', clearly favours A flat only at the start (Fig. 13): its reliance on the 'rocking' chords of the initial Shelley setting guarantees a high degree of tonal flux. And the Owen and Keats settings are allusive to the point where even the principle of extended tonality is difficult to apply. Owen's 'The Kind Ghosts', avoiding triads in its apparently simple chordal accompaniment, does move away from, and around, an E: but there is a key signature of one flat, and the later stages lean more towards a minorish D. No. 7, from Keats's 'Sleep and Poetry', has a two-flat signature, but this setting comes closest to tonal clarity when it reasserts the basic C of the whole work at Fig. 30, though D has been picked out for at least passing emphasis in the earlier stages. That reassertion of C is, however, only the first stage of the rich exploration of tonal ambiguities in the final movement, the setting of Shakespeare's Sonnet 43. Music from the end of the work's first section (Ex. 33a) is reproduced at the end of the Keats setting (Ex. 33b). In the first section the opposition of C and D flat prepared the strong B flat minor emphasis of 'The Kraken': in other words, the C-as-tonic proposition had been decisively rejected. As the Shakespeare setting begins, however, it becomes clear that the C is more stable than the D flat to the extent that the three-flat signature implies a tendency to either E flat major or C minor. Indeed, it seems in the early stages that in spite of various chromaticisms, a relationship between a 'tonic' C and a 'dominant' G is emerging. The harmony brightens still further with the emphasis on D at Fig. 36. But then, to the line 'Then thou whose shadow shadows doth make bright', the clash of D flat and C is renewed, and although the increasing harmonic tension of the second half of the setting moves towards a C minor dominant (one bar before Fig. 38) the sonority which embodies that essential confrontation is reasserted as the bass moves down from G, through G flat, on to F (one bar after Fig. 38). The effect, if retrospective, is to create a sense of an extended F minor tonality for the whole movement, in spite of the absence of any root position tonic chord. In the coda, from Fig. 39 to the end, the vocal line inverts the intervals of the first song's concluding phrase, 'Nurslings of immortality'; but the C/D flat conflict is given a new guise, ascending and finally dying away so imperceptibly that it seems permissible for ears which feel that a final C major chord is 'missing' to provide it (Ex. 33c).

With hindsight it is tempting to give the *Nocturne* special treatment, seeing it as Britten's most crucial transitional work. It reasserts the

Ex. 33a Britten, *Nocturne*

Ex. 33b Britten, *Nocturne*

Ex. 33c Britten, *Nocturne*

functional concentration of the James opera and Canticle III, but with
the even more vital, forward-looking element, seen embryonically in the
Chinese songs, of a tonal ambiguity so pervasive as to make it more
difficult, if not actually impossible, to resolve the issue at the end. In
Billy Budd, controversy centres not on which of the two centres, B or B

174

flat, is ultimately 'the winner', but on how hollow is the victory which the resolution on to B flat represents. In the *Nocturne,* however, the C/D flat polarity is just one factor in a motion away from traditional triadic and cadential practice: away, in fact, from 'progression' itself. Such a development, however 'inevitable', would nevertheless be profoundly uninteresting were it not for the increased expressiveness which it yields. In the *Nocturne* the vocal line has supreme flexibility and purpose-fulness, moving from arioso to more balanced rhythmic phrases with no crude changes of gear. Britten never surpassed the economic emotional force of his word-setting in this work, and the presence of a poem by Wilfred Owen inevitably foreshadows the emotional crux of the *War Requiem,* to be completed less than three years later. Economy and expressiveness were carried over immediately into the *Six Hölderlin Fragments* op. 61, first performed in private only a month after the *Nocturne* in November 1958, but not published until 1963. In an interview of this period, Britten described the Hölderlin settings as 'probably my best vocal works so far'.[1] This was to be his only venture into setting German poetry, and it was designed, like the final 'German' opera, *Death in Venice,* specifically for Peter Pears. When writing a song-cycle for Dietrich Fischer-Dieskau in 1965, Britten chose English texts by Blake.

In one important sense, the Hölderlin cycle is a reversion to the mode of *Winter Words*: the individual songs are not linked together or motivically interconnected in any explicit sense. Nor, in spite of the con-centration, is there that sense of floating away from any clear tonal centre in places which the more strongly shaped large-scale scheme of the *Nocturne* had made possible. Hölderlin's verse is more elusive in meaning than Hardy's, of course, but there is a fundamental, positive sense of a divine benevolence – the 'treuen, freundlichen Götter' of 'Die Jugend' (No. 4), so that the grief and shadows of life so powerfully evoked in 'Die Heimat' (No. 2) and 'Hälfte des Lebens' (No. 5) are offset by the 'Harmonien und ew'gem Lohn und Frieden' – 'harmonies and eternal reward and peace' – which God (or a god) offers ('Die Linien des Lebens', No. 6).

All but one of the songs have formal schemes in which completion is achieved through varied restatement: Nos. 3, 5, and 6 are essentially bipartite structures consisting only of statement and variation. But the first song, 'Menschenbeifall', has clearer central contrast, and the fourth is notably free in its use of metrical stress to contradict 'natural' verbal metre. No. 4 also has a freer form, dividing into two main parts, the second for once not leading to an explicit return of the first, though, as if to compensate, the overall G major is emphatically reasserted.

With its chromatic and canonic features, the Hölderlin cycle is very much of its period in Britten's development. Thus the basic fourths of the first song's accompaniment have accumulated a complete twelve-note cycle as early as the second line of page 2, though without eliminating the F major emphasis. In No. 3, 'Sokrates und Alcibiades', the tonally directed twelve-note cycle is still more evident when the first half's totally chromatic piano monody, spread out under the voice's recitative with many repetitions, returns in the second half: here it moves to the voice part, and is underpinned by thirteen major triads, the first and last of D major. The fifth song is a reminder that the most intense expression can be generated by a 'pure' melody with a motivically independent accompaniment, the consistency and contour of which may even recall Britten's very early Belloc setting, 'The Birds' (1929). In the final song, however, the 'lines' of the text are realized in a contrapuntal, canonic texture of three, expanding to four, parts whose total thematicism and tritone-spanning phrases are still more conclusive evidence of increasing concern with tensions between tonal and serial, hierarchic and symmetrical elements than the more 'orthodox' twelve-note occurrences in the James opera and *Noye's Fludde*. Britten's interest in the serial principle related as much to the pervasive motivicism which it seemed to promote as to its capacity of regulating a succession of twelve different tonal centres across large structural spans. The former possibility was, of course, much more genuinely Schoenbergian: it signified nothing less than the awareness that, with the loss of tonality, hierarchic means of harmonic organization were no longer to be found. But if tonality, however extended, was *not* lost, the sense of harmonic hierarchy could combine with intensified motivic processes to give new vitality to the traditional musical language.

In the *War Requiem* Britten was to achieve a remarkable extension of the pervasive tonal ambiguity and sectional interconnections of the *Nocturne*, a work whose own special tensions might seem to have developed ultimately from the relatively simple tritonal oppositions of *Les Illuminations*. The more rigorous, concentrated, thematically determined textures of the final Hölderlin setting were, moreover, to underlie many of the heterophonic yet tonally centred procedures of the final decade. And even in a lightweight, perhaps overlong, *pièce d'occasion,* the *Cantata Academica, Carmen Basiliense* op. 62 (1959), Britten felt free to indulge his increasing liking for primes and inversions in both juxtaposition and combination. The triadic underpinning of the actual 'Tema Seriale' is more directly comparable with the third Hölderlin setting, but even the primes and inversions of the ensuing fugue, entering on the successive pitches of the twelve-note theme, and changing places for the cumulative stretto, still contrive to retain toe-holds in tonal progressions. The clearest blend of simple triadicism and simple twelve-

Ex. 34 Britten, *Missa Brevis*

(i) Sanctus

(ii) Trichord forms

(iii) Kyrie

(iv) Gloria

note cycles is, perhaps, that found in the Sanctus of the *Missa Brevis,* which was finished on Trinity Sunday 1959, a few weeks after the *Cantata Academica.* The prominent fourths of the set inevitably recall *The Turn of the Screw,* and the first treble part at the start of the Sanctus (Ex. 34 (i)) can be reordered into two forms of that 0, 2, 5 trichord (Ex. 34 (ii)) which is so prominent in both the Kyrie and Gloria of the Mass (Exx. 34 (iii) and (iv)).

When Britten began work on *A Midsummer Night's Dream* in October 1959, five years had passed since the completion of *The Turn of the Screw.* Rumours of a very different Shakespeare opera – a *King Lear* for Fischer-Dieskau – were rife in the early 1960s; it might well have been undertaken had not Britten been deterred by the very strength of the rumours. His first Shakespeare setting, of Sonnet 43 in the *Nocturne* of 1958, had been one of his finest inspirations, and the emphasis on night and dreams in it seems a clear pointer in the direction of the next opera. *A Midsummer Night's Dream* was apparently the most rapidly composed of all Britten's full-length stage works – he wrote it between October 1959 and April 1960 – and it may well seem that the music skates too rapidly over the surface of the play for enough of substance to accumulate. In some respects, certainly, the music for the mechanicals on the one hand and the lovers on the other is relatively thin. The music is better the farther it gets from either the jolly or the passionate, and the varieties of serenity in the work are considerable, and convincing.

The musical heart of *A Midsummer Night's Dream* lies in its particularly direct use of consonant harmony within the orbit of extended or floating tonality. This technique is suggested even in the shadowy slitherings of the opening bars, which use the G major triad as their principal point of focus and move to several other triadic or fifth-based harmonies while shunning the diatonic, cadential confirmation of G.

Perhaps the best example of a section of lucidly extended tonality in the opera is the fairies' song – 'On the ground sleep sound' – which ends Act II (from Fig. 102). The harmonic basis, the four chords which divide the twelve semitones in an order and layout which stress the linear unrelatedness of the resulting 'progression', is governed by the framing recurrence of the D flat major triad, and by the obedient gravitation of the fairies' melody, which is as homogenous in texture and narrow in register as the chords are diverse and dispersed. The rotation of all four chords ensures the total absence of diatonic progression in D flat major, and the use of a mirror motion for the words

> And the country proverb known
> In your wakings shall be shown

enables the voices to build stronger connections between the elements of the first and last chords than the orchestra is ever prepared to do. The orchestra insists on an 'anti-cadential' ending to the act, for although the harmony which Britten provides between the final elaboration of the high fourth chord and the final D flat major leans in context towards that key, its register is so remote and its tone colour so rarified as to reinforce dissimilarity. The D flat major chord functions conclusively because it links back to all its punctuating predecessors. It is a large-scale point of focus which can disdain the local relations of more traditional tonal continuity (Ex. 35).

Ex. 35 Britten, *A Midsummer Night's Dream*, Act II (conclusion)

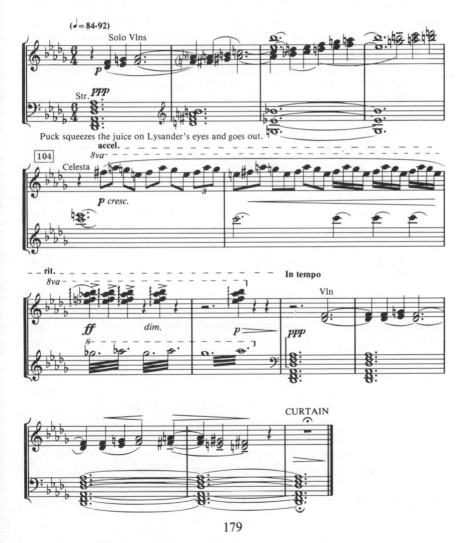

A Midsummer Night's Dream was first heard at the 1960 Aldeburgh Festival, and in the following year the new Britten work was his first composition for the Russian cellist Mstislav Rostropovich, the Sonata in C op. 65. The title is unprecedented in the Britten canon, and it was the first work to include an identifying tonality in its title since the String Quartet No. 2 (also in C) of 1945: it was also the last work to which Britten would accord so precise an identity.

With its five individually titled movements – 'Dialogo', 'Scherzo-pizzicato', 'Elegia', 'Marcia', 'Moto Perpetuo' – the sonata could equally well have been called suite. But its principal tonal centre is not in doubt. The first movement establishes that 'C' means a chromatically extended rather than even predominantly diatonic C major, whose tonic and dominant triads are first touched in as arpeggiations (from Fig. 1) and are never brought together in cadential harmony. The final cadence of the movement, just before Fig. 8, characteristically approaches the C in the bass by step rather than by leap, and the upper harmony completes a 'higher consonance', with E, B and F but no G present. The only other movement to centre on C is the finale, and here the dominant note is given stronger emphasis, even though no dominant triad appears. But the exuberant coda expands the essential C in a riot of goal-directed chromaticism which uses G as one of its principal subsidiary pivots *en route* for its final root-position tonic triad, the only such chord in the entire work. The three middle movements are stylistically consistent with these principles. The scherzo centres on an A major–minor mixture but excludes the dominant from any structural function. The 'Elegia' and 'Marcia' are both less intransigent, the former becoming quite deeply involved with the special ambiguity of whether D or A is the true tonic, the latter using stresses on and reiterations of A flat and E flat as part of its sardonic, anti-militarist harmonic vocabulary.

The Cello Sonata is a superb and demanding display piece, strongly built and showing the instinctive rapport with instrument and player which would stimulate the composer to four more substantial works for Rostropovich over the next decade. But by the time of its first performance, in July 1961, Britten was deeply engaged with the work which was to prove his most successful outside the theatre, and in many ways his most 'representative' in any genre. The *War Requiem* had long been contemplated: hence the sense of its summing-up all Britten's most essential concerns, both musical and extra-musical. It is indeed a work with a wide range of reference, and some have seen it as almost too anxious to ensure universal appeal; for example, by means of direct parallels with Verdi. Anticipations of its music in Britten's own earlier works are also easy to spot: the Cello Sonata's 'March' is one such forerunner. There is a clear anticipation of the 'Quam olim Abrahae' (deriving, of course, from Canticle II) in the recorders at Fig. 90 of *Noye's Fludde*; nor is the *Nocturne* – not merely the Owen text, but the sound of 'Midnight's Bell' – far away. But it is perhaps in the revived cantata form of the *Cantata Academica*, and in the liturgical text of the *Missa Brevis*, as well as of the brief *Jubilate Deo* for choir and organ (February 1961) that we can almost begin to speak of preliminary sketches for the *Requiem*.

The central structural element of the *War Requiem* is the tritone C–F sharp, and the work as a whole is concerned with two fundamental issues: the extent to which the tritone's parent tonality of G, and G's close relative D, are emphasized or avoided; and the degree to which its separate pitches, and those of other tritones, can be treated as tonal centres, or be triadically harmonized. Many of Britten's other works had shown much concern with the perspectives created by a single tritonal opposition or alternation. But the *War Requiem* reveals a particular intensity in the way that tritones link or permeate passages of extended tonality which may or may not involve twelve-note successions.

The first two sections of the work will serve as examples. The first part of the 'Requiem Aeternam' will seem to most analysts to relate to a D minor 'background', but, in the absence of triads and cadential progressions, the degree of extension is clearly very great. There are in fact no 'roots', but rather points of focus: in the bass, the pedal A, which is virtually constant save between Figs. 1 and 2, and in the upper registers, the 'bell' tritone (F sharp–C) which is taken up by the chorus. The main melodic line, in the orchestra, has its own points of focus – D, E, F, and A up to Fig. 2, then E between Figs. 2 and 3; and the 'harmonization' of this melody is more a matter of doubling and parallel melodic movement than of any independently functioning chordal support. There is a stronger sense of harmonic relation between the bass pivot A and the points of focus in the evolving melodic line in the orchestra than between the bass pivot and the tritone. This forms a 'neutral' diminished triad with the pivot, and so it may be felt to inhibit realization of the diatonic implications of the rest of the texture.

From Figs. 3 to 7 ('Te decet hymnus') slightly overlapping alternations of C and F sharp in the strings of the main orchestra hover above the twelve-note prime and inversion melodies in the boys' choir, which are harmonized by appropriate triads in the organ. Each melodic segment moves from C to F sharp and back again, and the harmony progresses from a C major triad at the end of each segment to a second inversion F major triad at the start of the next. Moreover, at the centre of each segment there is a corresponding dominant–tonic progression in B minor. This technique of expanding a tonic to include its tritonal opposite creates a rather different situation from that in the first section; there, not only was the tritone in effect excluded from the harmonic structure, but that structure itself depended on the suppression of the 'true' tonic triad (D minor) in favour of its dominant note. The 'Te decet hymnus' does not end with the F major dominant–tonic progression, however: it dissolves with alternations between F major and B minor – the Cs and F sharps in the strings again overlapping – and the more fundamental non-triadic language of the movement is then restored (Ex. 36a).

Ex. 36a Britten, *War Requiem*, I Requiem Aeternam, 'Te decet hymnus'

The pedal-based harmonic structure of the opening section is the precedent for the more elaborate, if (apparently) less chromatic, harmonic scheme of the concluding 'In paradisum', where an entire chord, consisting of A major's subdominant, dominant and supertonic (the $0, 2, 5$ trichord), recurs as a non-resolving pivot. But the work's great climax, at Fig. 116 of the 'Libera Me', does reveal that a strongly prepared perfect cadence in the principal key, G minor, can be integrated into the music's prevailing extended tonality without strain or incongruity. The *War Requiem* makes the maximum possible use of triadic harmony, even when diatonic triadic progression as such is little in evidence. Hence the nature, and the effectiveness, of the contrapuntally expanded chromatic motion which forms the work's poignant refrain (Ex. 36b).

The *War Requiem* may seem to have been painlessly processed and 'used up' by the contemporary machine for the digestion of socially significant cultural artefacts. But while its troubled exploration of the irresolvable conflicts which persist even when warring nations are reconciled may be too disturbing for permanent contemplation, the conflicts themselves will not go away. The 'irresolute' tritone, wavering between its function as the agent of tonal resolution and its alternative function as the definer of symmetries, is the perfect musical symbol for the persistent psychological and political problems of modern times: a warning indeed. The work of Tippett's first performed at that same Coventry Festival in 1962 is far less obviously a tract for the times: but warfare and violence are crucial to its theme, and their unsparing depiction provoked a remarkable change in Tippett's style.

Ex. 36b Britten, *War Requiem*, I Requiem Aeternam, 'Kyrie eleison'

183

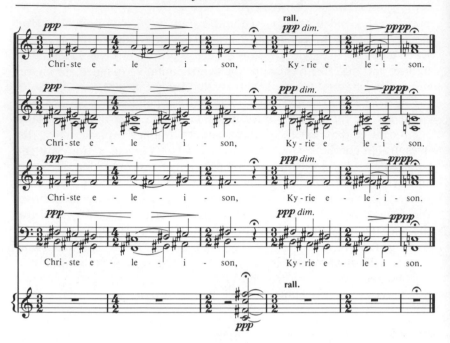

19 Tippett: *King Priam* (1958–61)

Six years (1952–8) separated the completion of *The Midsummer Marriage* from the commencement of work on *King Priam*, and these years can already be seen as particularly important for the development of modern British music. With the death of Vaughan Williams in 1958, the last significant links with the 'folkloristic symphony' were cut. Not only were Britten and Tippett becoming 'senior' composers; a new generation was emerging, with Peter Maxwell Davies to the fore, and their starting point was the serialism of Schoenberg, Webern, Boulez and Stockhausen, as well as the still developing, highly personal style of Olivier Messiaen. Messiaen, like Stravinsky, had moved beyond even the extended tonality of his earlier music to explore a more austere, radical manner involving serial processes; and although British composers in general were slow to react to the new varieties of radicalism emanating from both Europe and America, which were concerned as much with the increased freedoms of indeterminacy as the increased strictness of total serialism, they had begun to catch up by the late 1950s.

For Britten, as we have seen, the response – however instinctive – to the climate of the time was to bring an element of twelve-note thinking into the orbit of his extended tonality. In the 1960s he would also take significant note of indeterminacy, in the limited form of inexact co-ordination of polyphonic lines. For Tippett, however, 'total chromaticism' did not inevitably mean the sort of ordering principle pioneered by Schoenberg. What it did make possible was the complete dissolution of the principle of polar attraction: in music where 'harmonic progressions' were not the result of any 'technique' of organization other than that of contextual appropriateness, whether purely musical, or musico-dramatic, the need for tonality in any shape or form was never paramount.

Tippett has provided a neat link between his first and second operas by pointing out that the 'essence of *King Priam*' is to be found in some lines from *The Midsummer Marriage* which were 'always at the back of my mind while composing the second opera'.[1] The lines, in the version Tippett quotes, are

> Fate and Freedom are a paradox,
> Choose the fate but yet the God
> Speaks through whatever fate we choose.

(The lines come from an ensemble which is usually cut in performance.) The connection is indeed a striking one, since *Priam* deals with Fate and Choice in a very direct and potent fashion. But the worlds of the two operas could scarcely be more different. Of all Tippett's dramatic works, *King Priam* is the most directly concerned with war: indeed, it may almost seem like a pacifist's calculated response to the decade of Korea, ·Hungary and Suez. Because of the urgency of the issues facing the characters as war presses around them it seems inevitable that there should be relatively little time or place for lyric expansion, even though there is time for chorus-like commentary on the action. The most extended lyric episode – Achilles's song with guitar, 'O rich-soiled land' (Act II Scene 2), looks forward, with a melodic line whose opening recalls the arching fourths of *The Midsummer Marriage* and its satellite works, to what might happen 'after the war'. But the allusive, atonal harmony here strongly reflects the present unease rather than the possibility of future peace (Ex. 37a).

King Priam is a work of exploding energy which expands within its economically shaped structure to produce a remarkably coherent solidity. Unlike *The Ice Break,* Tippett's later treatment of the theme of violence, it ends with little or no sense of a new beginning, of that rebirth and regeneration which is normally such a central image in Tippett's subject-matter. Tippett has claimed that, at the end of the opera, Priam is allowed 'a direct moment of vision, a visionary perception of the inner

Ex. 37a Tippett, *King Priam*, Act II Scene 2

life'.[2] But even this moment of self-discovery may have come to seem too negative; 'the dark forms of creation' which Priam sees just before his death might even be essentially destructive forces. They do not lead on to 'the light', and although the audience has already been consoled by Hermes's message concerning the power of music to 'melt our hearts' and 'renew our love', Priam's own inexorable fate cannot be charmed away by any 'stream of sound': indeed, the music which ends the opera, the music of Priam's final disintegration, is Tippett's most bleak and disembodied: he calls it 'a few curious sounds that might represent *our* inward tears'.[3] The war music itself may rely a little too much on distorted fanfares, but these reach a degree of horrific intensity in Achilles's war-cry, and while the climactic encounter between Priam and Achilles could seem too understated from the purely musical point of view, its restraint probably brings out the intense humanity of the scene more effectively than would any breast-beating histrionics.

The range of the music beyond the more specific wartime aspects is in any case extremely impressive: the vital role of lyric contrast is evident not only in Achilles's song already mentioned, but in the set-pieces for Helen and Hermes in Act III. There is also a passage of pointed parody in the trio for Paris, Hector and Priam in Act II Scene 3, where the absurd pretensions of war-like ambition are sharply mocked. This passage is exceptional, however: Tippett's compassion for his characters is far more evident most of the time. In an uncharacteristically laconic note on the opera the composer has said that 'the theme of *Priam* is the mysterious nature of human choice, seen in the relations between Priam, King of Troy, Hecuba his wife, his sons Hector and Paris, and their wives Andromache and Helen'.[4] This emphasis on family rather than nationality is crucial, for it follows that the Trojan war is simply the means whereby the prophecy that Paris will cause his father's death is fulfilled at the hands not of Paris himself, but of Achilles's son, who plays no other role in the drama: the mechanics of the action are indeed inexorable.

Inexorable action could still be forced into an episodic form, however, and in view of the most obvious contrasts between the music of *King Priam* and that of *The Midsummer Marriage*, it might seem that in his search for explosive immediacy – for a 'spare, taut, heroic and unsentimantal' music, with 'a much more hard-hitting rhetoric'[5] – the composer had abandoned the essential richness and continuity of his earlier music. That Tippett was aiming for more than a merely negative sense of the inevitability of death and destruction in the work is clear from his comment that 'being . . . neither Christian nor Marxist, I am unrepentantly certain, from some deep intuitive source, that tragedy is both viable and rewarding. That when audiences see Priam's death at the altar as Troy burns, they will feel the old pity and terror and be uplifted by it.' Tippett's references to Brecht's epic theatre, and also to the Claudel-Milhaud *Christophe Colombe*, as providing precedents which 'pare away all the dross of the story, so that only the essentials – those scenes essential to *this* work – are there',[6] clearly did not imply any comparable, or parallel musical influences, however, and while the musical language of *King Priam* is by no means absolutely novel, it is a good deal more than a mere paring down of the language of his earlier works. Repetition, exact or varied, remains the essential structuring principle, and perhaps the most remarkable thing about *King Priam* is that, in spite of the large amounts of repetition, and the strong textural contrasts, the effect is genuinely cumulative. This is evident at once in the Prelude, which is built entirely from reiterations of the fanfare figures, and material so vividly characterized by tempo and tone colour may well have a more direct impact on the listener when repeated than a structure planned along the lines of tonal symphonic process, where themes evolve against a background for which tonal harmony provides the basic unity. When Tippett's material is freed of harmonic function, it becomes, in a sense, totally symbolic: it takes the form it does primarily to represent something in the most direct, effective manner. In fact, it can have a double symbolism: 'the opening prelude to the opera is both a symphony of war and an agonized image for the birth of Paris'.[7] Of course, there is always an extraordinarily powerful sense of freedom in all Tippett's best music, and that freedom has resided in the sheer exuberance of a thematic process which has carried texture – harmonic and contrapuntal content – along with it. That thematic process comprises all the traditional techniques – variation, extension and contraction, ornamentation. And *King Priam* provides clear evidence that such techniques do not depend on the presence of a single principle of harmonic organization to function effectively. From the harmonic point of view, *Priam* is indeed heterogeneous. Key signatures are not excluded – the first one provides a D major context for Hecuba's tirade at Fig. 35 – and because of the prevalence of repetition both within and between sections, the harmony almost always seems focused, though often on sonorities which are dense, discordant, dramatically highly effective (as in the three bars immediately preceding the first use of the two-sharp signature). The kind of fifth- or triad-based complex harmonies so important in Tippett's earlier and later works are not strongly or consistently in evidence: perhaps their most important use is, once again, in Hermes's 'hymn to music'. But, however simple or complex the texture, the ear is normally able to distinguish between what is fundamental and what is ornamental, and the kind of melodic ornamentations favoured by Tippett with their echoes of Monteverdi or Purcell continue to give his music what seems in the broadest sense a neo-classical quality.

One of the clearest examples in the work of the powerful eloquence which the composer generates from this highly individual neo-classicism is the arioso in which Priam appeals to Achilles for the body of Hector: Act III, Scene 3, Fig. 506. The texture is not typical of much of the work in that it is purely contrapuntal, suggesting a baroque aria with its urgent, instrumental line in octaves against which the voice moves in broader phrases. The instrumental line evolves through variation of its initial two-bar phrase, which centres on E flat, but the variations move away from this centre. The vocal line begins with a clear focus on B, but unfolds more freely, apart from the repetition of 'Think on your father', with none of the obvious motivic features of the instrumental parts (Ex. 37b). It is the fusion of the fixed and the free into a coherently evolving contrapuntal form which is so crucial here, and, as always, the result is intensely expressive, even without a harmonic logic defined more clearly than by the composer's instinctive sense of intervallic tension and relaxation. The music needs to be formally coherent, but it needs no other meaning than its expressive aptness. Thus, at the end, the return of the fanfare music from the very start of Act I is formally satisfying because it completes a process of thematic restatement which has functioned throughout the work and with particular consistency in Act III. But the final chords, enigmatic, atonal, apparently completely new, represent the freezing and dissolution of the action. Tippett has 'chosen' them for this symbolic purpose, as well as to suggest the audience's 'inward tears'. There are no words to tell us why they take the form they do, and so we feel them to be appropriate or redundant: we can only 'deduce' them from the earlier music by devious, dubious methods. This ending confirms what is, in fact, the major achievement of *King Priam*: even its most obviously neo-classical techniques serve expressionistic ends. The highly original, deeply satisfying musical language of the work brings these 'incompatible' principles together. *King Priam* is one of the most formidable demonstrations in modern music of a personal, eclectic idiom

Ex. 37b Tippett, *King Priam*, Act III Scene 3

in which the composer can choose and integrate the elements, however disparate, rather than work from a comprehensive structural system to musical material which seems to represent that system most effectively.

A musical language which combines freedoms of this order with distinct allusions to stylistic traditions obviously has much to offer a composer to whom 'complete' novelty is an illusion, and rigid systematizing anathema. But it is not without its technical problems, nonetheless. In Priam's plea to Achilles, the shape and tessitura of the vocal line have presumably been chosen for their dramatic appropriateness and practicability. But if we attempt to analyse the relationship between the vocal line and the accompaniment in other than rhythmic terms we can say little beyond the fact that unisons are on the whole avoided. When the confrontation between a 'traditional' texture and style and an atonal language is as acute as it is here, it is not easy to avoid all sense of conflict between the two. Perhaps the problem is in the 'pure' counterpoint, for later on during Hermes's 'hymn' (from Fig. 544), there is an independent harmonic accompaniment which, while not setting up a tonal structure, supports the melodies in voice and flute, making the distinction between fundamental and ornamental crystal-clear (Ex. 37c). As noted above, Priam's plea is atypical of the work as a whole, and it is so, most essentially, in being all-thematic – more precisely, in being bi-thematic. Simply because Tippett has so little need of traditional, functional harmony, the contrast between elaborately burgeoning melody and basic chordal support is the feature most essential to his music. It is even more

Ex. 37c Tippett, *King Priam*, Act III, from Third Interlude

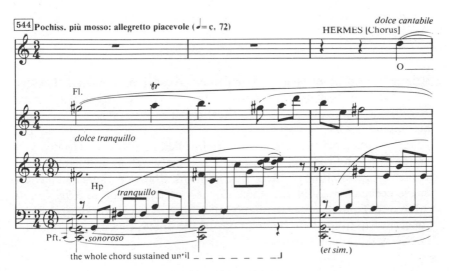

strikingly evident in Helen's often florid Act III monologue, 'Let her rave', and all-thematic passages like that after Fig. 384 are the more effective as contrasts to the basic texture. The most refined, amelodic accompanimental figurations in the work are probably those in the guitar commentary to Achilles's 'O rich-soiled land', while Hecuba's D major-oriented tirade seems to function equally well as all-thematic and as theme-plus-accompaniment. But points like these give some indication of the complex possibilities which the new concentration of *King Priam* offered to Tippett: understandably, therefore, his next works were to be concerned not only with the methods of the opera, but, at least to some extent, with its actual materials.

20 Tippett: After *King Priam* (1962–3)

'With *King Priam'*, one reviewer exclaimed, Tippett 'stands forth as a composer of unmistakable world stature.'[1] Most other reviewers were more cautious, more reserved. Even though *The Midsummer Marriage* itself was still inadequately known, and the works which followed it were scarcely less unfamiliar, it was widely recognized that the new opera initiated a new phase in Tippett's development, which would take time to establish itself, and more time still for critics and listeners to come to terms with.

Tippett himself began to work out the implications of *King Priam* in the most obvious way possible: by continuing to use its music. Almost a year before its first performance, the *Songs for Achilles* for tenor and guitar were heard at the Aldeburgh Festival in June 1961: the first of the three was abstracted from Act II of the opera. Then, in two works written during 1962 and 1963, Tippett made use of some of the instrumental material from the opera, while at the same time pursuing its formal and stylistic implications. Both works were premièred at successive Edinburgh Festivals, the Piano Sonata No. 2 in 1962, the Concerto for Orchestra in 1963.

Tippett comments on the sonata that, 'as in the opera, everything . . . proceeds by statement. The effect is one of accumulation – through constant addition of new material: by variation and repetition. There is virtually no development and particularly no bridge passages. The formal unity comes from the balance of similarities and contrasts.'[2] The sonata ends with a coda in which 'the bits of addition and repetition are made very small and the resulting mosaic therefore more intense'. Intensification, accumulation: these terms indicate very clearly that the sonata is a highly dynamic work: but not in the sense that it presents a connected harmonic argument. True, statements tend to recur at the same basic pitch levels throughout, and some are less ambiguous or allusive with regard to possible tonal identity than others. But for all the hint of a Stravinskian C major at the opening – another echo, perhaps, of that composer's Violin Concerto, a work deeply embedded in Tippett's consciousness – there is little point in attempting to trace a harmonic process through the sonata. Tippett verges on a style in which 'the actual notes' could genuinely be held not to matter, beyond the extent to which they facilitate the identification of 'similarities and contrasts'.

The consequences of this approach to atonality are still more start-lingly evident in the Concerto for Orchestra, perhaps of all Tippett's works the least appropriate to be dedicated to Benjamin Britten. But with Britten's fiftieth birthday in November 1963 imminent, the dedication was duly made, and Britten reciprocated a year later with *Curlew River*. One possible link between the two works is that both are relatively exploratory: the years 1962–4 were indeed crucial for both composers, and, if neither exactly 'came to the aid' of the other, it is notable that they should have acknowledged their mutual respect and admiration with two such powerful and uncompromising examples of their art.

The first movement of the Concerto for Orchestra, scored for wood-wind, brass, harp, piano and percussion, is Tippett's most complex exploration of the interaction between diverse thematic elements, an extreme from which he was to learn, and to retreat. It involves not merely the shifting contexts of varied thematic juxtaposition, but an elaborate kaleidoscope of superimpositions: a new polyphony. The movement can therefore be considered from several different though interdependent formal standpoints. It falls into two parts: the first presents the nine different thematic components, and the second (from Fig. 38) provides the sequence of varied, developmental superimpositions. Yet the first part itself divides into three, with each group of three successive statements being presented in contrapuntal combination before the next is exposed. Where timbral and thematic contrasts proliferate, tempo can perform a unifying function, and Tippett employs only two main tempos throughout the movement: the one change in the first part comes with the start of the third group of ideas at Fig. 25. Yet the nine thematic components are not as contrasted in their internal structure as they are in their overall timbral and rhythmic character. All are substantial enough to subdivide; all contain clear evidence of internal variation; and most of them also contain clear internal *contrasts*. The first element (A) for two flutes and harp, which seems to have grown out of Hermes's hymn to music near the end of *King Priam* (see Ex. 37c), has an important subsidiary thematic phrase (Fig. 1, see Ex. 38a). Element C, for three horns, concludes with new material in close canonic formation (Fig. 11). As for Element B, for tuba and piano: the tuba's four phrases all relate to one another by variation, but there is clear contrast in the piano part between the triplet arpeggiations and the descending scales. Only Element D, for timpani and piano, whose use of fourths recalls the earlier Tippett, lacks such explicit motivic contrast. This cadenza-like figuration is scarcely melodic at all, and its focus on the tonic, dominant and sub-dominant pitch-classes of C sharp seems like an ironic reference to a simpler past. It provides a perspective which points up the prevailing atonality of the movement.

Ex. 38a Tippett, Concerto for Orchestra, first movement

With such a wealth of material from a composer whose music had developed certain very clear and attractive stylistic fingerprints, it would be surprising if some links between the nine thematic elements could not be observed: for example, the fourths already mentioned in Element D crop up elsewhere. More significant from the point of view of form are recurring textural features: canonic imitation, for example, which has been noted in Element C, is also important in all the members of the third group, Elements G, H and I. The last is, in effect, the largest of all the elements, containing at least six distinct ideas. Thus motivic diversity, 'traditional' polyphony (canon) and 'new' polyphony (superimposition for reasons of colour and contrast rather than because ideas fit together according to certain harmonic rules) are all present in the first half of this movement. And one final aspect deserves mention here, which is also important in the second half: instruments may be temporarily 'loaned' from one group to another in order to double parts and clarify or enrich sonorities. The first, simple example of this is at Fig. 12, where the piano reinforces the start of the harp accompaniment figure at the first recurrence of Element A. The piano is something of a special case anyway, because it participates in three of the initial elements: B (with tuba), D (with timpani) and G (with xylophone), as well as being involved in part of Element I (with two trumpets).

In the second half of the movement, from Fig. 38, the superimpositions begin in earnest, crossing the hitherto separate borders between the three thematic groups. It could even be that the technique here provides evidence of the impact of indeterminacy on Tippett: specifically, of the kind of controlled aleatory counterpoint used by Lutosławski for the first time in his *Jeux vénitiens* (1961) where the conductor can cue separate thematic elements spontaneously, their character being such that the combined effect can always be foreseen by the composer even when precise synchronization is avoided. If so, there is some further point to the dedication of the Concerto to Britten, since in *Curlew River*, completed in 1964 and dedicated to Tippett, it is possible that a similar stimulus is at work. As Lutosławski's music shows, however, the material best suited to such aleatory contrapuntal treatment is often ostinato-like: and of Tippett's ideas in this movement only Element D (as it happens, the least used) is of this kind. So, although the pattern of entries and points of contact may seem random, precise synchronization is essential. This is polyphony in which the ear can follow degrees of intervallic and registral change in the individual textural components (a process of variation) as well as the various shifts of tone colour. The degree of concord or discord at any one point, or the relation overall between degrees of concord and discord, is no longer as relevant as individual thematic differences of shape and colour.

Tippett may indeed revel in his new freedom from harmonic constraints, and manipulate his thematic combinations with complete spontaneity, but the second half of the movement certainly has a form, which indicates that 'tradition' has not been wholly jettisoned. The superimpositions of Elements A, B, C and D, E, F from the first part are recapitulated, at Figs. 56 and 60 respectively. In general, indeed, the recurrences of A, which combines in different places with all the other elements (some more briefly than others), define the principal subdivisions of the form. Two other examples will indicate the organizing mind at work. First, during the early stages of this second part of the movement (Figs. 38 to 42), all the elements except F occur. Between Figs. 41 and 42 a climax is built with A, B, C and I combined; then, at Fig. 42, Element F is heard, briefly, in splendid isolation. Second, during the main body of the 'recapitulation' (Figs. 56 to 65), all elements except G are employed. And then, from Fig. 65 to the coda (dominated by Element A) which starts at Fig. 66, a variant of Element G is heard on its own, as a short transitional episode.

The nature and degree of the variation processes applied to the initial elements on recurrence are motivated, it would seem, by a concern to avoid actual transformation. The elements remain identifiable as themes as well as tone colours, but the richness of combinations and contrasted successions is matched by the moulding of the material itself. This movement is malleability incarnate, but the freedoms it explores are supported by the composer's innate coherence of style and movement. The music never lurches, even if, like the second sonata, it lacks such 'bridge passages' as, in tonal music, are the principal agents of harmonic change as well as formal continuity: nor does it lose momentum. It flows as effectively through its totally chromatic, yet locally focused, atonal contrasts as the first movement of the Piano Concerto does through its tonal, sonata-derived processes.

The second movement of the concerto, Lento, has far less diversity, of both tone colour and thematic material, than the first. That is not to say that its textures, for strings alone, are monotonous or unvaried, however. The movement simply seems both more economical and more expansive than the Allegro, and the swooning glissandos and rapidly turning ornaments of the main melodic line – the glissandos a feature which becomes a persistent Tippett fingerprint, as a similar effect in the Triple Concerto confirms – show that even with harmonic focus reduced to a minimum the necessity for a fundamental basis against which to project ornamentation remains as strong as ever. The repetitions, variations and contrasts of the Lento produce a structure which is none the less well-balanced for being conventional, but the ending, with a fragment of what was originally a much more extended phrase serving as coda, seems

Ex. 38b Tippett, Concerto for Orchestra, third movement (finale)

the more abrupt in view of its own basis in 'higher consonance'.

The finale reverts to the patchwork technique of the first movement, and, although the different thematic elements are not actually super-imposed, their own textural and timbral diversity makes for ample linear variety. Since untransposed recurrence is the rule, there is an almost tongue-in-cheek quality about the use of material to end the movement which so portentously prepares and sustains octave E flats, only to allow the music to wander away from their prolongation and stop on the verge of no-man's land (Ex. 38b). To use abbreviated restatement as a means of enforcing ultimate disintegration rather than resolution is a strikingly modern technique. But it raises questions about the value of 'collage-variation' form, at any rate for composers who regard unification and integration as vital psychologically, as well as technically.

As already suggested, the Concerto for Orchestra is something of an extreme case; Tippett was not normally to allow so consistent a loosening of the harmonic control and textural continuity which constant super- '

impositions promote. Since his earlier works explore the interaction of vertical and horizontal so vitally, it is not surprising that he should normally prefer to work in terms of harmonic points of focus which, if not triadic, are something more than the aggregates of thematic elements first established separately. Gradually, therefore, some sense of a return to earlier techniques, seen afresh as a result of the experience of these more radical works, would become apparent.

III PATTERNS OF TRANSFORMATION

21 Britten: The Cello Symphony and *Curlew River* (1963–4)

Britten was fifty on 22 November 1963, and although significant musical events marked the occasion, including first performances of the *Cantata Misericordium* and *Nocturnal,* a new production of *Peter Grimes* at Sadlers Wells and a concert revival of *Gloriana,* there was no serious attempt at an extended appraisal of his achievement, on the lines of the Commentary which had preceded his fortieth birthday. In an issue of *Music and Musicians* devoted largely to Britten, Hans Keller argued with his customary pugnacity that Britten was 'the greatest composer alive' – greater even than Stravinsky – 'for three very simple reasons: he says more that is new; he says it, by now, with more continuous mastery of expression; and he says it more directly'.[1] There was also a double number of *Tempo* which took close looks at various works or parts of works. Keller contributed a more general piece to this symposium; in it he touched on the issues of success and fashion, noting that Britten, while 'still partly inaccessible to the vaguely musical, and indeed to some highly musical conservatives . . . is too accessible to be comprehensible to the genuine avant-garde, especially on the Continental mainland'.[2] Keller noted a heartening change of attitude on the part of one fairly radical British composer, Peter Maxwell Davies: but it may well have been Britten's rapid and continuing productivity, rather than any sense of new and still imponderable historical perspectives, which discouraged Mitchell and Keller from producing an anniversary updating of their earlier study. The new perspective from which Britten's music could then be seen can be sensed in *The Musical Times* for November 1963. Britten was not discussed at all in the long editorial by Andrew Porter, though at the very end Porter did introduce 'two articles to mark the 50th birthday of our greatest composer'. The first was an interesting but slight account of 'Britten and Documentary' by the celebrated film-maker Basil Wright, the second a useful but summary study of the recently published *Hölderlin Fragments* by Hugh Wood. The issue also contained an enthusiastic review of the Promenade Concert performance of the *Cantata Misericordium*: but the musical supplement was a setting of Blake by the young, radical Cornelius Cardew.

Of course, there were many appreciative essays on Britten in the newspapers and journals, and a substantial part of the October issue of *The London Magazine* was given over to articles by, among others, Norman Del Mar, Basil Coleman and William Plomer. Faber and Faber even published a complete volume of tributes, though this was more scrap-book than *Festschrift*. In as much as those closest to the composer him-self were likely to be most aware of his own dislike of 'analysis', this apparently rather evasive response to the fiftieth birthday is understand-able. But it also suggests the extent to which, by this time, Britten could be taken for granted. Even those music-lovers who readily acclaimed him as 'our greatest living composer' would probably have found Keller's criteria puzzling. Britten's admirers tended not to expect anything very novel, or – at least in the technical sense – anything very profound from him. He was thought likely to continue in much the same way. And in any case listeners and students whose appetites for Schoenberg, Webern, Boulez and Stockhausen were, with the appointment of William Glock as Controller of Music at the BBC, being satisfied for the first time, were not to be diverted by a composer whose conservatism seemed to them distinctive, but dull.

During the remaining thirteen years of Britten's life, composers and, to a certain degree, audiences continued to explore the work of the great early twentieth-century radicals. It was therefore possible for Tippett, who appeared to move rather more with the times, to make more new converts than Britten, in whose music the basic formal emphasis remained very much what it had always been: a predominance of vocal works, whether operatic or in cycle or cantata form. But stylistically Britten moved into a new phase of working out the implications of the confrontation between diatonic and chromatic, dissonant and consonant features which had begun with the twelve-note orientation of *The Turn of the Screw*. In this sense, therefore, Keller was right: there were to be new things, and they would be said with greater directness and concentration.

At the very beginning of this period, in 1963, Britten completed a work which might have heralded a new interest in traditional instrumental forms – the Cello Symphony. But all his remaining instrumental pieces – there is only one other purely orchestral work, *'A Time There Was . . . '* – shun the three- or four-movement sequence of sonata tradition to an extent which, especially in the case of the String Quartet No. 3, is a matter of some debate. In vocal music, too, the period began with novelty in the shape of the three parables for church performance, and it was the new aspects of texture and thematic process which emerged in this trilogy which had the greatest influence on the most distinctive aspects of almost all the other late vocal works, from the Blake cycle to *Death in Venice* and *Phaedra*. There were still 'occasional' pieces to be written — *Voices for Today, The Building of the House,* the *Gemini Variations,* and, at the very end, the *Welcome Ode*: children continued to play a crucial part, as in *The Golden Vanity* and *Children's Crusade.* Formally, however, the most important distinction in his non-operatic music is between those works which employ single spans – notably Canticles IV and V, and *Phaedra* – and those which preserve the multi-movement suite or cycle form. Britten continued to make arrangements, and to compose for admired performers – Pears, Rostropovich, Vishnevskaya, Fischer-Dieskau, Osian Ellis, Janet Baker. From 1969 onwards he began to resurrect, and refurbish, some of his earliest compositions, and one, *Paul Bunyan,* from a later period. But the most significant 'resurrection' was undoubtedly his return to more conventional operatic devices and dimensions, in *Owen Wingrave* and *Death in Venice.* In the late works, the language is intensified, rather than purified, and one becomes increasingly conscious of the very special blend of sophistication and naivety in the material and its presentation which is Britten's most personal attribute. The incorporation of quasi-popular tunes, as in *Death in Venice* or the last quartet, is an inheritance from Mahler which Britten made very much his own, and it contributes much to the far from tranquil or resigned impression of his later works.

There can be few apparently more extreme contrasts between adjacent major works in Britten's output than between the Cello Symphony op. 68 (completed on 3 May 1963) and *Curlew River* op. 71 (completed on Maundy Thursday 1964). The symphony, while highly personal in texture and timbre, preserves the traditional symphonic procedures of a thematic and tonal process in which precisely notated and exactly synchronized rhythmic figures play the decisive role. The church operas, although (by the avant-garde standards of the 1960s) almost entirely 'determinate', have a fluidity which is most immediately apparent in the absence both of pervasive time-signatures and of a conductor. Of course, the absence of time-signatures does not necessarily imply the absence of all regular pulsation and accentuation: it is more significant as a means of promoting contrasts between textures which are exactly co-ordinated and those in which material moving at different speeds is superimposed. In earlier Britten such superimpositions have a precise local dramatic function – for example, that of the dance and the menacing Essex theme at the end of Act II of *Gloriana* – and Britten's awareness of the effect possible when different note-groups are freely combined within circumscribed limits has as long a history as his interest in heterophony. Whether or not the composer was aware of, or even influenced by, the new notational freedoms of Lutosławski and others in the early 1960s, however, he clearly sensed that such techniques were incompatible with traditional modes of phrase structure and harmonic organization, insofar as these two entities interact to produce balanced formal elements. He was presumably as opposed to extending the role of quasi-improvised display (in which thematic development may be intensified but the formal process as such suspended) as he was to allowing music to submerge its thematic identity in 'textural' alternations, combinations and successions. Yet there was a dramatic appropriateness in using heterophonic interaction to illustrate the communal nature of the enactment in the Church Parables, with their highly personal blend of ritual and spontaneity; and the idea of making the music grow naturally from plainchant also gives dramatic force to the blend.

It is perhaps in the nature of basic thematic material that an important connection between the Cello Symphony and the Church Parables may be observed: the initial ideas in each case are very simple. While Britten in his later works may indeed have had points of contact with his more radical contemporaries (after all, the Church Parables indicate a distinct disenchantment with the environments traditionally thought appropriate for musico-dramatic enactments), the loss of triadic functioning in the music was not so much the outcome of a substantial change in the essential character of his thematic material, but rather a refinement of his typical methods of thematic treatment.

It has been argued above that Britten's harmony had always involved very crucial tensions between triads and other constructs, and those tensions were reflected in the broader conflict between a tonality extended to embrace strong chromatic motions, and a language in which chromaticism was so pervasive as to ensure a virtual suspension of tonal identity. The Cello Symphony is consistent in being concerned most fundamentally with such an extended tonal vocabulary, in which tonic chords are rarely preceded by orthodox cadential preparations, and in which the role of chromatic, contrapuntal bass-lines is particularly crucial in ensuring that extension is not a mere matter of ornamenting the upper parts.

The Cello Symphony is certainly not an all-thematic work. But its purely harmonic aspects, as embodied more in doublings and inner filling-out than in purely harmonic bass-lines, are given unusual textural prominence in a score where colour and density are particularly important participants in the symphonic process. The precise degree of doubling, for example, and the exact nature of how a texture is filled out at any given point, shows how far from the routine elaborations of many post-Romantic symphonies is Britten's presentation of his thematic and tonal argument.

In the absence of generating harmonic progressions which are basically diatonic it is easy to sense that tonality-disrupting forces are more positively at work than tonality-establishing ones. Britten's most effective dramatic device here is still the 'dominant preparation' – the first as early as Fig. 1 of the first movement – which pins down the melodic motion of the bass line, but whose resolution on to a tonic is, most typically, dissociated texturally, or otherwise made into an incidental rather than an essential event: in the case of this first preparation in the symphony, the resolution at Fig. 2 launches a new texture and section, but does nothing to bring greater stability to the harmony (Ex. 39a). A similar situation occurs at the equivalent point in the recapitulation of the first movement (Fig. 19). In both cases it is only the dominant note which is stressed, not the dominant triad, and this emphasis returns a little later in the recapitulation (at Fig. 22) to prepare a resolution on to the tonic note at the beginning of the coda (Fig. 24). It is an appropriate and satisfying conclusion of the movement's processes that the D major

Ex. 39a Britten, Cello Symphony, first movement

205

triad which the solo cello achieves in the very last bar of the coda should be so very palpably a resolution on to the tonic, yet so distant from any explicit dominant preparation: the cadence is decisive, but hardly 'perfect' (Ex 39b). As for the final cadence of the whole work: in a finale whose major-triad consonances certainly contribute to the genial, forthright atmosphere of the music, this contrives to be structurally

Ex. 39b Britten, Cello Symphony, first movement

decisive and satisfying without eliminating the powerful chromatic extensions which continue into the very final bars. The cadence, with the dominant note typically overlaid (seven to eight bars after Fig. 80), occurs in the middle of the final variation of the Passacaglia, with the remaining music prolonging the D major tonic chord.

The two middle movements of the symphony are even less concerned with suggesting conventional cadences and harmonic progressions. In the scherzo the punctuation of the texture by chords which verticalize the pitch content of the motives which precede them helps to render triads, if not tonal references, redundant; while in the Adagio the chords enhance tonal conflict and provide a background for chromatic prolongation rather than progression, without any compensating clarification or resolution. The major–minor synthesis (both varieties of E) which provides the movement with its two climaxes (after Fig. 51 and at Fig. 60) can easily seem more a textural than a structural feature, too powerful and pungent in itself to relate easily to surrounding events, still less to promote them. Certainly the semitone clash receives some unusually harsh presentation in the cadenza, and offers an interesting anticipation of the final song of the Blake cycle, where the same major and minor third of F are projected across the uneasy surface of the music. In the Cello Symphony Britten's decision to run slow movement and finale together might seem particularly satisfying in view of the extreme contrast between them, but the material of the finale penetrates that of the Adagio too fully for the enthusiastic presentation of it in the Passacaglia to seem like a genuine revelation. It is not merely hinted at at Fig. 53 of the Adagio, but stated in full. When the trumpet takes it up at the start of the finale, the plain rhythms and narrow intervals may seem the agents of light relief, but the transfer is entirely justified; there is still enough chromaticism to prevent any sense of incongruous harmonic stolidity, or any firm focusing around a diatonic perfect cadence. The tonic note, even the tonic triad, may be unambiguous, but the general harmonic character of the music is not so firmly focused. Contexts are never sufficiently diatonic or stable for one to feel that the structural weight of the D major triads could survive a determined challenge. And so the ending, though brilliantly coloured, is only precariously triumphant, with its thematic density and avoidance of mere figuration evidence of the seriousness as well as the grand scale of the whole enterprise.

The two principal works which come between the Cello Symphony and *Curlew River,* the *Cantata Misericordium* and *Nocturnal* for guitar, have obvious and strong differences: moreover, the first tends to look back to earlier Britten while the second looks forward. The subject of the cantata – the New Testament story of the Good Samaritan – links the miracle-play theme of *Noye's Fludde* with the biblical material of the second and third parables: and the choral framing and commentary on an action presented through two male soloists (one, the traveller, a familiar figure in late Britten subjects) is also close to the resources required in the parables. But the neatly sectional form, and the style of the music itself, recalls the more 'occasional' Britten in its relaxed but rather formal vein. The work is often seen as a kind of appendix to the *War Requiem,* not least because it brought Peter Pears and Dietrich Fischer-Dieskau together again; but its text, compiled by Patrick Wilkinson, is wholly in Latin, and even when that text offers parallels – 'Let us sleep now' in the *Requiem,* 'Dormi nunc' in the *Cantata* – the music of the latter seems closer to the positive expansiveness of the 'Green leaves' hymn from *Gloriana* than to the uneasy peroration of the *War Requiem*'s 'In paradisum'. The instrumental introduction presents a relatively brief moment of concentrated working with the *Cantata*'s most important motive, a close relative of the second main theme of the Cello Symphony's first movement. But the extended triadicism of the harmony later on, and the presence of conventional accompanimental figuration, are both more typical of the work. Semitonal clashes between the roots and thirds of adjacent triads are certainly not excluded, however, and reach some intensity in the central episodes of the attack on the Traveller (for example, four bars before Fig. 10), which culminates in a choral statement combining prime and inverted lines in a totally chromatic phrase (three bars before Fig. 13, see Ex. 40).

With its continuous form comprising clear, separate sections, the *Cantata* comes closest to those cycles – the *Nocturne,* the *Songs and Proverbs of William Blake* – in which transitions between sections are the focus for thematic development. But the major-third relation (which provides the foundation for the harmonic essence of what is, after all, a story with a happier outcome than most of Britten's non-biblical works)

Ex. 40 Britten, *Cantata Misericordium*

can hardly offer the same degree of structural tension as more prominent
tritones or semitones: nor would such tensions be appropriate here. The
message is summed up in Patrick Wilkinson's phrases: 'Disease is
spreading, war is stalking, famine reigns far and wide. But when one
mortal relieves another like this, charity springing from pain unites
them.' Britten's choral writing avoids too naive a sense of stern,
sermonizing exhortation, but it is the rewards of charity rather than the
sufferings of those who need it which sound most clearly through the
gentle oscillations of the closing bars.

From the public face of a work first performed in Geneva at 'the
solemn ceremony of the commemoration day of the centenary of the Red
Cross' to the intimacies of an extended piece for solo guitar ought,
perhaps, to produce extreme contrast between assertion and allusion.
But the *Cantata Misericordium* is far too gentle a work to assert, while
Nocturnal is very precisely constructed, not in the least vague about its
essential processes. It was Britten's second night-piece of 1963 (the first
was a short test-piece for the Leeds piano competition) and his second
treatment of a Dowland song, coming some thirteen years after *Lachrymae*.

The pure major tonality of Dowland's music emerges only in the quotation of the original song in the final stages of the work. This is a very
different proceeding from the immediate statement of the fundamental

material in its original form in the Church Parables, or in any set of conventional variations; but there is a significant pointer to the technique of the parables in the fact that time-signatures (in brackets) are only used occasionally, and bar-lines are irregularly placed. With its freer approach to metre, its less insistent use of triadic harmony, coupled with an increased intensity of thematic manipulation, *Nocturnal* adumbrates many of the elements of the 'late Britten' style which are more fully set out in *Curlew River*; and, like that work, it has no very evident concern for the exploitation of tonally-centred twelve-note cycles. The character of *Nocturnal* stems rather from a particularly intense and subtle development of an even more well-tried device, the interaction of notes, chords and keys a semitone apart. Indeed, the interaction expressed in the first section of the work is unusually direct, with E major and F minor synthesized around the common tone G sharp/A flat, and the interaction intensifying when F minor changes into F major. Although it would over-simplify greatly to discuss the whole work solely in terms of this one relationship it does indicate how remote Britten's variations are from the actual harmonic idiom of the original song. As in the later cello suites, the resourcefulness of the instrumental writing cannot always compensate for the limitations the medium imposes – the absence of a strong melodic build-up in the Passacaglia, for example – but the ending, fading out on a G sharp major chord in mid-phrase, is magical enough to counteract the memory of more workaday moments.

The subject-matter and dramatic atmosphere of Britten's three parables for church performance may seem very remote from that of all his earlier dramatic works, except *Noye's Fludde*. 'Parable' must in effect mean sermon, and the only sermons widely appreciated in the modern theatre are psychological or political. Religious sermons, however secularized, may be frowned on if they are delivered outside the pulpit. But stylization as a form of dramatic presentation is much more acceptable. Art forms in modern times have moved between varieties of naturalism and abstraction, and while opera can probably never get particularly close to the essence of either, the effect when a plain basic point about human behaviour and relationships is made in a ritualistic rather than a realistic way can be powerfully original and intense: Stravinsky's *Oedipus Rex* has already been mentioned as a crucial prototype.[3]

The group of 23 performers needed to present *Curlew River* have to undertake a commitment to the spirit and style of the work which would not necessarily be expected in conventional opera. As the producer, Colin Graham, wrote in the score, 'the cast of the original production underwent a strenuous course of movement instruction and physical education before the rehearsals began and this training was maintained throughout the engagement'. This suggests a discipline not so dissimilar from that demanded by Stockhausen from the much smaller ensembles required for such works as *Plus–Minus* (1963) and *Stimmung* (1968), and the close relationship of singers and instrumentalists is also comparable to that demanded in music-theatre works by the younger British composers of the 1960s. The stylization of movement and gesture which is required in the Church Parables (an explicit debt to the Japanese Nō-plays which are the parables' most direct theatrical ancestor) is in essence not just a matter of economy of movement but of making the most intense, expressive gesture in the most effective manner. When Colin Graham writes that 'the miming . . . is symbolic and should be pared down to its quintessence' he is simply indicating a mode of performance which is the essential complement to the nature of Britten's music. Up to that point in his career, Britten might seem to have had little time for ritual, but the most important technical features of work after work are of the kind which could only find fulfilment in concentration, not in further expansion or diffusion. To this extent, the priorities have nothing to do with the theatre as such. Operas need time, and while it would be dangerous to assert that the greatest operas are the longest, it is safe to claim that there are more great long ones than short ones. *Curlew River,* like its two successors, cannot be described as expansive, but its compressed and repetitive form accumulates as much tension as any 70-minute single span could hope to do. At a time when the mere mention of T. S. Eliot's verse drama *Murder in the Cathedral* could produce shudders in the sophisticated, and garbled memories of pretentious blank verse in an all-too appropriate ecclesiastical setting, Britten's new venture impressed by its purity, as well as its intensity. Its critics may accuse it of eccentricity, but never of blandness. And the most serious charge of all, that it is an evasion of the problems and challenges of a truly modern music theatre, cannot survive the experience that, in the music of *Curlew River*, Britten reached a new level of integrated, functional expression. The medium is obviously a more restricted one than that of either 'grand' or chamber opera, but in such a special, confined arena Britten's music could make some distinctive technical advances.

The framing plainchants of all three parables are not just an accompaniment to the processions; they are the source, in rhythmic and intervallic character, if not in mode or timbre, of much of the works' materials. They are nevertheless not 'sets' from which all else stems. With its span of a perfect fifth and its use of both kinds of seconds and thirds, the original 'Te lucis ante terminum' can be held to provide *Curlew River* with all the basic intervals except the tritone; but for that very reason the chant can only exercise a genuine influence if more general features of its shape and contour are explicitly employed. Many pages of the score can be quoted as evidence of such connections, though when characteristic intervals are superimposed they accumulate clusters extremely remote from the cool monody of the original. But contrasting thematic shapes are also apparent: for example, the arpeggios associated with the Traveller (Fig. 13) or the cry of the Madwoman (Fig. 20) introducing the 'devilish' tritone. What links all the thematic ideas, whatever their closeness to or distance from the contours of the chant, is their extreme concision and plasticity. Because of this wealth and immediacy of themes and motives, the composer seems to have experienced a renewing sense of freedom, and his combinations of thematic elements are remarkably flexible and inventive. But combinations produce counterpoint, and counterpoint, whether strictly synchronized or not, creates harmony, vertical successions. Had Britten wished to underline the specifically pitch-based, structural role of the chant he could have chosen to focus all the harmonic processes and tendencies of *Curlew River* around its central F sharp. But it is an A, first imperiously asserted by the Ferryman's horn at Fig. 8, which is the most evident, if far from all-pervading, tonal centre, and its importance is reinforced by its reassertion at the musical climax of the work, at Fig. 90. These assertions occur within the work rather than at either end, however, and the tonality of the whole generally expands or even floats free of any purely diatonic or modal structure. The pervasive chromaticism can lead to twelve-note accumulations, as in the chant-derived lines for viola and double-bass from three bars after Fig. 84, but these are no more rigorously pursued than is pure diatonicism or modality. Peter Evans has discussed how the process of composing the Church Parables seems to have led Britten into a more systematic use of certain 'Modes of Limited Transposition'[4]; but the ground between diatonicism and total chromaticism which these define is, as in Messiaen's earlier works, placed at the service of extended tonality. What is most significant in all the parables is the transparency of texture and the minimal role played by the triad as a point of focus (it returns as a 'motive' in *The Prodigal Son*). After the very early years, Britten's preference for textures which did not explicitly aspire to the 'all-thematic' had encouraged him to retain the ultimate 'security' of the focal triad, even when that security was represented as highly precarious. But now its almost complete banishment had become dramatically as well as stylistically appropriate.

Britten's resourceful use of his limited instrumental colours in *Curlew River* is immediately obvious to the ear. He is also resourceful in his use of unsynchronized superimpositions which are not merely 'representations of chaos': at Fig. 49, for example, the density of piled-up canonic interactions, rooted to a dissonant organ cluster and propelled by sup-

Ex. 41 Britten, *Curlew River*

porting harp and viola ostinatos, is offset by the utter simplicity of the recurring melodic shape, which has been made familiar to the listener before the ensemble itself begins. But the most impressive examples of compositional virtuosity can be found in two very different episodes. First, the Ferryman's long narration as he poles the boat across the river, from two bars after Fig. 57 to Fig. 67. On the page this looks like sparsely accompanied recitative, but it is shaped with such sensitivity to verbal rhythm, colour, and large-scale linear contour, that neither focus nor momentum slacken for a moment. At the other extreme, the Mad-woman's two ariosos (at Figs. 33 and 81) are perhaps the most obviously all-motivic passages in the work, and among the most concentrated music Britten ever conceived. Anticipations of such intensive intervallic working can be found, for example, in the very different context of the Cello Symphony's first movement, where the plangent major and minor seconds in the solo part just before the coda (between Figs. 23 and 24) are comparable. But it is the impact of a moment like 'with silence ev'ry room was full' (Ex. 41) which demolishes any vestige of doubt about the purpose, or success, of Britten's move from 'grand' opera to church parable. If a composer can create this effect from one interval, one voice and four instruments, his impatience with more inflated resources can easily be understood.

22 Tippett: *The Vision of Saint Augustine* (1963–5)

At the end of *King Priam*, when Hermes appears as a god, Priam describes his vision: 'I see mirrors, myriad upon myriad, moving the dark forms of creation.' The vision is intense but obscure, a matter of reflection rather than of illumination, a helpless striving for a clarity worthy of the moment of death. A similar intensity, centring on personal vision, is expressed by Saint Augustine with the words 'intravi in intima mea, et vidi lucem incommutabilem': 'I went into myself and saw the unchange-able light.' Tippett himself has described *The Vision of Saint Augustine* (1963–5) as 'a special case of the same expressive need' for approaching that visionary element which is evident 'in much of my music, and which finds its first full flowering in *The Midsummer Marriage*'.[1] Tippett makes clear that, in the case of Saint Augustine,

I did not . . . come to the subject through faith . . . Just as I see, with my theatri-cal eye, Faust (or Priam) blind at the end to all but the inner vision, so I see Augustine and his mother standing at the window into the inner garden, wrapt out of time into eternity. The difference is that with Augustine it actually happened. There is a plot of earth in Ostia now where he and Monica actually stood.

Another fundamental difference between *King Priam* and *The Vision of Saint Augustine* is that the visionary image – 'I went into myself and saw the unchangeable light' – is positive, jubilant. The Augustinian progression – love, truth, light, eternity – is beyond Priam and, perhaps, beyond drama. Certainly it makes *The Vision of Saint Augustine*, perhaps Tippett's most ambitious and most abstract statement and structure, seem almost a necessary consequence of the opera. *The Vision* may be dramatic to the extent that it displays a quest for belief, for certainty. But its concern with the limitations of temporality inspires a remarkable formal stylization, with soloist and chorus dividing a text, and sharing the roles of narration and meditation, without 'dialogue' in the conventional sense at all. As Tippett put it, 'I found myself "wrapt away" for a while into this mystery of past and present, time and non-time, so powerfully that I was even able to use Augustine's method of word-association to construct a libretto by matching Latin to Latin. The result was a beautiful text which I eventually set to music.'

Tippett describes Saint Augustine as 'a priest, not a poet', and it may seem surprising that a composer not noted for his religious orthodoxy should find a priest so sympathetic. But it is evident that there is much more to Augustine's thought than theological, Christian dogmatics. His whole life was 'a progress towards certitude and faith', and even the unbeliever can be fascinated by the nature of that progress, if not accepting, or sharing in, its outcome. The common ground between the modern agnostic, sensitive to mysticism, and the medieval philosopher is likely to be a belief in the need for, and possibility of, regeneration. For Augustine, God's existence could be adduced from 'the Ideas residing in the soul', and it was an 'illuminating inner light which enables the soul to recognise them . . . The soul of itself is unable to see an intelligible truth; it is . . . dependent upon an illumination from God'.[2] For Augustine, understanding was impossible without righteousness, and righteousness impossible without God's grace. For the Jungian, understanding is impossible without illumination, and illumination impossible without the 'grace' of a mature, fully realized 'soul'. Knowledge of the shadow and the light makes the whole man. For the Christian, regeneration is the key to knowledge: for the Jungian, knowledge is the key to rebirth, and art may perform the crucial psychotherapeutic role for modern man as effectively, if not more so, than religion.

Jung referred to religions as psychotherapeutic systems. He might equally well have used the same phrase about works of art. Nowadays, more people gain what Jung would have called experience of the Self from one or other of the arts than they do from religion. The picture gallery and the concert hall have replaced the Church as places where the 'divine' can be encountered.[3]

215

In spite of his eloquent epigraph from Eliot's *Burnt Norton* – 'And all is always now' – Tippett has not accomplished the miracle of contriving a 'present tense' music without past or future in *The Vision of Saint Augustine*. There are recurrences, resemblances which reinforce the awareness of something passing through time. But the dominant sense is less of 'progression' than of an ecstatic expansion of the 'now': a spiritual 'trip', or '*Erhebung* without motion' as Eliot described it elsewhere in *Burnt Norton*. For this reason the cross-references in *The Vision*, the musical equivalents of Augustine's 'method of word-association', are a direct stimulus to the evolving musical process which circles around them: and that process itself is the conveyor of some of Tippett's most remarkably diverse and imaginative material. There is no place here, in his first major work to use texts not his own since *Crown of the Year*, for thumping Jungian slogans; and the arrangement of the text, as well as its language, directs attention away from its sense to its atmosphere. Freed from the operatic need to make what the listener sees relate to what he hears, the composer encourages in the listener a 'vision' – an unmistakable aural awareness – of the ecstasy of contemplating eternity, not as something which is empty of life, but as something full of spirit. To this extent, the line which appears at the end of Part II – 'O eternal truth and true love and beloved eternity' – is especially resonant.

The mere juxtaposition of contrasted elements is the surest way in which a composer can remind the listener that time is passing in a succession of distinct 'nows' which may be briefly prolonged and in certain respects related and connected, but which serve 'the triumph of time'. In *The Vision of Saint Augustine*, however, Tippett attempts to create a cumulative interaction of elements whose diversity is the justification for the kind of elaborately contrived superimpositions and interconnections which reveal the work as a true successor of, and an advance beyond, the Concerto for Orchestra.

The principal portions of text are taken from the later stages of Book IX of the *Confessions* – chapters 10 to 14. For Part I the solo baritone is allotted the first paragraph of Chapter 10. In itself, this is already allusive, in that it contains three biblical quotations, but in Tippett's structure it forms a background which flowers into a rich complexity as the chorus provide an overlapping commentary, sometimes amplifying the information given by the baritone with lines from elsewhere in the *Confessions*, sometimes seizing on a crucial word – 'garden', 'forgetting', 'panteth' – to provide an elaboration of the image, with words from the *Confessions*, from the Hymn of Bishop Ambrose (as quoted in the *Confessions*), or from the Bible – the Song of Solomon, the Psalms.

This fusion of 'exposition' with 'development' is at its clearest at the very beginning, where the baritone's statement (from the beginning of

Chapter 10) – 'When the day was approaching on which she was to depart this life' – is interspersed with the choral 'gloss' – 'on the ninth day of her illness, in the 56th year of her life, and the 33rd year of my life, that religious and devoted soul was released from the body' – words found at the end of Chapter 11. The effect of the choral interjections on the thread of the baritone line is to provoke frequent repetitions of words and phrases, as though new ideas and memories are continually inter- rupting a meditation. On the large scale, the work is integrated by several substantial passages of 'recapitulation', but the more immediate con- tinuity provided by the 'retakes' of the baritone line – in contrast to the self-contained statements of the chorus – provide the essential structural propulsion of the work. Continuity is further increased by the extent to which the musical material now overlaps the carefully graded contrasts of tempo which is another technical feature carried over from *King Priam* and its successors. Although the table of fourteen distinct tempos set out at the beginning of the score might seem to imply a highly sec- tionalized form of juxtaposed 'blocks', it is the evolutionary interaction rather than the contrasted juxtaposition of materials which dominates.

An early example of the degree of polyphonic complexity which the music can generate is found after Fig. 7 (Ex. 42). The choral tenors and basses chant St Ambrose's Hymn, doubled by the second horn, and there are three other, decorating lines: the solo baritone, the female chorus, and the orchestral cellos and basses, each with various, occasional doub- lings. As is to be expected, the force of the linear momentum ensures that each line has a shape, and a goal, but in combination, they do not cohere into a clearly defined tonal or harmonic structure. This is not to argue that all the notes are somehow equal in structural significance, since, as is consistently the case with Tippett, tonal or atonal, very clear distinc- tions between 'ornamental' and 'fundamental' features may be detected. But in the absence of triadic harmony, a very wide variety of sustained chords (like that of the very opening, with prominent octaves and fourths) assume the role of generating or cadential sonorities without in any sense fulfilling the larger pivotal function of triads in more tradi- tionally harmonic music.

This is the sense in which, even during Tippett's most radical phase, the 'actual notes' – the actual intervals – still matter. The composer con- trols his harmony through his sense of style, and through a sense of the relative weight, the degree of tension or repose, in those vertical con- junctions of a primarily polyphonic texture. There may be certain pas- sages, especially in the Concerto for Orchestra, where such significant vertical combinations are difficult if not impossible to detect. But since Tippett's rhythmic exuberance relies so consistently on small-scale repeti- tion for the building of phrases, the value of a sense of cadence, simply

217

Ex. 42 Tippett, *The Vision of Saint Augustine*, Part I

as a local release of tension, remains as strong as in tonal music – and that release can be obtained through melodic direction and rhythmic articulation, even without harmonic 'resolution'.

In this way, Tippett seems to have the best of both worlds: a means of communicating a sense of tension and relaxation without needing to summon up the tired formulae of styles and techniques foreign to his own. In this respect the slow, steady nature of his evolution has yielded rich dividends. It can be said of few other modern composers that they have achieved so complete a departure from tradition and yet remained so close to the essential dynamic forces of that tonal music which still seems to many the most natural, as well as the most appealing, which man is ever likely to devise.

23 Britten: Blake, Pushkin and the second Church Parable (1965–6)

During the last decade of his life Britten pursued the tension, ambiguity and potential inherent not only in sparse textures, but in the single musical line, with great persistence, and nowhere more rigorously than in his contributions to a medium to which only Bach had previously brought major distinction, the suite for unaccompanied cello.

After the 18-minute Cello Sonata of 1961 and the 34-minute Cello Symphony, Britten went on to compose 65 minutes or so of unaccompanied music in the three suites for Mstislav Rostropovich, which date from 1964, 1967 and 1971 respectively. A player of such gifts can sometimes promote shallow music simply because the technical challenge stimulates the composer's ingenuity rather than his imagination. Britten does not always sustain a high level of invention in these substantial works: the two weakest movements are probably the rather laboured 'Bordone' of No. 1 and the dry Fugue of No. 2. But even though textural manipulation can easily submerge thematic spontaneity, the first suite, op. 72, demonstrates the renewed vitality which the challenge of the single instrument could bring to a favourite form-scheme.

The work is cyclic, with pairs of contrasted movements – 'Fuga', 'Lamento', 'Serenata', 'Marcia', 'Bordone', 'Moto Perpetuo' – alternating with and, finally, in the 'Moto Perpetuo', being penetrated by varied recurrences of a sonorous 'Canto'. The very first clause of the 'Canto' is pointedly, passionately oblique, using a five-note collection (E, F sharp, G, A, B) to focus not on the E minor triad but the sixth A–F sharp. The principal tonality of the work as a whole is however not D but a pungently extended G, though even the neo-classical start of the 'Fuga' misses the pure major or minor mode by several semitones and all movements favour ambiguity rather than explicitness. The shortest movement – 'Lamento' – is of particular interest in offering a concentrated yet clear example of how extended tonality (the centre is the triad of E minor) can be presented through pure monody. The beautifully balanced miniature variation form centres firmly on the twelve E minor triads which punctuate the phrases; however, the final, expanded cadence is not a diatonic dominant-tonic outline, but the semitonally separated chords of D sharp minor and E minor. Eloquence and economy find a perfect match (Ex. 43).

Ex. 43 Britten, Suite for Cello No. 1, II Lamento

In the twelve years between *Winter Words* and the *Songs and Proverbs of William Blake* op. 74, Britten completed only one song cycle for voice and piano, the *Six Hölderlin Fragments*. Interestingly enough, this fallow period was one during which he worked with particular intensity with Peter Pears on performing and recording the major Schubert and Schumann cycles, notably *Die Winterreise*, which they tackled in public for the first time in the early 1960s. But the return to the medium in 1965 initiated a new flowering, with the Pushkin, Soutar and Burns cycles – the last with harp – providing some of the most characteristic music of Britten's final decade.

There are two important, and (for the medium) novel, features about the Blake cycle, apart from the fact that it is designed 'for baritone', rather than tenor, or high voice. First, it is constructed continuously, with the Proverbs linking the Songs and using related material in a manner recalling the variations of *The Turn of the Screw*. Second, the basic material presented in the first Proverb is not modal, like the generating chant of *Curlew River,* but twelve-note: a concept of inclusiveness which may represent Blake's 'infinity' held 'in the palm of your hand' (Proverb VII). The significance of this return to emphasis on a twelve-note pattern is considerable, though less for its revival of associations with the earlier Henry James opera than for its anticipation of the procedures of the two major dramatic works of the last years, *Owen Wingrave* and *Death in Venice*. Certainly the Blake cycle is far from a small-scale repetition of the basic structure of *The Turn of the Screw*. In the opera, the scenes themselves are to a large extent independent of the theme used in the variations, while having a logical basis in their own stepwise succession of tonal centres. The Blake cycle has no comparable symmetry, and the Proverbs do not significantly interact with the Songs until the seventh and final Song. Moreover, two of the Blake Songs contain twelve-note features employing different successions from those of the Proverbs.

Seen in this light, the Blake cycle is still a long way from the totally unified, tonally centred serialism to which a more theoretically minded composer of Britten's temperament might have aspired. Each of the song melodies is indeed unified in itself, but by different motives, with occasional cross-references, as between 'A Poison Tree' and 'Every Night and Every Morn', tending to point up the essential contrasts, as the motivic cross-references do in *The Turn of the Screw*. In both works the unifying element represents a relatively small proportion of the whole, but it provides an 'anchor', itself a process of variation rather than of repetition, in a form which involves a succession of separate, yet occasionally related, entities.

The presence in the Proverbs and the final Song of a fundamental pitch-sequence rather than some kind of motto theme perhaps reflects the fact that, while the Proverbs are all of the same type, their actual meaning is elusive, and difficult to illustrate through obvious musical imagery. The Songs, by contrast, cover a wide range of subject-matter, with the first two offering compassionate social comment, the third and fourth narrowing down to personal expressions of hate and fear, the fifth stressing the vulnerability of all living things, the sixth expressing a kind of death-wish, and the seventh revealing an ambiguous degree of acceptance of the fate to which all are predestined. Blake's meaning here is certainly ambiguous – 'some are born to endless night' (as opposed to 'sweet delight') but 'God is light/to those poor souls who dwell in Night' – and the music seizes on the doubt as to whether this message is consoling or alarming. It is a profoundly uneasy song, making the obsessiveness of its blanketed, stifled tonality almost unnervingly appropriate. Musically, as well as 'thematically', it provides a culmination; the subject-matter reaches its crucial issue and the music its most concentrated treatment of the work's essentials.

Since this is the work from Britten's later years in which system and freedom seem most concentratedly involved with each other, a detailed consideration of some of the consequences of that involvement is justified. In Proverb I the piano presents three groups of four different notes, centred on E flat, C and A respectively, and elaborates them in turn in arch-like shapes; a rapid ascent, then a more measured descent in octaves using for the most part the same octave positions. As presented here, and indeed as 'basic shapes', the three groups are different in interval content, apart from the initial ascending or descending semitone, but the melodic possibilities of this diversity are not explored until the final pair of sections. Permutations of the three groups, which never overlap with each other, recur (in the piano) in different ways in all the Proverbs:

I	a b c
II	a b
III	b c
IV	a b c a
V	b c a
VI	c a b
VII	c b a c

Just as the relationships within the groups change, so does the relationship between the voice and piano. Throughout the cycle, in the Songs as well as the Proverbs, one is acutely conscious of the extent to which voice and piano are 'consonant' or 'dissonant' with each other. Consonance here can take two basic forms: the traditional one, where the voice doubles or adds to a consonant chord in the accompaniment; or a form in which the voice, in a manner relating to the heterophonic practices of the church operas, draws its notes from the 'repertoire' provided by the piano. In this second sense, the Proverbs progress from complete dissonance to complete consonance, a progress in which the two participants also exchange roles as carriers of the melodic line. Thus in Proverb I the voice reiterates dissonant single pitches against each of the piano's note-groups, and the voice's pitches group themselves into a whole-tone scale-segment which is carried over, and filled in, in the first vocal phrase of the first Song – evidence of a Proverb generating an initial aspect of a Song which then goes its own way. In Proverb II, the voice again reiterates dissonances, each a semitone higher than those provided for the same groups in Proverb I. In Proverb III a process of overlap begins, with some pitches duplicated between voice and piano, and in Proverb IV this process continues, the vocal line becoming more explicitly melodic, and so motivically 'integrated' that it would only need a final three-note group of C, D flat, and B to complete a new twelve-note set of Webernian invariance. In Proverb V, for the first time, the voice has more notes than the piano, and the phrases, moving away from the ascending-semitone/descending-tone motive of the previous Proverb's vocal line, are subtly balanced, the second a simplified retrograde of the first, the third a varied transposition of the second. Proverb VI increases both the melodic emancipation of the voice and the voice's 'consonance' with the supporting groups in the piano, so the complete unanimity of the final Proverb is not totally unprepared; the piano is now completely unmelodic, with tremolandos replacing the pervasive ostinatos, while the voice makes full use of the variety of interval offered by the twelve-note cycle (Ex. 44a).

The double role of consonance in the cycle as a whole can only be touched on here, but the indications are that a study of Britten's music which concentrated on this issue of complementation would yield many points of interest. The first Song, 'London', is one of the two to include a further twelve-note element, in that the first-inversion or root-position major or minor triads, into which the agitated scale-plus-arpeggio figuration periodically freezes, use twelve different triads in a manner recalling music from *A Midsummer Night's Dream* and the *Hölderlin Fragments*. This succession of chords does not conform to the Proverbs' serial cycle, however, and the function of the triads in the Song is all the more disturbing in that they are not arrived at by any kind of conventional progression (the Song's extended tonality is G minor). The frantic ostinatos which precede and connect them may represent the 'mind-forged manacles', and the voice in general picks 'consonant' pitches, which belong to the various collections employed by the piano. This is not surprising, since the collections contain so many different notes: but it does establish a criterion of 'unanimity', makes 'dissonant' deviations from it significant, and creates a sense, not of the piano accompanying

224

the voice, but of the voice clarifying the outline of the accompanying texture.

The second Song, 'The Chimney-Sweeper', extends its essential B major–minor through a fairly high degree of consonance between voice

Ex. 44a Britten, *Songs and Proverbs of William Blake*, Proverb VII

and piano, and pure triads do occur. They occur again in the third Song, 'A Poison Tree', but here the extended E flat minor is the background for some fairly determined 'serialism'. Two distinct twelve-note sets are presented successively: the first, in the piano, consists of three 0,2,5 trichords and an 0,3,7 trichord – the triad of E minor. The second of these trichords is given the form of a 'partial' dominant seventh in E flat (B flat, F, A flat), and leads to the first presentation of the second twelve-note set in the voice, accompanied by full minor triads in the piano. As a melodic outline, this declares a tonality of E flat minor though, naturally, it is extended: there are no diatonic progressions. In spite of its emphasis on the interval of the minor second, this second set has no more extensive invariances, nor are its trichords or hexachords arrived at by reordering those of the first set. The first set is used only three times altogether, before and after the first phrase, and at the very end. The second, after the first nine notes of an inverted statement to the words 'I was angry with my foe: I told it not', becomes the source of thematic development rather than serial patterning, until a full inversion appears in the piano to prepare the climax.

The texture throughout the central part of the Song is intensely contrapuntal, and there is a minimum of purely harmonic filling-out. But the various repetitions help to keep the tonic of E flat clearly in view, and this is reinforced with the return of the complete statement of the second set's inverted form in the left hand of the piano part at bar 39. This prepares the climactic statement of the Song – 'glad I see/My foe outstretched beneath the tree' – in which major triads support an eleven-note sequence over a tonic pedal (Ex. 44b). (If one of the D flats were a natural, all twelve notes would be involved.) Clearly, as a systematic exploitation of the potential of its twelve-note material, this song is extremely limited. But its material provides the basis for the musical portrayal of the growth and fulfilment of violence, and in its Claggart-like implacability it is one of Britten's most powerful and disturbing achievements.

The climactic consonances of 'A Poison Tree' set the seal on the essential unanimity within which the entire structure has been unfolding. There is also a high degree of such consonance in 'The Tyger', whose B major tonality recalls that of 'The Chimney-Sweeper', even though the texture and atmosphere are utterly different. The extended G minor of 'London' is likewise hinted at in the fifth Song, 'The Fly'. Voice and piano shadow each other throughout, and in this, the least assertive of all the Songs in the cycle, the simple rhythms, narrow intervals, and uniform texture provide as suitable a basis for the chromatic activity within the harmony as the more dramatic and varied elements of the other Songs. Nevertheless, 'Ah! Sun-Flower', which comes next, is a

Ex. 44b Britten, *Songs and Proverbs of William Blake*, 'A Poison Tree'

powerful contrast, and the way in which dissonance and both kinds of consonance are played off against each other is, dramatically, remarkably apt. The thematic use of an outlined diminished triad could suggest a link with the material of the previous Song, and the B flat tonal centre is a close relative of the G minor of 'The Fly'. But even without any apparently pre-planned twelve-note patterns, 'Ah! Sun-Flower' is among Britten's most rigorously chromatic pieces; the ruthlessly sustained distinction between the febrile bass-line and the rest of the texture offers a metaphor for the 'shrouding' image which is as applicable to the concept of tonality here as to the 'pale Virgin' of the text.

The final Song has a much more obvious emphasis on unanimity, both in its textural homogeneity and the pervasive consonance between voice and piano. The predominant material is the last of the Proverbs' three four-note groups (F, G sharp, A, B flat), but the other two groups appear as part of the inexorable linear motion of the music. Group C

227

remains a point of focus around which other chromatic tones can be introduced, and from which a suitably tentative resolution on to just two of the four pitch-classes, F and A, can finally be extracted. In context, this sounds like a retreat from decisiveness into exhaustion, and the total absence of diatonic harmonic progressions in such an intensively linear texture makes the question of whether or not the song is 'in' F major particularly crass. The associations are there for those who can hear them, but the more essential relationships between the central, focused dissonance and everything else provides more than enough logic in view of the directness and immediacy of what is expressed.

After the innovations of *Curlew River* and the renewed involvement with twelve-note features in the *Songs and Proverbs of William Blake*, the next three years (1965–8) were, essentially, a period of consolidation. Britten's main concern was to provide companion pieces for the first Church Parable, and to establish a repertory within which the value of certain associated performance conventions could be demonstrated. The three parables, whose durations are given in the scores as 71, 64 and 72 minutes respectively, really need to be performed on separate occasions for their full effect to emerge, however, and they are probably more suited to 'festival' circumstances than to conventional seasons of operatic and concert performances. As for the conventions which the parables employ, these are most obviously of form, texture and presentation; but the musical materials are manipulated in comparable fashion in all three, the framing chants providing background and foreground patterns whose very simplicity stimulates such highly imaginative and concentrated musical developments.

Before composing *The Burning Fiery Furnace* Britten wrote two short pieces of very different kinds for very different occasions. The anthem *Voices for Today* op. 75 offers rather faceless music for a highly auspicious event, the twentieth anniversary of the United Nations. By contrast *The Poet's Echo* op. 76 was a very personal response to a very personal event, Britten's visit to the House of Composers, Dilhizan, Armenia, in August 1965. Dedicated to, and first performed by, Galina Vishnevskaya and Mstislav Rostropovich, it has moments of that impassioned rhetoric which Britten provided for the Soviet soprano in the *War Requiem*, but the music in general has a relatively 'pared-down' texture: perhaps Britten was thinking of Rostropovich's possible limitations as a pianist!

The challenge of setting Russian may also have induced a degree of caution: but although the ideas and atmosphere in the settings of poems which tend more towards the 'conceit' than Britten normally favoured may seem slightly frigid, the tonal techniques are of considerable interest. There are no free rhythms, or 'curlew' signs allowing one performer to 'mark time' until the other has reached a specific point, and so the heterophonic texture of the first song comes even closer than usual in Britten to traditional canonic device. But the absence of 'free' rhythm is paralleled, or complemented, by the absence of complete twelve-note patterns. The first two chords of the first song each use eight different pitches altogether, and the third chord provides three more. Only D natural is missing, so the 'total chromatic' is only just evaded, but it is enough to indicate a distinct difference in emphasis from the Blake settings. In the third song, again, where the tendency of the accompanimental phrases to cadence on major or minor triads recalls the first song of the Blake cycle and, in character, the engine whistles of *Winter Words*, these triads do not employ all twelve roots. But the absence of relative 'strictness', or completeness, is balanced by a tendency, in several of the songs, for the music to progress towards a degree of tonal centrality, rather than to state and 'prolong' its tonal bases from the outset. The very first song, 'Echo', does begin with, and returns to, its 'dissonant tonic sonority', whose bass note of F is the principal point of focus, achieving maximum clarification at the climax, where the singer's high A flat is supported by a chord which includes an F minor triad. But the second song, 'My Heart', though its broken-chord accompaniment is rather routine, progresses from tonal indistinctness to a decisive resolution into B major. The added notes in the final triad and the avoidance of a plain diatonic perfect cadence ensure that the tonality is extended, but it is definite nonetheless. Progress towards clarification is even more explicit in the third song, 'Angel', where the skilfully deployed contradictions of the early stages are replaced, after the words 'a strange confusion at the sight', by a chromatic but firmly focused A major. And the finest song of the set, 'The Nightingale and the Rose', moves delicately but decisively from ambiguity towards its clarification of E major, a subtly ironic effect, since the reiterated words are 'there's no answer', and the song ends with a haunting, disintegrating prolongation of the final tonic sonority (Ex. 45). The brief 'Epigram' is centred on C, and the concluding 'Lines written during a sleepless night' hints in its first bars at a G which achieves a precarious triadic security in the final stages. Perhaps it was the decision to end the cycle with the poet's cry, 'voices, make your meaning clear' which led Britten to emphasize the progress towards a degree of relative tonal clarity in several of the songs. But the clarity is far from absolute: it is hinted at rather than asserted.

In Britten's second Church Parable, *The Burning Fiery Furnace* op. 77 (1966), there is one very striking deviation from the convention established in *Curlew River*. At the very end, the composed Benediction and Amen uncannily disturb the modal purity of the recessional chant

Ex. 45 Britten, *The Poet's Echo*, No. 4, 'The Nightingale and the Rose'

(Ex. 46), as if to remind the listener that intolerance and crude paganism have not yet been removed from the face of the earth. The effect may also be a reaction to the more evident tonal unity of the work, since this is the only one of the parables to use the final of the chant, D, as the principal tonal centre. As later in *The Prodigal Son*, the nature of the

Ex. 46 Britten, *The Burning Fiery Furnace*

(Sá - lus ae - tér - na,   in - de - fí - ci - ens mún - di   ví - ta),
lux sem - pi - tér - na,   et   re - dém - pti - o   vé - re   nó - stra.

God_____ be   with____ you___ all!___   A - men.___

biblical story involves the kind of direct confrontation between good and
evil which is very different from the central issue of *Curlew River*. It
follows that extremes of musical characterization are more evident,
exoticism more determined. In *Curlew River* it is present in the treatment
of the Madwoman, with her keening, cavorting flute, so poignant not
least because it totally escapes all Donizettian associations. In *The
Burning Fiery Furnace* the brazen alto trombone is the principal representative of the pagan practices of the Babylonians. The second
parable also involves less narration, less arioso, and more ensemble.
But even though textures may often be more dense then in *Curlew River*,
the music is not noticeably more chromatic: indeed, it is particularly rich
in prolongations of such fundamental harmonic elements as the root and
fifth of the D major tonic triad.

An impressive example from early in the work is the Herald's first
statement (Fig. 7 to Fig. 9) in which the various strands of texture serve
the same structural purpose in different ways. The double bass is confined to the tonic and its lower neighbour-note C, while the viola, also
in a subordinate role, moves away from and back to the D two octaves
higher. The main melodic lines are provided by the trombone and the
voice: the trombone prolongs the same D as the viola by unfolding an
ascending major seventh and then, after Fig. 8, follows the horn in
descending to the middle octave D. The voice achieves the same essential
motion, but in a very different way: it concentrates throughout on the
notes around and below the initial D, and even moves briefly below the
lower D which is its goal at one point (two bars before Fig. 8).

Only one other example relative to the tones of the tonic triad can be
instanced here. At Fig. 76, the three brothers have a passage of long,
complex motion from D to the A above. Nebuchadnezzar's angry reaction immediately outlines the octave descent from the higher A, and
follows this with a prolongation of, and strong cadence on, the higher D,

which remains the central tone until Fig. 80. All these details are of great significance in indicating the positive role which tonal elements retain: and, as with the Ferryman's narration in *Curlew River,* the positiveness is matched by a melodic simplicity and strength which gives dramatic life to what might so easily have become austerely episodic recitative.

24 Britten: From *The Prodigal Son* to *Who are these children?* (1967–9)

Britten composed two substantial pieces between *The Burning Fiery Furnace* and *The Prodigal Son*: *The Golden Vanity* op. 78, 'a vaudeville for boys and piano after the old English ballad', and the second cello suite op. 80. In spite of being written for the determinedly loveable young professionals of the Vienna Boys' Choir, *The Golden Vanity* gave him ample scope for his special technique of providing simple, even folk-like tunes with disruptive if not actually destructive accompaniments, after the model of his arrangement of 'The Ash Grove'. The second cello suite is quite distinct from the first: there is no recurring 'Canto', the familiar genre-titles are avoided, and it displays touches of that austerity and asperity that were to become more common in the works after *Death in Venice*. These qualities are also to be found in the arrangement of 'Hankin Booby' written for the opening of the Queen Elizabeth Hall in 1967; Britten later incorporated it into his final orchestral work, '*A Time There Was . . . '*.

The prompt completion of *The Prodigal Son* op. 81, in April 1968, indicated that once again Britten had been fortunate enough to find the ideal subject for the kind of technical and formal features that he wished to exploit. In the fundamental sense of its tonal organization, *The Prodigal Son* is perhaps the most satisfying and characteristic of the three parables. The principal tonal centre, B flat, is fairly remote from the F sharp of the chant, and the distance from the one to the other is covered with graphic clarity in the organ at an early stage (Ex. 47a). But not only is the B flat more consistently in evidence than the A of *Curlew River* or the D of *The Burning Fiery Furnace*: it is often present as a major triad, not merely as a single, stressed note. The programmatic appropriateness of this is obvious, since it evokes the security of the family home as well as the warmth of the father's personality: indeed, the expansive intervals of his melodic material seem to reach back through the serene affirmations of the brothers in *The Burning Fiery Furnace*, and the gentle Samaritan in the *Cantata Misericordium*, to the solemn

Ex. 47a Britten, *The Prodigal Son*

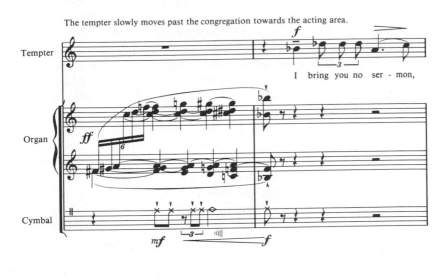

homage of the 'Green leaves' chorus in *Gloriana*. The possibility that the triad of B flat symbolized the idea of peace for Britten has often been mooted, since it occurs in such crucial places as Captain Vere's moment of apparent understanding near the end of *Billy Budd*, and Wingrave's 'hymn to peace' in the television opera. But more significant than any such local symbolic associations is the effect of the increased perspective brought to the tonal language of *The Prodigal Son* by the presence of a triad which, while it is not made the justification for a return to diatonic harmonic progressions (there is no music in the key of B flat major), acts as a splendidly explicit foil to the corresponding and complementary increase in chromatic, and at times twelve-note, activity. The colourfully uninhibited celebration of the delights of the flesh in the central stages is notably vivid, given the nature of the work in which it occurs, and there is certainly more than a hint of the terrible sensual temptations which will rise to the surface in Act II of *Death in Venice*. Yet the style of that work is perhaps more directly foreshadowed in the Younger Son's lament, 'With joy I sowed' (Fig. 63), whose narrow chromatic phrases, in canonic inversion with the viola, and evolving into deeply eloquent arioso, seem like a preliminary study for the tortured economies of Aschenbach's lyricism, as well as a close relative of the Madwoman'sariosos in *Curlew River* (Ex. 47b).

The Prodigal Son employs the conventions of the parables pointedly and powerfully. There is nothing in the least cold or evasive about the stylizations of the genre, and yet the limitations of its possibilities and properties must from the beginning have suggested that the genre was only a specialized sub-category of theatrical, operatic, music drama, rather than a complete alternative to it. And Britten, of all composers, could only be satisfied with such 'remote' subject-matter for as long as he felt able to make it genuinely immediate through his music. So his next major work seems almost like an explicit rejection of the ethos of the parables: a declaration of intent that his themes would now be urgently contemporary.

It could seem eccentric to call the *Children's Crusade* op. 82 (1968) a major work, since it lasts only nineteen minutes and was composed for a public occasion, the fiftieth anniversary of the Save the Children Fund. The idea of setting Brecht's ballad in an English translation for children's voices might seem fraught with problems, and to tend inevitably to a lightweight result. Certainly all the expertise of the Wandsworth School Choir in their recording cannot completely dispel a sense of incongruous good taste and lack of emotional involvement from singers more at home with the *Ceremony of Carols* or *The Golden Vanity*. The ballad itself does not imply that it is actually being narrated by a child or children: the only 'I', as at 'Whenever I close my eyes/I see them wander/There from this old farmhouse destroyed by the war/To another ruihed house yonder', is the poet himself. And yet the simple, direct nature of the poem makes the use of the children's voices by no means inappropriate. If anything, it ensures the avoidance of what might become an all too easy display of emotion. In the circumstances, Britten's music is extraordinarily uncompromising. Doublings and anticipations in the instruments give the singers every assistance in pitching

234

Ex. 47b Britten, *The Prodigal Son*

and sustaining their notes and intervals, but the music is highly chromatic, with much use of twelve-note cycles, several of which stress the 0, 2, 5 trichord. The 'chant' style and flexible rhythms of the parables are evident. But this is possibly Britten's least lyrical vocal work, and the A major ending towards which it progresses inevitably disintegrates (like those other A major endings from *Peter Grimes* to *Death in Venice*) under the influence of Brecht's laconic final lines (Ex. 48). The sheer length of the text, and the concentration of the music, may promote a somewhat episodic effect in places. The form of the work, for all its

Ex. 48 Britten, *Children's Crusade*

cumulative progress towards resolution and disintegration, is not as satisfactory as in most of Britten's other later compositions, but it clarifies and confirms just what the elements of that late style would be.

Even before illness finally ended Britten's career as a pianist, the harpist Osian Ellis had begun to share the composer's recitals with Peter Pears, performing folk songs and other appropriate arrangements, like Schubert's *Harfenspielerlieder*. Eventually, Britten composed two works especially for Pears and Ellis – Canticle V op. 89 (1974) and *A Birthday Hansel* op.92 (1975) – and he also made several special folk-song arrangements. But first Britten provided the harpist with a short five-movement suite op. 83, which Ellis first performed at the 1969 Aldeburgh Festival.

Like the cello suites, it avoids the dance forms of baroque precedent, and includes several of Britten's favourite genre pieces: toccata, variations on a 'ground' ('Nocturne'), fugue, and theme and variations

('Hymn'). The suite begins with an Overture whose resonant C major triads offer a timely reminder that timbral appropriateness could be as compelling a reason for Britten to use a particular sonority as any technical or structural principle. The Overture is nevertheless consistent with Britten's style in extending its basic C major to the point where no conventional harmonic progressions occur, and the rest of the suite conforms to this model, despite the extreme contrasts in texture and character of the various movements. The 'Nocturne' is especially subtle, with its cross-rhythms and evolving patterns in the bass, while the 'Hymn' offers an initial harmonization of 'Saint Denio' whose clashing sevenths and seconds make the occasional, cadential tonic triads sound eerily disembodied. The melody is itself disoriented to begin with, starting on the 'wrong' degree of the scale. When it finally reaches the correct pitch-levels for a C major harmonization in the last variation, diatonic triads are not shunned, but firm cadencing is, and the suite ends, like the *Nocturnal* for guitar, with dissolving motion on to a final chord (G major) which sounds too insecure to be a tonic, but too passive to promote further search for greater finality.

1969 was a particularly traumatic year for Britten. In particular, a disastrous fire occurred at the Maltings, and he had to put all his energies into urgent fund-raising for its rebuilding. It was also around this time that he began to turn back to the music of his childhood. In 1966–7 he had revised three carols originally composed between 1929 and 1931. In 1968 he refurbished some de la Mare settings, *Tit for Tat* (1928–31), and in the spring of 1969 came rewritings of the still earlier 'Five Walztes' [sic] for piano (1923–5). By far the most substantial of these exhumations were still to come: the D major String Quartet of 1931, and his first stage work, *Paul Bunyan* (1940–1), both revised in 1974. Not surprisingly, then, several of Britten's later works seem still more involved than formerly with the fascinating inaccessibility of childhood. Less than a year after completing the *Children's Crusade* he was working on what was to be his last substantial song cycle for tenor and piano: *Who are these children?* op. 84, Lyrics, Rhymes and Riddles by William Soutar.

There is much more to the subject-matter of these poems than the obsession with juvenility which the title might suggest: but there can be little doubt that the extreme simplicity of the verse forms, even when the sentiments and images are complex, was deeply attractive to a composer who was at his freest when simple material could be placed in an aura of ambiguity. Even the most complex of the Soutar poems, 'Nightmare', whose central image of the tree recalls the most intense of the Blake songs, 'A Poison Tree', is economical in form and, for the most part, straightforward in rhythm. The contrast between the violent, war-scarred images of 'Nightmare', 'Slaughter', 'Who are these Children?', and 'The Children', and the whimsy of the dialect riddles and rhymes, is unusually acute even for Britten; indeed, the overall contrast is much greater than that between the Songs and Proverbs of the Blake cycle. To some extent, there is a synthesis in the implacable repetitions of the final song, 'The Auld Aik', but in any case degrees of formal similarity and parallels of style ensure that diversity creates no solecisms. The central theme, war and the pity of war, could easily seem diluted by the Riddles and Rhymes. But their role as a consciously contrived escape from the horrors of reality gives them a contrasting relevance of no little power.

The first song, 'A Riddle (The Earth)', is in a characteristically extended G major, with a neat tripartite form. But the first rhyme, 'A Laddie's Sang', is in a saturatedly diatonic, by no means untriadic D major: there is only one chromatic note (the A sharp/B flat in bar 8) and both stanzas end with perfect cadences. In 'Nightmare' the voice's initial heterophonic presentation of the piano's ostinato matches effects in the Pushkin and Blake cycles, but, for all the final return to the initial A and the key signature of one flat, the frequent clashes between semitones help to prevent the emergence of any but the most precarious centrality for the note A. The form of alternating textures for alternate lines of text is simple, but variation and contrast ensure that evolutionary process overrides small-scale sectionalism. The final A of 'Nightmare' is the centre for the straightforward expansions of 'Black Day', but the two stanzas of 'Bed-Time' each progress towards a G major triad with two transpositions of a single, tonally remote statement and a final, complementary descent, with no orthodox cadential preparation. 'Slaughter' has a rhetoric which has sent commentators reaching as far back as the *Donne Sonnets* for comparisons: so disturbed is its surface that it can only confirm its ultimate concord by means of contrary motion whole-tone scales. The vocal line is by no means wholly 'dissonant' with the accompaniment, but the persistent rhythmic patterns provide an implacable regularity for this central and most violent number in the cycle. Gentle simplicity seems the only possible consequence, and No. 7 – 'A Riddle (The Child You Were)' – is unusual in being based entirely on an E/B drone. It is therefore strongly centred, but far from diatonic, and the same is true of No. 8, 'The Larky Lad', whose insistence on F as pivot makes the final flourish – A to D – such a surprise. But it is A and D which provide the first sound for the title-song, No. 9. The accompaniment is intently focused on repetitions of distorted fanfares which evolve into more conventionally pianistic shapes for a while and which initally seem to pivot on an A/E fifth, with F sharp and G sharp superimposed, as a central pivot, though the F of the previous song is not without some influence; nor is the D of that song's final cadence. The economy of it all is haunting. The passing hunt seems as disquieting as a half-remembered nightmare, the staring faces of the children as quietly horrific as the suffering ghosts of M. R. James.

As already noted, it is one of the miracles of this cycle that the riddles and rhymes offset the lyrics without incongruity: it is the pervasive simplicity, the disturbed pivots common to the harmonic character of all the movements, which provide the essential unity. No. 10, 'Supper', is another short movement which centres entirely on an 0, 2, 6 trichord with E and A sharp alternating in the bass, a tritone which is carried over from the previous lyric. There is some motion around this unstable entity, but no resolution. No. 11, 'The Children', has a particularly substantial structure, with room for two powerful if not exactly expansive climaxes. Though centred on E, this is one of Britten's least obviously tonal songs, its tritones, minor thirds and seconds creating octatonic, twelve-note and whole-tone areas within which only the occasional hint of triadic progression can operate. At the end, three minor thirds combine into a Mode II hexachord, and the final vocal phrase presents a pure Mode II statement: for this reason, 'extended modality' might seem a more appropriate term for the language of the piece than 'extended tonality', not least because Mode II gives Britten's favourite 'bi-modal' tonic triad. It is nevertheless satisfying that the ending of this song can be felt to 'resolve' triadically into the opening of the final rhyme, 'The Auld Aik' (Ex. 49). On paper, this short setting looks like one of Britten's simplest, and its form – a verse and its varied restatement, each verse with clear internal relations outlining smaller-scale ABA schemes – is indeed simple. But the registral displacements of the accompaniment, and the intense instability of the motion towards the cadence chord of each phrase, somehow emphasized by the full triadic writing, make this an appropriately disturbing conclusion to the cycle. It celebrates destruc-

Ex. 49 Britten, *Who are these Children?*

(i) No. 11, 'The Children'

(ii) No. 12, 'The Auld Aik'

tion (Britten may have had the Maltings in mind, for all its miraculously rapid rebuilding) and, as in the equally memorable *Winter Words*, the ultimate major triad has a chilling rather than a comforting finality.

25 Tippett: *The Knot Garden* and *Songs for Dov* (1966–70)

In 1963 it could be claimed that *The Musical Times* had underplayed Britten's fiftieth birthday. In January 1965 it rose to the occasion of Tippett's sixtieth with an article by Alexander Goehr, and a drawing of the composer by Guy Worsdell on the front cover. The Faber and Faber *Symposium* celebrating the event was also a more substantial affair than the Britten equivalent: as the editor, Ian Kemp, explained, 'it celebrates Michael Tippett's sixtieth birthday traditionally, with contributions from his personal friends and, it is hoped, practically, with a critical examination of his music'.¹ The most enthusiastic critical acclaim for Tippett was still three years away, however, for it was only with the second production of *The Midsummer Marriage* at Covent Garden in 1968 that most if not all of the old reservations were dismissed. The ground had been prepared for this reappraisal by a broadcast of the opera on 13 January 1963, conducted by Norman Del Mar, and the impact of the work in the theatre under Colin Davis was not only sufficient to cancel out most of the old doubts, but also to justify Covent Garden's daring in commissioning a new opera from the composer. *The Knot Garden*, first performed on 2 December 1970, had been begun four years before, and Tippett's only other works during this time were *The Shires Suite* for the Leicestershire Schools Symphony Orchestra, and a variation on a Welsh tune as part of a collective celebration for the opening of the Severn Bridge in 1967.

The Vision of Saint Augustine might seem, in its jubilant elaboration, to be the very reverse of 'Eliotesque'. Yet the tone of Tippett's introductory note in the score, as well as his chosen epigraph, make clear the extent to which the style as well as the thought of the poet, who had died during the year in which *The Vision* was completed, still mattered to him. It may well be that Eliot would have been disturbed by Tippett's agnostic approach to Augustine: in view of the poet's belief that 'without a religious basis in the society no culture is possible', and the corresponding, inevitable fact that 'fundamentally, Eliot had no faith in modern civilisation',² the manner and matter of Tippett's affirmations might well have offended Eliot deeply. Yet it is difficult to exaggerate the depth and power of his influence on the composer, not in his role as a pessimistic observer of modern society – here there is a more direct link with Britten – but as an evoker of archetypal images. And it is lines from *Burnt Norton* which provide a transition from *The Vision of Saint Augustine* to *The Knot Garden*:

> To be conscious is not to be in time
> But only in time can the moment in the rose-garden . . .
> Be remembered . . .

Not only does the opera concern a garden, where Thea prunes the roses, but the images associated with it become steadily more extended until, at the climax of Act II, the musician Dov sings, in very un-Eliotlike phrases:

> O hold our fleeting youth for ever
> O stop the world I want to get off
> O honey, honey, make love to me
> Now (O Boy!) now (how play it cool?)
> In the fabulous rose-garden.

Other commentators have discussed all the various sources and associations which lie behind *The Knot Garden*, from Mozart to Shaw to

Virginia Woolf to Pasternak: as *Burnt Norton* pertinently has it, 'other echoes inhabit the garden'. The musical and literary quotations create the most direct links with Schubert and Shakespeare, for, just as quoting the Bible came naturally to Saint Augustine, so Tippett makes liberal reference to the sources of his own inspiration. Flora's quotation of Schubert's 'Die liebe Farbe' may be evidence of several different things: her immaturity, her sexual insecurity ('But that's a boy's song'), her liking for the 'bitter-sweet'. Musically, its chaste but intensely expressive minor–major tonality – the same key-centre of B as that alluded to at the beginning and end of the opera – is worlds away from the jaunty, expansive chromaticism of Dov's ensuing song about the 'big town' and the 'golden Californian west'. So it functions as a facet of characterization as well as offering a vision of a musical past which is no longer accessible save in quotation marks.

But Shakespeare is a good deal more central to *The Knot Garden* than either Schubert or the author of the other quoted song, 'We Shall Overcome'. To begin with, Tippett's epigraph is Parolles's line from *All's Well That Ends Well* (Act IV Scene 3): 'simply the thing I am shall make me live'. In isolation, this seems a positive, euphonious, perhaps rather vague assertion. But the overtones, the implication that a full sense of personal identity can only be based on realistic understanding of one's whole being, explain the appeal of the line to the creative artist whose early experience of psychoanalysis, as explained earlier, was itself a prelude to a period of intense self-analysis. The character of Mangus in the opera, who eventually assumes the guise of Prospero, is described as an analyst, and may indeed represent those aspects of the creative personality which are not present in the self-confessed composer Dov. (The occurrence of the line 'Men are to mell with' a little earlier in the same scene of Shakespeare's play, may also have helped to suggest the name Mel for Tippett's homosexual Negro writer.) As for Parolles, the context of his comment is not the elevated one which might be expected: 'the thing I am' is, in essence, shabby: 'live safest in shame! . . . by foolery thrive!' It is a modern, anti-heroic stance, with the kind of tone that seems somewhat dissonant with Tippett's far less down-to-earth enactment. But in so far as Parolles learns to be realistic through some unpleasant experiences, his affirmation does become relevant to Tippett's own characters.

The principal Shakespearean association in *The Knot Garden* is in any case not with *All's Well That Ends Well* but with *The Tempest*. For most of Act III of the opera, the garden gives way to the island. To wish that Tippett could have emulated several other composers and simply turned Shakespeare's play into an opera is to miss one obvious point: the music of Shakespeare's poetry. Tippett had indeed set Ariel's songs, in 1962, but he no doubt felt that the kind of selection and juxtaposition which he could employ with Saint Augustine's *Confessions* was not possible, and not relevant to his dramatic purposes. His modern characters learn through contact – even in a charade – with the memorable archetypes devised by Shakespeare. *The Knot Garden* argues that self-discovery is as possible through play as through more serious actions, and as Tippett grows older the virtues of rediscovering child-like qualities assume a greater resonance. Even so, it is as adults that the characters re-emerge from the charade, some old relationships restored, some new relationships established. The 'issue' of *The Tempest* is described thus by Gonzalo:

> Thus in one voyage
> Did Claribel her husband find at Tunis,
> And Ferdinand, her brother, found a wife
> Where he himself was lost; Prospero his dukedom
> In a poor isle: and all of us ourselves,
> When no man was his own. (Act V Scene 1)

At the end of the opera, only the composer Dov seems to need pitying. And even he, as Ariel, has been set free: free, perhaps, to discover the music of the opera.

'Confrontation', 'Labyrinth', 'Charade': the act-headings of *The Knot Garden* seem to stress tension and artificiality. The effect of the work is certainly no more naturalistic than the sound of its music, with prominent wind, percussion and electric guitar, is warmly Romantic or soberly classical. The whole opera is so concentrated and so fast-moving that the characters scarcely develop at all: they are constantly confronted with new aspects of themselves, and their own most essential attributes, which range from the cosseted repressions of the garden-loving Thea to the agonizing self-analysis of the freedom-fighter Denise and the self-parodying homosexual caperings of Dov and Mel, are stressed at the expense of any attempt at fully rounded characterization. The characters might be those conjured up in an uneasy sleep by a work-weary analyst, for although at the outset Mangus believes himself to be a 'man of power', he ends with the appropriate note of self-parody: 'Prospero's a fake, we all know that: . . . I'm just a foolish fond old man, just like the rest of you.' Even so, Tippett is presumably not arguing that the human, all-too-human analyst is useless, with no role to play, any more than the composer is useless. Both must discover their roles, and the best ways of playing them. Here the difference between Augustine's 'vision' and Mangus's 'practice' is most clearly shown. The scene has changed from the mystic-spiritual location of fourth-century Ostia to the urban psycho-social labyrinth of the late twentieth century. 'Each character had learnt' – thanks to Mangus? – 'that the acceptance of all we contain is the only hope' Tippett proclaims;[3] in Shakespeare's terms, they have all found themselves. Nothing, it seems, must be rejected – that way lies destructive repression: everything must be admitted, integrated, and exploited.

In musical terms such comprehensiveness could be a recipe for utter incoherence, and we may indeed sense in the later Tippett a less immediate and obvious concern with unity, that most classical and traditional of aesthetic virtues. But his music never aspires to the state of a random collage, even when it includes elements as disparate as the Blues and a Schubert *Lied*. Its pre-eminent concern with evolutionary continuity is apparent at the opera's outset, when the orchestral prelude to Act I presents its two ideas in an expanding tripartite form – A, A^1, A^2. The 'twelve-note' tempest-theme which dominates this prelude is, it would seem, simply a way of getting the work launched. It may evoke the 'whirling storm' described in the stage directions, or even represent the kind of totality which Tippett regards as the aim of life and art, and it recurs – for example, in retrograde at the end of Act II. But it is the three-fold developing-variation form which is the more significantly Schoenbergian feature of the prelude, and of the opera as a whole.

Subdivision of acts and scenes, for example the ternary structure of the Blues ensemble which concludes Act I, is straightforward enough, and the repetitions in the music function as the most basic structural device in the absence of an all-determining harmonic system. Tippett is not particularly concerned to differentiate his characters consistently in vocal style – or, for that matter, to distinguish between different kinds of vocal statement. The pervasively florid, heightened vocal utterances do duty alike for such conventional exchanges as that between Thea and Mangus at the beginning, and for the much more poetic moments in Denise's Act I aria, or Dov's Act II song. The vocal writing is far from monotonous or unvaried, but the composer uses the orchestra as the principal means of effecting the many sudden changes of mood and manner on which the structure depends. The most obvious recurring element is purely orchestral and theatrical – the dissolve – and this music, with its shifting superimpositions, is representative of the polyphonic priorities of later Tippett in all save its lack of distinctive thematic elements: in a sense, as the composer admits, it is 'non-music'.[4]

The Act I finale has great cumulative power, but ensemble as such plays relatively little part in the opera, and its use in the later stages of Act III may even seem a little perfunctory. The heart of the work is found in the extended solos, which are granted to by no means all the characters, but in which the late-Tippett style is heard at its richest and most original. In the case of Dov, this glorification of the solo voice extends beyond the confines of the opera into a separate, splendidly idiosyncratic composition, *Songs for Dov*, which was actually given its first performance before the opera, and which has a sweep and power anticipating the second part of the Symphony No. 3. But in the opera the most powerful antidote to the prevailingly terse confrontations of the characters is the long aria for Denise which precedes and prepares the Act I finale. Its grand rhetorical phrases (Ex. 50a) stand out the more powerfully because warm lyricism is used so sparingly in the work. The eloquence of a line like Thea's 'I am no more afraid' (Ex. 50b) nevertheless confirms that there is much more to *The Knot Garden* than a rather attenuated 'camping-it-up', even though the element of game- and role-playing is important, and anticipates the equally ritualistic but more menacing celebrations surrounding Olympion in *The Ice Break*.

The Knot Garden is not primarily a study of the character and sources of creativity, but about problems of personal development and association which are common to all, creative artists or not. And, as already noted, these collective issues are more important than the individual traits and 'histories' of the individual characters. In deciding to extend the char-

Ex. 50a Tippett, *The Knot Garden*, Act I Scene 13
(accompaniment omitted)

Ex. 50b Tippett, *The Knot Garden*, Act III Scene 7
(accompaniment omitted)

acter of Dov the composer outside the opera, therefore, Tippett might have been expected to fill out Dov's background in a more conventionally narrative way, to tell us more about who he is, where he comes from, what the influences on him have been. In *Songs for Dov*, however, the musician remains to a large extent a mythic figure, a projector of symbols, a cross between pop-star and preacher who gets his message across even though we do not really get to know him. Indeed, it might well be the case that he communicates so effectively because of the larger-than-life air of mystery which surrounds him. Dov's experience ranges from the 'big town', the 'home without a garden' of his birth, through the promised land of California to the bleak wastes of Siberia, and back home. In *The Knot Garden*, Shakespeare's Ariel is Dov's alter ego, and Ariel's words recur in the second song of *Songs for Dov*; but the larger presence here, in Song 3, is that of Boris Pasternak's hero Dr Zhivago. Song 3 ends with lines from one of the poems of Zhivago which are printed as an Appendix to the novel:

> Then why does the horizon weep in mist
> And the dung smell bitter?
> Surely it is my calling
> To see that the distances do not lose heart
> And that beyond the limits of the town
> The earth shall not feel lonely?

This seems an inspiring affirmation: but it is followed in *Songs for Dov* by the half-cynical, half-questioning 'Sure, baby' which Dov has borrowed from his *Knot Garden* friend Mel. And Tippett himself has written that 'Pasternak's trope for Zhivago is all rhetoric' – the kind of rhetoric which, according to Yeats, poets make out of their quarrel with society. 'So we know that Dov must turn his back on it and peer into himself to find his poetry.'[5]

This effect, of certainty and completion called into question, is frequently found in Tippett's work from the final, disintegrative chords of *King Priam* onwards – and anticipated as early as the end of the Symphony No. 1. The concluding whisper of the chorus in *The Vision of Saint Augustine*, and the last neutral chord of the Symphony No. 3 create a similar effect, though by no means all the later works follow their example. There is, however, a natural progression from Dov's 'I was born in a big town/Where the buildings grew so mighty high/(O boy!) high enough to scrape the sky' to Pasternak's 'The living language of our time is urban'. It is a huge distance from this back to the magical nature-language of, for example, the Ritual Dances of *The Midsummer Marriage*, whose 'Englishness with Greek overtones' seems completely excluded from the Russian–American emphasis of the *Songs for Dov*. This emphasis, in turn, is more fully worked out in *The Ice*

246

Break, where Solzhenitzin replaces Pasternak as a central source of inspiration. Such a change is part of Tippett's courageous attempt to give his archetypes a more directly contemporary tone and naturalistic context: from Dov to Lev is a much larger step than the similarity of their names and their common role as creative artists might imply. But Tippett himself, in his notes on *Songs for Dov*, is deeply conscious of the expressive gulf between the brash, conventional urban-American anti-lyricism of 'Talk that talk/Walk that walk/It don't mean a thing if it ain't got that swing' and the un-urban, and therefore passé, lyricism of Zhivago's verse.

Pasternak states that Zhivago wrote a line . . . which runs 'The living language of our time is urban' but that nothing of this supposed living language was found in Zhivago's poetry. So that Pasternak, through Zhivago, in a marvellous trope, suggests that one of the tasks of, shall we say, lyric poets of our period, might be just to sustain the pastoral metaphor, in its deep sense, against the ephemeralities of town fashions.[6]

It is not too difficult to see the task of synthesizing pastoral and urban as one which the lyric dramatist Tippett tackled most directly in *The Ice Break*. Dov, in Song 3, 'is now a grown man, a creative artist struggling with the intractable problems of "poets in a barren age"', and he finds, on his Siberian journey, that the lovers (Zhivago and Lara) have deserted their forest idyll and gone 'back to the town, she first, he after, each alone into the swarming city'. But Tippett nevertheless achieves, in his concluding setting of Zhivago's lines quoted above, a brief glimpse of the quality of exalted affirmation to which the traditional urban language can only react with scepticism: 'Sure, baby' (Ex. 51).

Tippett has explained his view of the interpenetration of American and European associations in Song 1, which is taken complete from the opera:

The timbre produced by the amplification draws our ear to jazz (using the term as a wide generality) and America, while the activity of the instrumentalist's fingers on the harpsichord or guitar (more obvious on the stage than in the concert hall) draws us to the European operatic tradition of the stage serenade.

Tippett was to achieve his most memorable synthesis between a popular form and idiom, and his own lyric intensity, in the Blues section of the Symphony No. 3. In the symphony, moreover, the technique of 'collage' is far less evident than in *Songs for Dov*, and, even more importantly, there is less reliance on the allusions set up by quotation, though Beethoven's Symphony No. 9 is not without influence. The reliance on quotation in *Songs for Dov* is greatest in Song 2, where Dov sings 'of the *Wanderjahre*, those years of illusion and disillusion, innocence and experience, which we all pass through to reach what maturity we may'. Someone as conscious as Tippett of the value of accumulated experi-

Ex. 51 Tippett, *Songs for Dov*, No. 3 (accompaniment omitted)

ence probably needed to get such an elaborate compilation of 'found objects' out of his system sooner or later, and, after the completion of *The Knot Garden*, which, in spite of its concentration, and a certain amount of rather 'dry' material, does achieve the first hints of a musical marriage between lyric and urban, he could perhaps relax sufficiently to do so. Goethe as set by Beethoven, Shakespeare as set by Tippett, as well as hints of *King Priam* and *The Flying Dutchman* rotate through the clear verse-refrain form. By contrast, the only quotation in Song 3 is a brief snatch from *Boris Godunov*, a 'wandering' viola line when Zhivago is 'scribbling in his attic'. But in Song 2 the range of allusion and quotation serves to stress the fact that Dov's experiences matter more as an example to others rather than for their effect on Dov himself. Tippett described the work as 'a cycle of songs which Dov is supposed to compose and sing': but they remain songs for, rather than by him. They are also, certainly, songs about him: but the work is less a biography of a composer than a portrait of a culture in a crucial phase – still searching for a synthesis, but self-conscious to the point of self-parody.

26 Britten: From *Owen Wingrave* to *Death in Venice* (1970–3)

In 1909, after reading *The Saloon*, Henry James's stage version of *Owen Wingrave*, George Bernard Shaw expressed to the author his passionate disapproval of the work's entire ethos: 'you have given victory to death and obsolescence: I want you to give it to life and regeneration'. In noting the disagreement between two such different major writers, Leon Edel has contrasted 'James's taking the world as he found it, and seeking to demonstrate its realities and existential absurdities', with Shaw's taking 'the world as a place in which art had to serve revolution'.[1] One would be wise to steer clear of the temptation to continue the discussion as if James were Britten, and Shaw Tippett, with the former exclusively the poet of death, the latter of life. But in its very intensity, Britten's own later music seems to confirm a conviction that the very idea of 'revolution', none the less dangerous for being vague and ill-defined, is inimical to art. There is certainly a greater reliance than formerly on those familiar procedural ambiguities to match an increasing sense of 'existential absurdities'. Reality is still explored, but beliefs can only be expressed with caution and circumspection. It is perhaps the case that certainty has become the prerogative only of the revolutionary or of the naive (Lechmere), and the family security which had triumphed briefly in *The Prodigal Son* already seems impossibly remote.

It is indeed a striking coincidence that, so soon after the composition of the third Church Parable, Britten should have embarked, in his most substantial dramatic work for virtually a decade, on the tale of a prodigal nephew and grandson, *Owen Wingrave*. Yet it was not a sudden, still less a new idea. Tippett believes that it may have been in Britten's mind 'even before he returned to England from America',[2] and it was certainly spoken of before the writing of the *War Requiem*.[3] But there were at least two strong reasons for the composer to turn to a subject so familiar to him and so close to his heart in 1970: first, he had only recently rejected what would have been a bold new venture, an opera based on Tolstoy's *Anna Karenina* for the Bolshoi; second, he was 'feeling strongly about the Vietnam war and the shooting of students at Kent State University'.[4] No wonder *Wingrave*, the opera for television, contains more of the despair of the pacifist who sees little hope of influencing the course of events than the hope of the humanist who believes that mankind is, ultimately, regenerate.

A possible alternative title for the opera, if rather inappropriately

249

ironic, might be 'The Family Circle', which, as Owen tells the tutor Coyle in James's story, is what his aunt calls the collection of family portraits which hang at Paramore. It is the thought of this collection which leads James's Owen to exclaim rather melodramatically, 'Ah, we're tainted – all!'; and the theme of the story, the oppression of the family which Owen can only escape by making himself an outcast from it, is one which Britten rarely tackled. Indeed, apart from Mum's tyranny over Albert Herring, and the Madwoman's frenzied longing for her lost child in *Curlew River*, parental claims and family ties do not feature prominently in his plots until, once more, *The Prodigal Son*. It is the merest speculation which might lead to the suspicion that there could be a hint of the relationship between Bridge and Britten in that between Coyle and Owen. As James says of the tutor, 'this young man's facility really fascinated him' – but the agonies experienced within the family circle after the exposure of non-conformity might have touched an area of personal experience. Maybe it was this which helped to attract Britten to a plot which is not without its weaknesses: in particular, the 'private' haunting theme blends a little uneasily with the 'public' pacifism theme. And yet those who criticize James may simply have failed to recognize the essential point of the story, which is not that war is evil, fighting futile. The point is that the true futility consists in the testing of courage for its own sake: perhaps even war is preferable to this? Does Owen invite death out of guilt and self-doubt rather than out of sheer unadulterated bravado, misplaced self-confidence? At the end, surely, he lacks the courage of his convictions: he is not certain that he is right, and so seeks to prove his courage by the sort of reckless deed which wins VCs. He does violence to himself.

Just as the least stable kind of tonality is that which gives the strongest evidence of anti-tonal tendencies, so the least stable atonality is that which seems predisposed to abandon totality for particularity. In the broadest terms, the musical content of *Owen Wingrave* could perhaps have maintained the balance evident in, for example, the *War Requiem*, where the disruptive forces of violence and destruction are, if not assuaged and dissolved, at least contained by the strength of the forces making for peace and tranquillity. The television opera, however, is about one man's unsuccessful fight to survive his decision *not* to fight. In place of the *War Requiem*'s hint of a world of peace beyond war and death, it offers no evidence that Wingrave's self-sacrifice has achieved more than his own personal and brief moment of truth.

If Britten had chosen to end the work with a reversal of the Prelude's opening processes, dissolving the relative stability of Owen's theme into totally chromatic chordal alternations, then a sense of futility would be much more difficult to resist. But this initial twelve-note idea still represents war and aggression in the most general sense (it surely cannot represent the dead weight of tradition!), and it ensures that the extensive use of background twelve-note successions elsewhere in the work creates an underlying sense of inescapable corruption (not least at Owen's apparently positive moment of self-realization). The specific 'curse of the Wingraves', which ensures that it is the locked room at Paramore which is fatal for Owen, rather than any battlefield, is represented by the Ballad, whose use as a frame for Act II introduces the new technical element of the 'disturbed' Mixolydian mode. This seems to match the 'out-of-timeness' of the dramatic device (the narrator) with 'out-of-style' music, and its function in the opera is too serious for it to be felt as a parody of traditional ballad music. Yet in its use of wider intervals, its reluctance to confirm or even clarify a tonic, the Ballad is not dissimilar to Lechmere's excitedly distorted version of 'The Minstrel Boy' (Fig. 15) – Lechmere is too impulsive to sing in tune – whose initial perfect fourth provides enough of a fanfare for much of the more martial music in the opera to seem associated with it (Ex. 52a(i)). Following this fourth, and detached from it in the accompanying melodic line, is the $0, 2, 5$ cell (B flat, C, E flat). This links the first two, 'atonal' chords of the work and the Ballad tune (Ex. 52a(ii)) as well as appearing in chordal form at one of the work's major climaxes, with Owen's words 'Come, turn your key' at Fig. 279 (Ex. 52a (iii)).

It would be satisfying if it could be claimed that the composer actually used this cell as his principal means of mediation between the apparent atonality of the initial chords, such moments of explicit tonality as the resolution on to B flat major four bars after Fig. 246, and the modality of the Ballad. But such a selectively focused interpretation runs the risk of obscuring the very subtlety of an interaction, hinted at earlier, in which 'atonality', 'tonality', and 'modality' are not exclusive abstractions but degrees of emphasis within the rich perspectives of Britten's late musical language. Of the three, it is naturally tonality as a pure, diatonically progressing phenomenon, which is least in evidence. Even the powerfully prepared and deeply satisfying cadence on to B flat major at Owen's words 'In peace I have found my image', introduces, not an extended passage in the key of B flat major, but – a rarity for *Owen Wingrave* – a passage founded on sustained major and minor concords which are enhanced rather than threatened by decorating dissonances. These chords range majestically across the tonal spectrum with harmonizations of, successively, the notes of the B flat, C, B and A major triads, until the scheme breaks down (A flat major does not harmonize an E) and is left incomplete; this confirms as surely as the celebrated chord-sequence in

Ex. 52a Britten, *Owen Wingrave*

Ex. 52b Britten, *Owen Wingrave*, Act II Scene 2

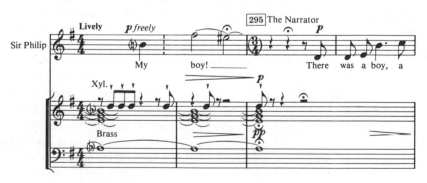

Billy Budd, that what is 'resolved' is the fact that the hero must die. Owen has not defeated the curse, but he has banished, if only temporarily, the mindless violence of the twelve-note chords. Fanfares remain to disturb the resolution of the ballad at the end of the work, but there is certainly a hint of resolution, and of true stability: the work does not simply stop (Ex. 52b).

In a sense, however, the 'resolution' of the work is not Owen's B flat, but the Mixolydian chord (G, A, C, E – a superimposition of two 0, 2, 5 cells) heard as he enters the locked room (Fig. 279). The B flat has explicitly resolved the first tetrachord of the basic twelve-note statement which, in its climactic presentation (just before Fig. 246) has a G added to it, thus further removing the chord from its basis as a 'pure' diminished triad. But the other two chords of the initial twelve-note complex are not treated in similar fashion. Even before the end of Owen's final scene with Kate when, at Fig. 273, she states the challenge directly with the words 'sleep in the haunted room', the 0, 2, 5 trichord is heard in a way which makes it appear to contradict rather than resolve the musical argument: an argument which thus far has not lost sight of the 'hopeful' B flat. This exchange is structured around transpositions of the 'ballad trichord'; and this, after Fig. 276, is clearly shown to be a partial inversion of Chord I. The twelve-note aggregate which emerges at Fig. 277 achieves the nearest thing to resolution when, after the interruption of the final passage of dialogue stressing the 'neutral' fourths (including B flat), the climax at Fig. 279 is reached. Through its clarification of those pitches from the twelve-note complex which are ultimately most important, this climax might seem to represent the establishment of G as a tonic, but that note is only the focus of modal priorities, rather than a genuine diatonic centre. The 'invariants' in the music between Fig. 279 and the end of the work expand on the shifting prolongations of the 0, 2, 5 cell which have been presented between Figs. 273 and 276. These basic shifts – from G, A, E to B flat, F, G, to A, E, F sharp, and finally to D, E, B – make it clear that there is no longer any attempt to generate the total chromatic by complementary transposition of the trichord. The issue is no longer that of what possible outcome may be deduced from a twelve-note complex, but of what can happen to a sustained D, E, B complex against which a G is repeatedly projected. What happens is that first the sonority dissolves into ostinato-like figuration (after Fig. 293); then the final chord of the opera, generated by overlapping fourths, offers a 'neutral' background of thirds – A flat, E, G, B flat – centring on the diminished triad, against which an upper third, D, is picked out for special emphasis, thereby perhaps recalling the pivot note of Owen's own theme as first presented in the Act I Prelude. As already illustrated, Sir Philip's final cry adds another third (E sharp) to the pile, so the chord which fades at Fig. 295 has touched on six different notes. But it is of course the D which cues the Ballad-coda, and the motion from D through F to G which ends the work has a multiple neutrality, fitting in view of the enormous range of technical possibilities which the language of the work has explored, and the bleak economy with which its most hopeful and expansive aspirations are blocked and set aside.

Between the completion of *Wingrave* during the summer of 1970 and the start of work on *Death in Venice* in October 1971, Britten composed two short pieces which added to 'collections' already begun. Canticle IV op. 86 was written between 12 and 22 January 1971, and the Cello Suite No. 3 op. 87 between 23 February and 3 March.

Canticle IV, *Journey of the Magi*, together with Canticle V, *The Death of Saint Narcissus*, written after *Death in Venice*, represents a long-delayed encounter with the poetry of T. S. Eliot – though the delay is scarcely to be wondered at in view of the obvious differences in syntax and style between Eliot and those English poets whom Britten had previously set. Tippett's early contacts with Eliot had not led to any direct collaboration, and by the time Britten came to set his poetry Eliot had been dead for six years; during Eliot's lifetime the only major composer to use a text of his was Stravinsky in his brief anthem, 'The Dove Descending Breaks the Air'. In his last illness, Eliot's poetry was 'one of the few things Britten felt himself able to read',[5] and these last two Canticles certainly seem to find the strength for their concentrated musical ambiguities in the careful, obsessive repetitions and strong cadences of Eliot's verse style. The progression away from Auden was complete.

Journey of the Magi is a treatment of the travelling theme which is present in all three Church Parables and *Death in Venice*; and its three male voices, at times seeming almost to parody popular close-harmony style, are a clear link with the three brothers of *The Burning Fiery*

Furnace. The chordal character of the 'travelling' refrain, supported by a percussive yet rhythmically supple ostinato, recalls the opening of *Owen Wingrave*, while the self-conscious pedantry of the verbal style even suggests a link with Aschenbach. Nevertheless, the true, individual character of the Canticle emerges not from its account of the journey, but from what it says about the permanent effects of that journey.

> We returned to our places, these Kingdoms,
> But no longer at ease here, in the old dispensation,
> With an alien people clutching their gods.

It is this unease, persistent, profound and unrelieved, which the music evokes most consistently. It is an unease consequent on the basic if hardly novel perception that birth and death are, in a sense, the same: part of the same process, and therefore to be equated.

> I had seen birth and death,
> But had thought they were different; this Birth was
> Hard and bitter agony for us, like Death, our death.

In Eliot's extraordinarily bitter poem, suggesting as it does that the conversion to a new certainty is as much to be feared and resented as welcomed with joy, Britten found a powerful expression, more allusive than he had previously encountered or exploited, of the theme of doomed youth. By introducing the Epiphany Antiphon 'Magi videntes stellam' into the later stages of the Canticle, Britten may actually have made the fact that the occasion of the poem is Christ's nativity more explicit than Eliot himself might have wished, but the extra literalness is musically justified by the way it focuses the purely musical issues in what is one of Britten's most radical pieces. The chant emerges with a 'perilous sweetness', prevented from establishing the purity of either the major key or Lydian mode which its monodic presentation would favour by the dissonant underpinning based on the G natural which is the recurrent though far from persistent tonic of the work (Ex. 53a). The power of G natural to disturb is strengthened by the fact that, during the episode of the chant's first presentation, the vocal repetitions of 'satisfactory' all employ G natural rather than G sharp. And so the work proceeds to its ending at a point of clarified ambiguity rather than either resolution or dissolution. Future hopes and present unease co-exist in the way the final phrase of chant circles round the major third while G minor persists beneath (Ex. 53b). The precise balance between hope and doubt is for each individual to decide.

Like Canticle IV, the third cello suite uses a chant as one of its thematic elements – the Russian Kontakion, or Hymn for the Departed – alongside three folk-tunes which Britten found in Tchaikovsky's volumes of folk-song arrangements. The suite resembles *Lachrymae* and the

Ex. 53a Britten, Canticle IV, *Journey of the Magi*

Nocturnal for guitar in that it ends with 'plain' statements of the themes which have been the sources of the earlier movements. There are nine distinct sections before this coda, and the whole work is based in an extended C minor which is clearest in the opening and concluding sections, and is supported not only by the general orientation of the rest of the work, but also by reference to the C minor dominant, especially at the end of the third section and the start of the fourth and sixth.

The presence of a 'death' theme in the work immediately preceding *Death in Venice* needs no labouring: nor does the appearance of the unusual genre-piece 'Barcarola' (Movement IV) with its hints of the rhythms found in the opera's 'Overture' (Fig. 41). There may even be a further tribute to Shostakovich, already the dedicatee of *The Prodigal Son*, in the C, B (H), C, E flat, D of the Kontakion's first phrase, since this alludes to the Russian composer's musical 'signature' – DSCH; if so, however, it makes the story, told by Britten in his preface to the score, of that composer's remark that he had been brought up on a different version of the Kontakion (with B flat, not B natural) the more touching. This occasion, in April 1971, was the last time the two composers met: it was also Britten's last visit to Russia. In October 1971, with Myfanwy and John Piper and Peter Pears, Britten travelled to Venice, and work on his final opera began.

Ex. 53b Britten, Canticle IV, *Journey of the Magi*

In *Journey of the Magi*, old men cast a cold eye on death-in-birth. In *Death in Venice* op. 88, Britten's great, persistent theme is once more made explicit. Indeed, some might feel it is uniquely unambiguous, since here youth, in all its beauty and inaccessibility, is not so much doomed as the cause of doom in those who seek to regain it. So often, in Britten's earlier dramatic works, the young find it easier to lose their lives because of their innocence, while the old can only lose youth – in either sense. Gloriana grows old, the Mother in *Curlew River* loses her son. Now, youth regains the mythic timelessness which it had in *Paul Bunyan*. Tadzio is not so much young as ageless, immune to mortality, a paragon conjured up by Aschenbach to bring an aesthetic intensity to his own death. The appropriateness of this subject for Britten is acute, and in a sense which has nothing to do with homosexuality. Throughout his life, Britten's greatness was founded on his ability to use an 'old' language freshly. No innovator, he was not concerned with staying young, but with keeping his creative 'oldness' vigorous and hale. So, in *Death in Venice,* the sexual and spiritual merge, and in their union the individual creator is dissolved, his never-aging conservatism perfectly poised to the last.

In *Owen Wingrave* the drama centres on a young man whose alien ideals provoke dark forces to shape his death: nevertheless, he is not killed by the forces of conformity so much as by his own inner disharmony. He may have 'found himself' in peace, but this discovery fails to save him from losing his life. The central conflict in *Wingrave* is not simply between youth and age: indeed, Owen's contemporary Kate Julian plays a more direct part in his downfall than his choleric grand-father. In *Death in Venice* it is the aging Aschenbach's longing for the provoking boy Tadzio which overrides caution and common-sense. But Tadzio does not kill Aschenbach any more than the Wingraves kill Owen: both deaths are made inevitable by the doomed one's realization of what separates him from what he desires most, and from the prevail-ing 'standards' of his time and place.

Early in Thomas Mann's story we read that 'forbearance in the face of fate, beauty constant under torture, are not merely passive. They are a positive achievement, an explicit triumph; and the figure of Sebastian is the most beautiful symbol, if not of art as a whole, yet certainly of the art we speak of here.'[6] For Aschenbach, the torture is to perceive Tadzio's beauty, yet to be unable either to possess it or, ultimately, even to reflect it. The Narcissus theme, which Britten was to follow up in Canticle V, applies not merely to Tadzio's image of himself, his self-love, but also to Aschenbach's hope that Tadzio might somehow see himself in Aschen-bach:

Just at this second it happened that Tadzio smiled. Smiled at Aschenbach, unabashed and friendly, a speaking, winning, captivating smile, with slowly part-ing lips. With such a smile it might be that Narcissus bent over the mirroring pool, a smile profound, infatuated, lingering, as he put out his arms to the reflection of his own beauty.[7]

Tadzio is therefore not simply the young man Aschenbach wishes he himself had been, but the young man he wishes to become, now.

Death in Venice is the work of Britten's which deals most explicitly with homosexual feelings. But it is *not* a work about an active, adult homosexual relationship – the contrast with Tippett's trendy, with-it pair in *The Knot Garden* is total. Nor does Aschenbach ever speak directly of his feelings to Tadzio. Yet the opera is far from presenting a mere fantasy: the sense of place and time is vividly actual, and this double sense contributes much to the crucial operatic dimension of the drama. Without the palpable presence of an inhabited Venice, the work might well seem more a secular Passion, almost too unified by its focus on the central character, who speaks more directly to the audience than to most of his fellow 'shades'. Gary Schmidgall has argued that the work remains focused on a 'universal level' which he identifies with Nietzsche's belief that 'man must not flee from the reality of his passions, for they may vanish and leave him permanently impoverished or break forth unpredictably'; no more than Mann's original novella does the opera 'merely communicate a moral tale for pederasts'.[8] Schmidgall rightly observes that 'the crux of the story is not sublimation of homosexual instincts, but more generally the sublimation of vital instincts – the instincts of life – which is a danger courted by the superior intellect'.[9] Hence its value in any interpretation of Britten which sees him as at heart an Apollonian artist, one who understands 'the power of reticence'.[10] And, of course, this reticence is expressed through a technique, not of positive indecisiveness so much as of functional ambiguity. *Death in Venice*, like all Britten's successful structures, balances its formal and procedural clarity with harmonic ambivalence: if simplicity is in the form, then subtlety is in the sound, as Myfanwy Piper's Aschenbach might have put it. And the use of a 'foreground' of rich motivic interactions to produce shifting degrees of tonal clarity and harmonic implications, rather than an all-thematic atonality is a powerful, and particularly subtle demonstration of the final stage of Britten's development as a composer. Not only is tonal organization dependent on thematic contour and character, but individual harmonic events are principally the product of thematic processes.

Like *Owen Wingrave*, *Death in Venice* 'modulates' from an initial twelve-note proposition to a modal 'resolution' which seems both ambiguous and inevitable. In both cases the initial twelve-note material evokes disturbance, discontent. But the third-based percussive chords of *Wingrave*, whose individual pitch components make little initial impact, are very different from the gradually accumulating collections of *Death in Venice*, founded though these, too, are on a diminished triad (F, A flat, B). The *Wingrave* material is initially divided into three; so is the first *Death in Venice* statement, but the pitch-classes are not grouped as $4+4+4$, but as $4+3+5$, an arrangement in which each group employs a collection of adjacent semitones (F, G, F sharp, G sharp: A sharp, A, B: E, D, C, D flat, E flat). The two complementary hexachords of this set are already articulated in such a way as to draw attention to the only leap – B to E – and this provides a rich store of tonal allusion, most immediately in the 'resolution' into E major at Fig. 3. Like the emergence of D at Fig. 11 of *Owen Wingrave*, this is of course only a relatively stable tonal focus, without substantial diatonic consequences: in both cases, long-term influences and associations count for more than any immediate, decisive contradiction of the prevailing chromaticism. It is also true that the conclusion of *Death in Venice*, like that of *Wingrave*, convinces because of the way in which generating material is ultimately transformed; yet once more the parallel is not exact. What precedes Aschenbach's final moment of illumination is not a climactic twelve-note accumulation but the very reverse – a final attempt to re-assert the E major basis of the opening declaration of self-respect and self-awareness: and this dissolves, not into an expansive but rootless affir-mation – a prelude to destruction – but into a poisedly ambiguous aesthetic disquisition, an acceptance of the inevitable. Remarkably, the chord which receives a threefold repetition at the words 'Socrates knew, Socrates told us' is none other than a version of the 0, 2, 5 trichord (based on C, see Ex. 54). Some parallels do indeed exist between Wingrave's determination and Aschenbach's enlightenment. Yet neither here nor later does the music attain any diatonic stability; there is a brief moment of pure melodic C major at the end of Aschenbach's 'Phaedrus' mono-logue, but this is discoloured on the final word 'too'; and the A major indicated by the key signature for Scene 17 remains oblique, as each suc-cessive phrase moves abruptly into darker regions. At Fig. 317 the repeti-tions of an F sharp in the bass offer a relatively stable focus, but once this has been replaced by the comprehensive accelerating progression of chords from Fig. 318 which turns into a dominant preparation of A, neutrality returns. The music of the children's game, after Fig. 320, like-wise seems suspended by the very clarity of its repetitions. It offers no roots, but seeks further clarification, rather than absorption into an undifferentiated atonal totality. Clarification is achieved at the point, after Fig. 324, where the sequential shifts float the music on to the Tadzio chord. With the end of sequential movement and variation, chro-maticism is reduced to a decorative role, and the final paragraph pro-longs the notes of the Locrian mode on G sharp (or A flat – 'As', for Aschenbach, in German); a refracted A major, as it is likely to sound to modern ears.

This extraordinarily atmospheric ending conveys the exaltation of Aschenbach's release into death, and shows the Locrian mode being treated to the same kind of lyric prolongations as the twelve-note ac-cumulation of the opening. The inescapable disquiet inherent in the total chromatic, however securely rooted, is dissolved into modal ethereality rather than resolved into the solidly hierarchic planes of the tonal system. We most definitely do not 'progress' from one to the other, but the music evolves the conditions whereby the transformation can be effected. Whether or not the use of twelve-note ordering to represent 'parched creativity' – as suggested by Peter Evans[11] – itself represented an in-creased determination on Britten's part to regard it as an essentially negative device, it is certainly true that its main function in the opera is

Ex. 54 Britten, *Death in Venice*, Act II Scene 16

not merely to generate motives but to provoke harmonic alternatives to which these motives may also relate. And in the works which Britten was able to complete during his years of severe illness the need to avoid disintegration into total chromaticism remained as strong as ever. His music continued to face its most challenging ambiguities with strength and resolution.

27 Tippett: Symphony No. 3, Piano Sonata No. 3 (1970–3)

In an early and bold statement about the conception of the Symphony No. 3, Tippett declared that 'it won't be a "Beethoven" symphony, I know that, but in it I will be attempting to resolve all over again what is the nature of symphonic music in our time'.[1] In the event, not only was Beethoven to be directly involved in a work which owes much to his spirit, if little to his actual symphonic processes: the 'resolution' was to hinge on recognizing the power of the irresolute. In Tippett's first two symphonies 'the nature of symphonic music' still depended to a considerable extent on a consistent tonal-harmonic scheme. In the Symphony No. 3 that is no longer the case, and a very different approach to both form and technique could be explored. The liberating figures of Mahler and Ives were also in Tippett's mind in varying degrees, and although the work does not quote from *The Knot Garden* it could almost be thought of as Dov's symphony. It has a predominantly 'urban' character; yet it looks forward to the ultimately optimistic sentiments of Lev in *The Ice Break*, rather than back to the self-conscious doubts of Mangus and his companions in *The Knot Garden*.

In other respects, the work looks back further still. For example, it is closer to the broader continuities of the first two symphonies than to the constant stratified contrasts of the Concerto for Orchestra's first movement. As before, procedural emphasis is strongly on variation: but in the symphony variation is, essentially, a means of achieving expansion, a higher continuity, and as strongly symphonic a sense of completion as is possible in the absence of traditionally tonal goal-directedness.

Tippett characterized Part I of the symphony – itself in two distinct sections – in terms of polarities.

At the start, the polarity, necessary to any symphonic argument, is between Arrest . . . and Movement . . . [These terms] are metaphorical, implying a compression of energy, and an explosion of energy: both positive . . . At the halfway point . . . the polarity changes to that between a pattern of discontinuous music 'in the heights' . . . and a flow of continuous music 'in the depths'.[2]

Elsewhere Tippett has specifically mentioned Stravinsky in connection with the 'block-like' construction of the first movement, as well as the type of 'Arrest' involved in the use of ostinati which preclude harmonic movement.[3] Clearly, there is no intention to use the term 'polarity' to imply the kind of tonal interactions and oppositions which Stravinsky usually had in mind, and from the tonal and harmonic standpoint, as we shall see, the Symphony No. 3 is one of Tippett's most complex and demanding compositions.

It may seem odd for Tippett to describe Part I of the work as an 'abstraction', since his essential metaphors are so concrete. Yet the issues which he expresses metaphorically are those of the great symphonic tradition: they concern different types of motion and different types of continuity. The composer must work with greater or lesser degrees of connectedness. So in spite of the distinction between the essential 'modes' of the two principal sections of Part I, there is also an important interaction. The 'Arrest' music, with its jagged rhythms, is less continuous than the jubilantly expansive 'Movement' music; while the high, discontinuous music is more compressed, more 'arrested', than the low, continuous music. But it cannot be denied that Part I as a whole moves from lesser to greater continuity, not least because the two types of music in the second half of Part I proceed at the same basic tempo.

If the end of the first part of the symphony seems inconclusive, therefore, it is not because the music has grown less integrated, or no more integrated, than at the outset: it is because the mood is a passive one. This is the least 'urban' part of the work, and Tippett's metaphors speak of a landscape, the 'windless night sky and the ocean currents': as yet, there is no specifically human presence. Part I prepares the stage for that presence by exploring the 'abstractions' most basic to life itself: motion as a progress through time which should involve a process of discovery; and continuity which, when sensed and controlled, gives a sense of the individual's role and destiny. Behind the abstract dualities of Part I, as Tippett suggests, and more explicitly present in the subject-matter of Part II, are the contrasted human qualities of innocence and experience, which are most challengingly represented by the power to love and the power to destroy. The 'trinity' of Schiller, Beethoven and Blake therefore provide the symphony with its dramatic theme, its conflicts and contrasts possibly encouraging us to recall that one of Tippett's earliest, and soon discarded works, was a setting of part of Blake's *The Marriage of Heaven and Hell*, called by Blake, with true Beethovenian directness, 'A Song of Liberty'. In his notes on the Symphony No. 3, Tippett argues that, in spite of our present 'Season in Hell', which calls Schiller's enlightened vision of universal joy into question, a 'dream of the peaceable kingdom' is still possible, still cause for celebration. Expressed in words, the sentiments seem trite, naive; but the music, above all in the progression through the work from the collective, 'abstract' background to the single singer articulating specific aspirations, gives the sentiments substance and power.

A true symphony, a substantial work of integrated contrasts, will display relationships between processes on the largest and smallest scales. So the 'Arrest' and 'Movement' musics, from the outset, are built up similarly by means of varied repetitions of small basic units. The symphonic argument does not have direct recourse to functional tonal relationships, but the initial brass progression, extending a higher consonance based on E major, and with tonic – dominant arpeggiation in the bass, indicates one area of emphasis which is part of the work's large-scale pitch-procedures (Ex. 55). The use of E major associations as pivotal disappears only after Fig. 268 of Part II, and by this time it is possible for ears which work that way to regard E as a dominant to a still more essential. A, which happens in turn to be the dominant of 'Beethoven's' D.

Ex. 55 Tippett, Symphony No. 3, Part I

As other writers have often pointed out, Tippett's later language appears to owe more to Ives than to Beethoven, and the 'analytical problems' presented if one wishes to proceed beyond the level of thematic, textural and timbral commentary are comparable to those present in Ives. But Tippett's great achievement – an especially remarkable one for a British composer – is that he has been able to make his progress towards a focus on the human presence (the singer of Part II), free of any need to 'resolve' the musical richness into a simple tonal affirmation. In *The Knot Garden*, the contrast between two particular allusions – an aggressively complex Blues and a 'pure' Schubert *Lied* – highlights the contrast between the bitterness of modern experience as it tends to isolate people from each other, and the pathos of modern innocence as it approaches some of the possible truths about love. In the Symphony No. 3, the quoted Beethoven seems to represent the intensely pure vision which must disintegrate, the broken dream which begins to be remade through the extraordinary transmogrification of the Blues: no longer bitter, but expressing a profound sense of the sorrows which modern generations inherit. The contrast between Tippett's capacity to transform the popular intensities of the Blues into his own idiom, and his inability to do more than quote Schubert, or progressively distort Beethoven (the *Grosse Fuge* aspect of the String Quartet No. 4 comes closer to genuine transformation), could be poignantly negative were it not for the sense in which the music relates Blues-energy and Beethoven-energy, and expands its tonal language to embrace both. Of course, the Blues and Schubert material in *The Knot Garden* are used to make dramatic points, and the drama does not call for the kind of interaction between them which the Blues-Beethoven material generates in the symphony. But the fact that a similar 'opposition' is dealt with so differently in the symphony is surely sufficient indication that the lack of contact in the opera provided the specific challenge to try out the possibility of interaction in the later work.

The nearest the symphony seems to get to a purely harmonic resolution is the relatively consonant chord which underpins the words 'heal' and 'love' in the final vocal phrases. The hint of A flat major which it provides certainly evokes the healing magic of *The Midsummer Marriage* and the Piano Concerto, and yet the quality of the chord, which presents a cycle of fourths (C, F, B flat, E flat, A flat), seems to detach it from the sharper, more dissonant characteristics of the prevailing harmonic activity: it relates more to the cycles of fourths in the second section of Part I. But the harmonic argument of Part II is more involved with the dynamism of the Beethoven material, and all Tippett's references to this are such as to give a sense of expectant irresolution: the dominant A is more in evidence than the tonic D. Three stages of the argument involve this factor. At Fig. 182, the first Beethoven quotation acts as a stern call to reality after the diverting 'irresponsibilities' of the purely thematic superimpositions and juxtapositions of the Allegro molto which opens Part II, and the emphasis on A which the Beethoven brings with it survives in the wind and brass chord which acts as a preliminary to the Slow Blues. The strong 'dominant seventh' quality of this chord is distantly remembered at the very end of the work.

The second Beethoven episode (Fig. 234) achieves a kind of progression from dominant to tonic, though the tonic D (from Fig 245) is cunningly caught up in reminiscences of the fourths-music from Part I, and is altogether too passive to survive for long in this new context. After the singer proclaims that 'my sibling was the torturer', stamping brass chords, which also recur at the end of the work, restore the prevailing dynamism. The final Beethoven allusion (Fig. 257) achieves particularly strong support for the emphasis on A in the voice, and since the context is that closest to a recapitulation of the material preceding the Slow

267

Blues, a decisive stage of potential closure in the form has been reached. This time, however, the Blues chord is transposed down a fourth, from A on to E, and the work moves forward from this point to its remarkable, radical ending.

The human presence in the Symphony No. 3 is, of course, female, and she seems to blend the essential qualities of *The Knot Garden*'s freedom-fighter Denise with those of *The Ice Break*'s black nurse Hannah. Tippett does not labour the obvious images of birth and nurture. Nor does he risk the suggestion that America is a more likely place to achieve the ultimate elimination of evil than Europe or anywhere else. (He gets closer to such a suggestion in *The Ice Break*.) Just as his compositional techniques reconcile opposites through common procedures of varied re-petition and linear projection, so his ideas, and the forms which embody them, now preserve an element of opposition to the end, though without leaving any sense of dissatisfaction or imprecision. Tippett's last major non-vocal work before this symphony, the Concerto for Orchestra, simply stops, in a way which leaves the piece coherently intact, while sug-gesting a radically new approach to forms which had traditionally pro-gressed to a culmination, or at least to a conclusive cadence. But the ending of the Symphony No. 3 – aggression alternating with tenderness, as David Matthews describes it[4] – works as a conclusion because it is 'thematically' and harmonically relevant. It is psychologically, as well as musically, appropriate, if not inevitable, since the object is realization, not resolution. The two sides of the human personality are here, the power to heal and love, but, in their shadow, the capacity to curse and torture. And so the music mediates between the present 'Season in Hell' and the dream of the Peaceable Kingdom. Both the final chords are higher consonances in the sense that each contains a triadic 'base', and the C which provides the bass of the aggressive brass chord shifts up two octaves to provide the top note of the withdrawn, tender string chord. The 'negative' and 'positive' poles are starkly, conclusively stated: through them, the implications of the whole work continue to resonate.

After the exalted visions of the Symphony No. 3, the Piano Sonata No. 3 may seem a necessary, valuable antidote. The sonata is, in every sense, more modest, even more conventional. But what is most interesting about it is the way conventions appear in the light of the 'abstract' es-sences so recently explored in the symphony. Tippett's own note on the sonata[5] shuns the metaphors and allusions with which he discusses the symphony, and stresses two points which make the greatest possible con-trast to that work: the presence of three traditional formal schemes in what he sees as 'a single, unbroken piece' – sonata-allegro, variations, ternary toccata – and the connection between textures and the 'layout' of both piano and pianist. The essential stimuli for the symphony – ideas of contained and projected energy, continuity and discontinuity – are translated into a different duality in the sonata, that of the pianist's hands 'and their possible perceptible independence in one compositional direction and aural unity in another'. So 'the independence of the hands is explored chiefly in the outer fast movements', where contrast is in any case formally admissible, and the unity in the slow middle movement, where variation involves elaboration rather than contrast.

The image of the two hands converging from the outer extremes to the centre, and moving constantly and variously in mirror patterns, explains such evident contrasts as the motion from beginning to end of the Allegro's first paragraph (bars 1-21) and the rapid, reverse fanning-out of the second paragraph's initial clause (bars 23-6). And although Tippett never resorts to the combination of lines in a literal mirror relation, the theme of symmetry as a means of dividing the octave, as well as the entire keyboard, evidently provoked the movement through minor-third transpositions in the central variations. Even more strikingly, the composer *does* resort to literal mirroring in the finale, where bar 352 marks the centre-point of a 130-bar palindrome which spans two-thirds of the movement. Since textural momentum seems to matter rather more than thematic characterization in this toccata, the technique is acceptable, though its literalness is disconcerting in a composer normally so committed to 'ongoing' variation. As an unbroken toccata, this finale shows Tippett's style in full retreat from the patchwork juxtapositions of the second sonata, and rediscovering the élan of his early fugal *jeux d'esprits*. Moreover, one passage – bars 323 to 338, mirrored in 367 to 381 – reapplies the formal outline of the central variations (partition of the octave by minor thirds) as the basis for a passage of almost blatant textural by-play.

The finale is generated by the same sort of textural devices as the first movement. Indeed, the initial left-hand statement of each is the same, allowing for octave displacements and differences of rhythm (Ex. 56a). The generating paragraph of the opening Allegro is a particularly impressive example of Tippett's most natural technique, using expanding variation to construct a tripartite statement. The two-part counterpoint is clear through registral separation and rhythmic contrast. No evident rules with regard to the vertical alignment of pitches seem to be in force, and this might seem to confirm that such interval control is not essential to all music, but only to functionally tonal structures; but the technique of variation itself, involving repetitions, ornamentation, displacement, and extension, carries the burden of sense which was once shared with the grammar of tonal progressions. Both the second and third thematic groups of the first movement proceed similarly: the second (bars 23-30) has only one variation, which the third (bars 39-55), like the first, has two

Ex. 56a Tippett, Piano Sonata No. 3

(i) opening of the first movement

(ii) opening of the finale

variations. And in spite of the silent bars which separate these groups, the essential continuity of the movement ensures that the principal return for decorated recapitulation (at the end of bar 111) enters with knowing unobtrusiveness. If this is indeed Tippett's 'late Beethoven' sonata, such formal sophistication is as indicative of the master as the trills and decorative elaboration. The String Quartet No. 4 takes up this textural thread.

The generative harmony of the sonata's slow movement hints at a common basis with the left-hand fourths of the two Allegros, and the arpeggiations and decorations of the seventeen chords whose four variations make up the movement provide a sustained example of Tippett's more restrained rhetoric, which is almost as remarkable as the slow movements of the Piano Concerto and the Concerto for Orchestra. The texture, though unremittingly rich, is diverse enough to enclose the imitative, quasi-canonic-by-inversion texture of Variation 2 (from bar 230) and the melody with accompaniment of Variation 3 (from bar 249). As for the chord which 'resolves' the outer sections, in bars 209 and 286 (Ex. 56b(i)), this offers, in its focusing on E and B, a hint both of the E which launches the outer movements, and of the A which comes into focus

270

Ex. 56b Tippett, Piano Sonata No. 3

during the toccata (bar 323, Ex. 56b(ii)), eventually underpinning the decisive final chord of the whole work (Ex. 56b(iii)).

This chord is more diatonic, and therefore may seem more conclusive than the A-based 'higher consonance' which ends the Symphony No. 3; but it is prepared, not by a dominant, but by a simple linear motion from the previous chord, in which the upper four notes move down a semitone. Analysis in terms of basic shapes (or pitch-class sets) reveals that the content of this final chord (A, B, C sharp, D, E) is anticipated by a similar configuration in the second left-hand group of the finale, but this is as much a further aspect of the 'cluster-harmony' used as early as bar 95 of the first movement as evidence of any kind of contrived hinting at tonal precedents. The final chord – arrived at, as Paul Crossley has revealed, only after some debate between pianist and composer – has the sound of the improviser's spontaneity, not the theoretician's calculation. But the sonata is satisfyingly proportioned, and planned carefully enough to make this affirmation seem as successful as Tippett's more familiar, more equivocal later endings. The apparent absence of quotation makes the work a no less effective musical tribute to Beethoven than the Symphony No. 3 or the String Quartet No. 4. Above all, the virtues of integration are now overt. Collage has had its day. Its 'aperient' qualities can still be acknowledged, and just as the exclusiveness of diatonicism is no more appealing to Tippett than the intolerance of organized religion, so the unambiguous unity of baroque counterpoint is no more appealing than the fragmented indeterminacy of the once-modern avant garde, whose 'motionless' measures so struck him at the 1965 Edinburgh Festival.[6] The process of discovery through transformation is all in music, just as the process of individuation is all in life. Tippett's musical discoveries can most effectively be explained through their relationships with each other, rather than through parallels with any other premises or procedures.

28 Britten: The final compositions (1974–6)

After *Death in Venice*, *The Death of Saint Narcissus*, dated July 1974. It is safe to say that Britten never set a more complex poem, and his choice of such an early, apparently unrepresentative work of T. S. Eliot's as a sequel to *The Journey of the Magi* may seem curious. The poem, as Lyndall Gordon notes, 'expresses a savage joy in pain'.

Narcissus sets out to win the glow of fervour through abuse of his body but whatever glow he achieves quickly subsides, leaving him exhausted and without grace. Like St Sebastian, St Narcissus represents an idea. He is not a realistic character and, of course, Eliot cannot be identified with him. But take away the caricature of twisted motives and excessive egotism and the poem reveals the consuming issues of Eliot's life – his longing for metamorphosis, his vision and loss of vision, and the avidity of his religious emotions . . . Eliot's heroes of the spirit genuinely experience the attractions of asceticism, they know dazzling glimpses of divine reality but these possess no decisive, life-transforming power.
Eliot's interest in St Narcissus lies chiefly in diagnosing the man's failure . . . He [Narcissus] wants to reform himself, to be more than himself, but instead of self-enhancement there is, at the end, the shock of self-loss.[1]

Whether any such perceptions were aroused in Britten as he read and set *The Death of Saint Narcissus* cannot be known. But in this interpretation it seems an almost frighteningly apt text for a composer conscious of his own sickness. So apt, indeed, that if such an interpretation had occurred to Britten, one can scarcely imagine him being able to set the poem at all. And there are other aspects of the poem, less devastating, more immediate, which the composer might well have found more striking.

Mann's Tadzio is not unlike Narcissus: Tadzio is certainly 'a dancer to God', if the God is Eros. Yet whereas in *Death in Venice* youth and age are crucially distinct, with contact between them apparently impossible, the Canticle V poem reveals them as aspects of the same individual. Above all, some lines from the second section of Eliot's poem seem to encapsulate the dilemma of the isolated, self-conscious modern artist: the outsider is still the dominant image for Britten.

> When he walked over the meadows
> He was stifled and soothed by his own rhythm.
> By the river
> His eyes were aware of the pointed corners of his eyes
> And his hands aware of the pointed tips of his fingers.
> Struck down by such knowledge
> He could not live men's ways, but became a dancer before God

The music of this extraordinarily concentrated piece seizes on the resonances and special tonal characteristics of the harp to enhance the ambiguous harmonic possibilities of 'unrelated' triads which coalesce around a single note. The aggregate at the opening – C major and C sharp minor, with their common E – provides a fruitful source of conflict, and although it is the C which receives the most explicit clarification and emphasis, first at the start of Section 2 ('He walked once' . . .), then at the climax of this section and again in the final section ('As he embraced them'), it is as a separate, pivotal chord rather than as the tonic of a diatonic tonality. The full triads of these climaxes – the sonority recalls the opening of the Suite for Harp – stand out strongly from the prevailing non-triadic or 'super-triadic' harmonic processes with their semitonal clashes and constant ambiguities, and there is, inevitably, a disintegration at the end, where the first and last phrases of the first section are recalled, and E emerges from the C sharp minor/C major complex as the only possible point of rest. The final vocal phrase outlines a Lydian E major, but the harp's 'shadow' retains more C major elements, and its final Es are therefore echoes which are already shivering into dissolution (Ex. 57).

The Death of Saint Narcissus is dedicated to the memory of the librettist of *Gloriana* and the Church Parables, William Plomer. The *Suite on English Folk Tunes, 'A Time There Was* . . . ' op. 90 has an unusually fulsome inscription, 'lovingly and reverently dedicated to the memory of Percy Grainger'. Grainger, who died in 1961, was, obviously enough, a very different character from Britten (though in all probability driven by some not dissimilar obsessions), and a far less important composer. Yet Britten's own creatively penetrating way with folk tunes links him to Grainger, and this suite, his last orchestral work, is therefore an appropriate tribute: economical, forceful and, in the final movement, which

Ex. 57 Britten, Canticle V '*The Death of Saint Narcissus*'

uses the tune 'Lord Melbourne' as collected by Grainger, deeply melancholy. It is this movement which justifies the Hardy quotation that pre-
faces the score and occurs in the poem set by Britten as the final song of
Winter Words twenty years before.

This last orchestral suite of five movements is followed by one of eight movements for unaccompanied voices, the *Eight Medieval Lyrics*, *Sacred and Profane* op. 91 completed in January 1975. For those to whom Britten's enthusiasm for the dialects of Soutar and Burns is something of a trial, the medieval English of these lyrics may be even more alienating. But if this barrier is penetrated, it can be seen that the poems offer the kind of unnervingly direct juxtapositions of concern with love, death, the delights of nature, and the power of religion, which more sophisticated poetry might disdain. The actual sound of the medieval English, with its frequent, explosive consonants, was also a stimulus to a composer dedicated to exploiting simplicity while rejecting the effete gentility of the partsong tradition, and the directness of style in this last of Britten's all too rare returns to the *a cappella* medium of *A Boy Was Born* and the *Hymn to St Cecilia* makes it as disturbingly memorable as many of his more ambitious and extended creations.

No. 1, 'Saint Godric's Hymn', expands its basic C major with a considerable number of triads, diatonic and chromatic, but few conventional progressions. The major–minor conflict is at the heart of it, with other semitonal clashes evident; but the C major triad, which Britten employed with notable frequency in these late works, is the unmistakable pivot, beginning each of the three main sections and ending the second and third. Such triadic explicitness is less common in the later lyrics. No. 2, 'I mon wax mod', is similar in form to No. 1, with two related verses and a coda, but its more open contrapuntal texture excludes triadic clarification of its tonal centre, A. No. 3, 'Lenten is come', is centred on D, and after two identical verses in which there is a diatonic cadential issue from all the incidental chromaticism, a third stanza develops material from the first two, turning the tonality towards a decisive assertion of a D minor triad, and then dissolving the texture around a dominant (A) pivot. The sense of pause rather than closure at the end of No. 3 is appropriate, for the first two lines of No. 4 – before the mood changes drastically – are set to a reminiscence of No. 3's opening. Thereafter, however, the 'severe' weather described in 'The long night' is matched by some severe counterpoint. There are two related sections, the first moving from its G starting point through D to an uneasy plateau on B flat; the second, developing material from the first, regaining the G (bar 36), but actually ending with a tentative G major first inversion. The way in which the original three-note descent of the movement's subject is given its most concentrated treatment in the final bars shows Britten's abiding relish for unifying economies which dissolve tonal certainties (Ex. 58). As the text of No. 3 expresses it, 'All this happiness will I abandon, And quickly in the woods be a fugitive'.

No. 5, 'Yif io of luve can', offers a dramatic change of texture, with two stanzas of four-part homophony, during the second of which a

Ex. 58 Britten, *Eight Medieval Lyrics, Sacred and Profane*, No. 4 'The long night'

descant floats above the narrow-intervalled theme. This is a particularly moving piece, the text a passionate contemplation of Christ on the Cross, the music moving intensely away from and back to its basic B major triads, the only pure consonances in the piece apart from a passing B minor triad in bar 15.

After this, the 'Carol' is light relief, for all its minor modality. The harmony is more diatonic, and much of the humour of the piece lies in the way the second, third and fourth stanzas progressively vary the first, while all returning to the same simple cadence-figure in conclusion. No. 7, 'Ye that pasen by', returns to Passiontide subject-matter, and to a simple yet expressive contrapuntal device, descending scales with decorating appoggiaturas. The piece is centred in A minor, but the tonic triad is clarified only at the end, and there are no diatonic cadences. It is a short movement, but its form is of great interest: two phrases related by variation (transposition), and with a short refrain borrowed from No. 6, are followed by two more phrases which are more determinedly developmental in character: the first is in essence an inversion, the second (including the climax of the lyric) welding an augmented version of the refrain on to the descending steps of the basic scale-motive. Finally, there is a coda whose pair of simple chromatic cadences supports final statements of the refrain, the second only a fragment.

The final lyric, 'A death', is the most extended, and is cast in a kind of miniature cantata form: there are three distinct sections, the second and third separated by a transition at 'Thanne lyd mine hus . . . '. The starting point stresses E, and the goal is an E major triad, but there is little triadicism, even though the last section regularly repeats and prolongs the basic E. The gallows humour of the text is matched by vivid musical imagery. The attributes of decay and death are listed; the kind of aging that Aschenbach sought vainly to counter, hence perhaps the use of 'his' E major! And there is no mention of the consolations of religion, only a hearty contempt for the whole world, 'al this world'.

It is only in the comic lamentations for the young ewe in 'My Hoggie' that death impinges in Britten's last song cycle, *A Birthday Hansel* op. 92, completed in March 1975. But the work is not without its touches of melancholy, particularly in the haunting setting of 'The Winter': 'now everything is glad, while I am very sad/Since my true love is parted from me'. Even in the final number, a delightful protraction of Burns's four lines (or three with one repetition), the tonally disorienting switches for the repetitions of Leezie Lindsay's name ensure a typically ambiguous ending (Ex. 59), appropriately for a cycle which begins with such explicitly clashing semitones, and which contrives, in what initially promises to be a rather bland setting of 'Afton Water', to suggest by chromatic inflections that Mary's dream is indeed somewhat disturbed.

Ex. 59 Britten, *A Birthday Hansel*, 'Leezie Lindsay'

Disturbance becomes the essence of *Phaedra* op. 93, which Britten described as a dramatic cantata, and whose central figure recalls the un-
canny intrusion of the line 'And I mon wax mod' ('and I must go mad')
into the second of the *Sacred and Profane* lyrics. Phaedra, as represented

in Robert Lowell's English version of Racine, may have rather too much of silent-film melodrama about her, and there is little point in labouring comparisons with Britten's other tragic female figures – Lucretia, Gloriana – which are both obvious and limited, if only because the musical characterization of each is so different. Since in *Phaedra* Britten chose to use only a small orchestra, the grand effects which the text makes possible can only be suggested. As in baroque tradition, the action occurs in the concentrated recitatives (with their prominent harpsichord – comparisons with Aschenbach's 'meditative' piano are shunned), and these dominate the flexible form of the work without making the more measured 'arias' seem in any way perfunctory. The deranged Phaedra, driven by a guilt which seems to have been wished on her by Aphrodite, finds relief in suicide, and the onset of clarity which this act provides is matched in the fine, expansive, final vocal paragraph. This is hardly 'cold composure', and at the last the nobility rather than the madness of the character comes through. In comparison, the earlier attempts to suggest consuming sexual passion – the repetitions of 'Fool, I love you' – seem awkward. Such sentiments were not Britten's element – he was far more successful with the frigid provocativeness of Kate Julian in *Owen Wingrave*. So for once the images of corruption do not wholly convince, because of the rhetoric through which the composer seeks to present them. Yet the grandly ironic resumption of 'purity' at the end, with a C major perfect cadence strained for and in a sense achieved, only to provoke the final disoriented collage before the C fades away in frozen isolation, is as graphic a musical evocation of disintegration as any modern composer has achieved (Ex. 60). Britten's admiration for Janet Baker's voice led him to attempt a tribute appropriate for her, but less so for him. One regrets that he did not compose something less 'dramatic', a song cycle, for example; but at its best, and especially at the end, *Phaedra* is certainly a disturbing work in the directness with which it focuses on disintegration.

It would have been impossible to conceive of a more appropriate tribute to another old friend of the composer's than the String Quartet No. 3, dedicated to Hans Keller. In returning to a medium last employed almost thirty years before, Britten must have been enormously conscious of 'expectations', and also, perhaps, of the fact that he had never directly followed up the new vein of mastery in instrumental music demonstrated by the Cello Symphony. The Quartet No. 3 is also, in certain respects, the perfect enigma. It has already inspired interpretation as a creative continuation of the true tradition of the genre in all its sonata-symphonic glory, while seeming to others simply another 'late' Suite (the work has five movements), with no particular concern for, or connection with, the tonal, formal and motivic integrations of the tradition extending from

Ex. 60 Britten, *Phaedra*

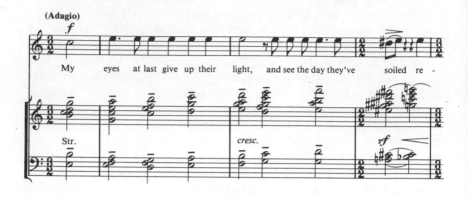

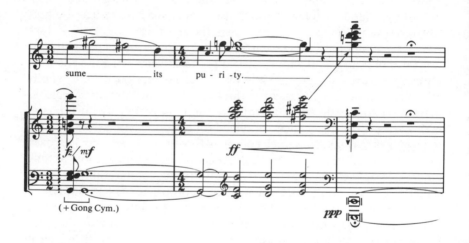

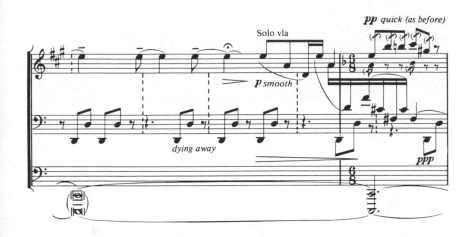

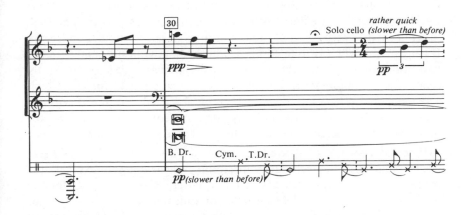

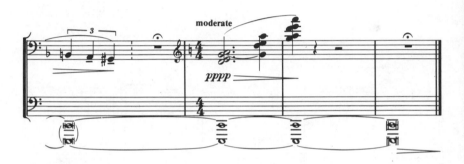

Haydn to Schoenberg and Shostakovich. As for Britten himself, he simply referred to it as his 'Divertimento'. What cannot be denied is that the allusive sonata form and floating tonality of the first movement are balanced by the explicit Passacaglia, centred in E major, of the finale. Equally explicit, in the title and material of the finale, is the link with *Death in Venice*. But enigma is not to be excluded here either. The Passacaglia theme, with its whole-tone rotations about E, always ends on a D natural, and when Britten composed his ending, with the final D in the bass and a non-cadence above, he provided perhaps the most perfectly economical example of his dissolving, inconclusive conclusions, in which a last page of pure diatonicism (the E major triad prolonged without actual progressions) is dramatically, determinedly 'corrupted', if not positively contradicted (see Ex. 2 in the Prologue, p. 7).

If this is evidence of Britten's irony at work (and that irony is never clearer than when the techniques are simple, the meanings unexplicit), the second and fourth movements of this quartet, 'Ostinato' and 'Burlesque', have a laconic ebullience similar in atmosphere to the last lyric of *Sacred and Profane*. But most remarkably ambiguous of all is the central movement, entitled 'Solo', a ternary design in which the first violin's extended meditation seems determined to shun both lyric efflorescence and clear-cut motivic working. The central cadenzas apart, it is indeed 'very calm', as marked. But how has such serenity come about? Hans Keller discusses the sense in which the work is an 'instrumental purification of opera', a work in which Britten reaches 'the height' of his 'symphonic thought'.[2] But in this central movement the 'soloist' achieves self-fulfilment through self-denial, and the musical result is not so much dramatic, still less symphonic: it is intensely, simply, ambiguous. Its meaning is its mystery (Ex. 61).

Ex. 61 Britten, String Quartet No. 3, III (Solo)

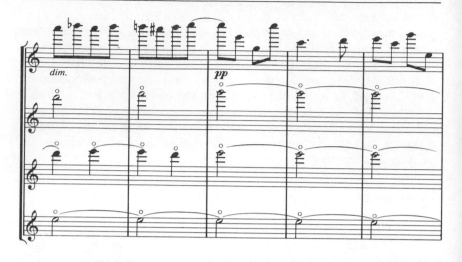

29 Tippett: *The Ice Break*, and after (1973–80)

The Ice Break is Tippett's fourth and shortest opera: at 75 minutes it is precisely half the length of *The Midsummer Marriage,* in the timings given by Eric Walter White.[1] Since many critics feel that it is also the least successful of the four, it should be stressed that in some respects it is also the most ambitious. The images of contemporaneity so crucial to *The Knot Garden* are enacted in the restricted environment appropriate to a family rather than to an entire society. Indeed, Tippett's first three operas are all in their very different ways concerned primarily with individuals, their relationships, motivations, needs and actions. Social circumstances are invoked rather than enacted, and the sense of the individual's vulnerability in the first opera's Ritual Dances, or of societies at war in *King Priam,* is the more effective for the background role which those factors play in the dramas as a whole. In *The Ice Break,* however, it is more as if the drama of individual relationships is taking place as a background to the social upheavals which dominate the action. The 'family circle' of Lev, Nadia and Yuri is shown sliding in and out of the public domain, and constantly under threat of dissolution; and although the opera ends with what might in isolation appear to be Tippett's most positive declaration of belief in the rebirth of the individual and his capacity to survive, that declaration provides only an epilogue to a series of events in which public destruction is more evident than public healing. The title, *The Ice Break,* and the music associated with it, provide an image of rebirth, and it is that image, of the 'exhilarating sound of the ice breaking on the great northern rivers in the spring', which is at the centre of the pastoral memories which fill Nadia's mind before she dies. Yet one of Tippett's purposes, in which *The Ice Break* evidently follows on from *Songs for Dov* and the Symphony No. 3, is to pursue the theme that 'the living language of our time is urban'. There is so great a tension between the kind of deep awareness of natural forces which the dying Nadia displays and the terrifying violence of the urban life which surrounds her, that survival for Lev, and for Yuri who almost dies through his involvement in urban violence, will depend on learning how to integrate something of the extremes.

Tippett is able to turn both the racist aggression of the mob and the effete indulgence of the flower-children into the positive 'huge, compassionate power to heal' of the nurse and the doctor. The price paid for the concentration with which these complex processes are presented is not so much the plethora of slang and swearing which has been widely noted, as the uncharacteristic sentimentality of the crucial image of rebirth. Yuri is cured in 'an alarming but healing ritual'[2] by the skills of modern urban society – one which can get an ambulance to the scene of a riot with remarkable alacrity. And at the point where he embraces his father the 'ice break' music is climactically reiterated for the last time. It seems that Yuri is now freed from commitment to those negative social ideas which led him to reject his old-fashioned dissident father. In acknowledging, accepting his father, and rejecting the 'new', negative dissidence, Yuri seems musically to be embracing the true reality of the nature images. What announced death to the mother offers rebirth to the son, and survival to the father. And so the living urban language absorbs the rich heritage of nature archetypes, just as the liberating society transcends the repressive society, destroying the prejudices which hectic urban life can so easily foster.

The central importance of the idea of rebirth should nevertheless not lead to an underestimation of the persistence of 'the dark' in *The Ice Break*. It may seem a small step from the turning of dark to light in *A Child of Our Time* and the cry of joy which, quoting Yeats, ends *The Midsummer Marriage,* to Lev's concluding quotation from *Wilhelm Meister:* 'Yet you will always be brought forth again, glorious image of God; and likewise be maimed, wounded afresh, from within or without'. But here, the light and the dark, the rebirth and the wounding, are seen as an eternal, cyclic progression, with the 'fall' as much a consequence of rebirth as a prelude to it.

That the full social optimism of the early Tippett is no longer possible is a result of the realities of the postwar world; this reality is surely the point of the epigraph which Tippett wishes to remain unattributed: 'Brother humans, who will live after us, do not harden your hearts against us.' But, it is when we come to consider the music of *The Ice Break* that we remember that, like all Tippett's operas, it entertains more vividly than it instructs. The images of construction and destruction which dominate the plot dissolve into the images of realism and sur-realism which pervade its stage presentation and into the distinctions between fundamentals and elaborations which characterize the music. The 'entertainment' aspect of the work has been stressed by Meirion Bowen in a brief discussion which argues that

The Ice Break is indeed a modern masque: . . . more than in the previous three operas, any number of liberties can be taken – musical and technical – to project the masque-like character of the work to the full. Realism is not its object. It would soon die, as an opera too much of our time, if that were so.[3]

It is significant therefore that the idea for *The Ice Break* may have come to Tippett not directly from reading Solzhenitzin, or seeing Mohammed Ali on television, but from a performance of Berlioz's *Benvenuto Cellini,* when he was 'struck by the effect of the masked revellers in the Roman carnival scenes. It occurred to him that there was a significant distinction to be made between the anonymity of these revellers and their charac-terization as dramatis personae when not in Carnival disguise.'[4]

Tippett has consistently shown that the connection between 'themes' of renewal and rebirth, and techniques in which evolving variation tends to force juxtaposed contrasts into a subordinate position is a powerful, viable one. The beginning of *The Ice Break* offers an arrestingly un-ambiguous example of it. There is a preludial pair of parallel statements of the 'ice break' music, the principal material expanding from minor thirds to major thirds. A third statement follows at Fig. 4, once Nadia's first paragraph is under way, and its strongly asserted bass note, G, prepares for the ensuing descent on to a chord which seems emblematic, not only of Lev's rather tortured nobility of spirit, but of the new resonances superimposed on traditional harmonic and tonal phenomena which emerge in Tippett's later music. The harmonic paragraph from the opening to two bars after Fig. 5 expands around a focal C, and the scene is concluded with the return to the initial pair of statements on C and B (Fig. 11), which, however, moves without transition into new, more contrapuntal music even before Scene 2 begins. Only the resourceful ostinato character of this new music seems significantly related to what has gone before.

Between these two assertions of C, the principal focus (at three bars after Fig. 8), is provided by a transposition of the C-based chord on to C sharp. The relation between triad-based chords a semitone apart is further stressed to accompany Lev's first words at Fig. 10. Here the minor-triad base in the orchestra conflicts strikingly with the voice's major intervals (themselves discreetly supported by a solo cello) (Ex. 62a).

Ex. 62a Tippett, *The Ice Break*, Act I Scene 1

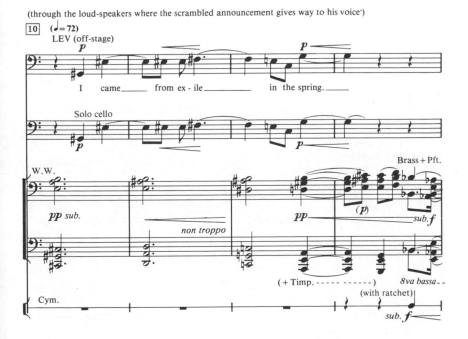

Ex. 62b Tippett, *The Ice Break*, Act I Scene 8

These essential elements are employed again at various stages throughout the work, and they seem fundamental enough for all the other
material, and all the work's processes, to relate to them in varying
degrees. Particularly close variants occur in Act I Scene 7, where the
passage first heard between Fig. 10 and three bars after Fig. 12 is extended and elaborated (Figs. 66 to 71); and the C-based chord is first
heard on its own at Fig. 77 when Lev quotes 'the earth was worth ten
heavens to us' (Ex. 62b). The essential bass progression in Act I Scene 7 –
from C to B and on to A – is the one which is itself elaborated under
different material to support the two main sections of the ensemble
which opens Act II, and this sequence returns (again under different
material) at Fig. 448 to accompany Lev's final Goethe quotation. (Lev
does quote once without this music: in Act II Scene 7, after Fig. 242).
The 'ice break' music itself occurs twice at climactic points of Act III: at
the climax of Nadia's death-aria (three bars after Fig. 340) the twofold
statement on C and B is heard, as at the work's opening, but with new
counterpoints; while at the moment of Yuri's 'rebirth' (Fig. 440) the version from Act I Scene 7 is presented.

The most volatile type of music in the opera is first presented in Act I
Scene 2, when the young and radical pair Gayle and Yuri are contrasted
to their idealistic, romantic seniors, Nadia and Lev. The form of the
scene is characteristic – a simple sequence of related phrases, expanding
and contracting, with no strong contrasts, but a less focused harmonic
character than the more 'stable', reflective material. As for the first

choral scene (Scene 3), the fuller harmony, simpler rhythm and even more explicitly repetitive form are not used to make any tonal focus explicit: under analysis, E flat may come to seem central, but it is deployed as a mark of formal division rather than of harmonic stability.

The concentration and economy of *The Ice Break*, and the tension between characters who only communicate obliquely, leads in Act I Scene 5 to a texture which, for Tippett, is unusually sparse and recitative-like: the contrast with the surrounding choral textures is obvious, but the effect is to create even greater tension, since the confident beat of the choral cries is suddenly withdrawn. Vocal characterization as graphic as this is vital in opera, and no character is as vividly drawn as the black champion Olympion. The fact that he does not survive long enough for us to learn more about him is one of the opera's weaknesses, but he is clearly not a simple 'villain', out to provoke the maximum hatred and violence. Tippett's use of his most exalted coloratura, attempting to outdo even *The Vision of Saint Augustine*, is appropriate to Olympion's good humour and idealism. His tragedy is that he cannot control what he has inspired, and in Act II his sentimental romanticism is cruelly contrasted with the mindless destructiveness of followers and enemies alike.

Olympion's 'private' music, in his love scene with Hannah (Act II Scene 3), could certainly be even more strongly contrasted with his public response to adulation. But whereas the potential in his music is swept away, as he is swept away by the mob, the reflective intensity of Hannah's phrases in the love scene flower fully in the opera's centrepiece and longest solo scene, Act II Scene 5. It may be accidental that the lamenting clashes in the orchestra at the start of this scene recall a passage from Denise's Act I aria in *The Knot Garden* (compare Fig. 182 of *The Ice Break* with Fig. 155 of *The Knot Garden*). But the image in *The Ice Break* is not solely of regret, of lament, but of reflection. Here, for once, a character explores and reveals herself – 'stranger, darker, deeper' – and undertakes, in 'real' time, the first stages of the Jungian voyage of self-discovery in her own words, her own terms. And yet – with what is perhaps the most powerful of all indications in later Tippett of a retreat from his own youthful optimism – Hannah finds that it is too soon to comprehend its possible consequences: 'No time is yet for sense.'

Hannah's aria is cast as a large ternary scheme: each of the three parts are of almost equal length (55, 54 and 55 bars respectively) and each subdivides into two principal sections. The first part comprises the orchestral introduction (Fig. 182 to Fig. 188) and the first vocal section (to Fig. 192), and the introduction itself subdivides further into two principal sub-sections, each made up of three related statements – the whole aria proceeds by evolving variation within its constituent sections. The second sub-section of the orchestral introduction begins one beat before

Fig. 185, and it is the return of this material at Fig. 205, with a vocal line superimposed, which initiates the final, recapitulatory part of the ternary scheme. In both these outer parts, each section employs different material. But in the central part of the aria, from Fig. 192 to Fig. 205, the second section begins as a repeat of the first (at Fig. 198), then moves at Fig. 202 into a transition to the final part of the aria.

The 'resolution' of the aria's harmony on to C major–minor harmony at Fig. 214 may or may not be the 'consequence' of an initial emphasis on C. But the associations of this chord in the work are such that it seems to represent the extent to which the black nurse is in touch with the not totally unrealistic idealism of the émigré Lev. And in general the music of this scene seems to flow from initial and recurrent clashes, a flow interrupted by chords which freeze the notes of the melodic lines into aggregates that have the character of higher consonances. The central section of the aria is more flexibly linear, and the ending of the whole, eliding as it does with the bald F major of the approaching chorus, is appropriately inconclusive. Hannah remains indecisive, knowing only what she cannot do.

The last four scenes of the opera confirm that the processes of harmonic focusing, and evolving variation, of the work's basic material are to be given a final clarification. Though ensemble textures remain as elaborate as ever, the formal repetitions are simple and clear, the initial focusing on a B minor triad at the start of Scene 6 a base from which the final, higher consonance involving B major can be sought out. The return of the chords which seem associated with Lev's learning from experience (Fig. 420) allow fifth- and triad-rooted harmony to increase its hold during the 'operation ensemble', and such harmony is still the foundation of the choral 'Hymn to Spring' which comprises the brief Scene 8. To some extent, as with certain works of Ives, it might be felt that the almost garish orchestral colours and bold textural superimpositions in these scenes distract from what could have been an even simpler harmonic outline. But the progression which does emerge at the end is all the more solid for the sense that it is not a simplistic rendering-down of a pervasive total chromaticism. The linear motion and characterization of the interacting textural strata produce a richly personal effect. Tippett does not merely 'speak through' Lev, but lets the music itself affirm its own essential motivation and meaning.

Tippett's second and third symphonies are radically different from each other: the second is a powerful and successful example of 'late' neoclassicism, while the third seems to invite the label 'neo-Romantic', or even 'post-Expressionist', to characterize its richly individual rethinking of the basic symphonic elements – progress, contrast, argument, affirmation. The contributions of Beethoven, and of the soprano singing Tippett's own texts, confirm the possible function of drama and of humanistic confession in a symphony. Given the composer's American enthusiasms, it might even seem an attempt at a 'Universe' Symphony: and while it may not entirely escape the charge of wanting to preach to, as well as embrace, the millions, its central message concerns the need for each individual to find and know himself – it does not offer a blueprint for collective action.

The 'birth to death' progression which underlies the Symphony No. 4 (1976–7) is similarly a characterization in individual terms of a universal experience. It is clear from both the Symphony No. 3 and *The Ice Break* that 'the huge, compassionate power/To heal, to love' is not a simple religious metaphor – however miraculous the rebirth, there is no immortality. But the scope of Tippett's late instrumental works makes clear that vitality may be enhanced rather than undermined by the acknowledgement of human contingencies. There may be a new 'realism', but there is no loss of richness or refinement.

In 1972, four years before concentrated work on the fourth symphony began, Tippett spoke of 'returning to the symphonic field' to explore 'the collage-concentration of the most diverse musics in a single-movement form'.[5] Those who regard the Piano Sonata No. 2 as the work of Tippett's with the least potential might have found this an ominous statement, and there is indeed a sense in the symphony of an unresolved tension between the strategic recurrences of the 'diverse musics' and the need for a strong sense of evolution over the surface of a single-movement structure lasting half an hour, if it is to seem truly symphonic.

The fourth symphony was Tippett's largest single-movement structure to date, and its seven-section design – Exposition, Episode I, Slow Movement, Episode II, Scherzo, Episode III, Recapitulation – evokes precedents as different as Schoenberg's first Chamber Symphony and Sibelius's Symphony No. 7. Neither the material nor the orchestration may always reveal Tippett at his best: indeed, it would be difficult to claim that any of the works he has begun in his seventies are the equal of earlier compositions. But the dynamism of the thematic processes, which at times refer to the more traditional imitative devices of Tippett's past – the fifth-based entries of Episode II (Fig. 78), the 'flying' counterpoint of the scherzo (Fig. 100) and Episode III (Fig. 129) – show the still undiminished fertility of his invention. It is the sheer diversity of thematic material in the symphony which, paradoxically perhaps, makes his decision to end the work with a section of selective recapitulation, rather than a finale with still more new ideas, so challenging: though not devoid of all recurrence, the work has shown little concern with the possibility of larger-scale integrations, save through tempo, up to that point, and even in the final stages neither integration nor resolution are the prime purpose. It is a recapitulation which reverses the forces making for growth in the exposition, rather than a finale which takes the work's materials and processes to the point where they find fulfilment and resolution. Hence, perhaps, the curiously understated effect of the return of the very opening music at Fig. 160: a decisive stage in a process of winding-down rather than winding-up.

The symphony achieves a rather uneasy balance between contrast and continuity, that alliterative pair of terms so beloved of commentators, yet so rarely given precise technical connotations. By contrast with the works of the 1960s, there may seem to be too little in the way of dramatic confrontation between distinct ideas, and even between the successive stages of the structure. But the recapitulation demonstrates in a very simple and effective manner how the expansive thematic prodigality of the work is gradually brought under control, and the final, mediating presentation of the opening material prepared. The concluding section (from two bars before Fig. 179) involves a clinching series of juxtapositions between two ideas, one associated with the first tempo, the other with the third. The first three appearances of the Tempo 1 material offer an expanding, soft chorale in the brass, which reaches its fullest expression in the first six bars of the last Tempo 1 section. The Tempo 3 material reduces, spanning four bars the first time, only two each the second and third times. And so the conclusion of the recapitulatory process is not so much a culmination along traditional lines as a defining of the limits imposed on the expanding material of the work. In the absence of underlying tonal logic there must always be something arbitrary about a decision to limit thematic proliferation. But Tippett's instinctive sense of progressive variation, operative from the initial three-stage first paragraph, and always controlled so that the final stage of one paragraph points firmly towards the first stage of the next, is capable of equally natural reversal: it is this tension between expansion and contraction which the concluding stages of the recapitulation reveals. Tippett's material is always dominated by a 'will to live', and so decline must not be into babbling incoherence but into a fierce focus on conflicting essences which provoke either a silent stasis or, as increasingly in the later works, a mediating and therefore, in a sense, inconclusive or irresolute coda.

As in *The Ice Break*, Tippett's harmonic strength here is less a matter of consistently planned progression than of the significant stabilizing presence of fifth-based chords. Since the ending of the fourth symphony is even more tentative than that of the third, the oscillation may even seem to end on the wrong chord: the favoured bass-note A is abandoned and the line moves back on to C sharp (Ex. 63). It is unusual to find so

Ex. 63 Tippett, Symphony No. 4

straightforward an image for beginning again at the end of a Tippett work, but it may simply be a determinedly personal allusion, like the use of the early fugal style and the reference to Orlando Gibbons in the third episode. In view of the composer's remarks about Strauss's symphonic poems and Elgar's *Falstaff* in connection with the piece, it is tempting to talk in terms of the life and death of a hero – or anti-hero. But the ending seems concerned neither with rejection, nor with transfiguration. Because of the nature of his language Tippett can round out a form (by returning to its initial material) without 'resolving' that material. So his version of 'from the cradle to the grave' is much less about the aging of ideas, about loss of definition and coherence, which would only be possible through an unacceptable degree of mimetic degeneracy, than about the senses of fulfilment and frustration which co-exist in old age. Tippett is rather cavalier about old age: since he himself remains so young for his years he is capable of ascribing it unconvincingly, as to Nadia in *The Ice Break*. But like any major creative artist, he has learned that fulfilment itself will be frustrated unless a balance is struck between whatever poles are in question at any given time. In purely musical terms, he has mastered the greatest challenge: the chance to mediate between the need for completion and the structures of the tonal system. Such a conclusion may need to be either tentative or decisive: but it must never be arbitrary. And that means that the processes whereby it is prepared must be coherent and consistent from beginning to end.

The appearance of a relatively conventional fugato in the Symphony No. 4, and the allusion to string music by an earlier composer, has been instanced as evidence of the wide-ranging, not to say confessional nature of that work's processes. But in the String Quartet No. 4 (completed in September 1978) fugue is notable by its absence, not simply in comparison with its pervasiveness in the String Quartet No. 3 of some thirty years before, but in view of the work's conscious and clear reference to the theme from Beethoven's *Grosse Fuge*. Just as the perspectives which the Symphony No. 3 offers on the 'Ode to Joy' reinforce the guarded nature of Tippett's latter-day optimism, so the fourth quartet's homage to the Great Fugue seem designed to point up the differences between Beethoven and Tippett, rather than any similarities. The almost nonchalant skill with which Beethoven draws an effortless tonal resolution from his striving polyphony is one of the pinnacles of the tonal art. The fugue theme itself expresses a turbulence which could just as easily lead to a Mahlerian collapse, a spiritual disintegration in which the preservation of tonal gestures seems poignant or hollow, according to taste. In Tippett the energy (both his and Beethoven's) provokes neither a 'conflict' which is resolved, nor a catastrophe faithfully mirrored in the music. It is simply placed alongside more reposeful gestures, and a final 'mediation' between the two is sketched out (Fig. 127), whose simple texture and tranquil character, together with the fifth-based higher consonances of the harmony, provide the sense of an ending, without for a moment eliminating all ambiguity (See Ex. 1, Prologue, p. 5). The ending is comparable to that of the Symphony No. 4, as are the principal, evolutionary, compositional processes, but the form of the quartet demonstrates a further accommodation with the past. The four movements are marked 'Slow' (crotchet 46); 'Fast' (crotchet 92) – a scherzo; 'Moderately slow' (quaver 112) – 'the emotional core of the work' according to the composer; and 'Very fast' (quaver 116). These combine into a single movement, and the reduced dependence on juxtaposition and superimposition suggests a link with the Piano Sonata No. 3, whose three sections each preserve their basic tempos throughout.

The introductory slow section of the work seems almost too literally generative at the outset, but it rapidly reaches the point of defining a typically florid idea which is presented as two duets (Figs. 9 and 10) and ends the movement as an 'accompanied duet' (Fig. 12). The first fast movement is very different in character from the central section of the Piano Sonata No. 3, but it borrows the basic idea of moving through a symmetrically divided octave: in the quartet there are three sections, each a minor third apart from the other (on D, B, and A flat). This is a rare example of Tippett's use of such symmetry, and on this occasion the 'circle' is not closed by a completion of the motion through the fourth and last minor third of the octave. This section is strongly evolutionary in Tippett's most direct manner, the material of greater rhythmic than motivic consequence. Hints of the 'old' style occur from time to time: for example, at Fig. 12 where the first violin and cello duet three octaves apart. Strong contrasts of texture and rhythm also appear (especially in the material first heard at Fig. 20), but the same pulse persists and the movement is notable for the amount of rhythmic unison it employs. Just before the end of the first main sub-section, at Fig. 27, an interruption does occur: a brief Adagio recalls the final phrase of Section 1, and a similar effect appears at the end of the second main sub-section (Fig. 42).

The slow movement is divided into two parts by the contrasts between relatively sustained and floating textures, but this is an episode which avoids the obvious parallelisms of large-scale repetition. As a result, its gradual build-up is particularly impressive, and its later stages anticipate certain aspects of the work's conclusion – the lulling fifth-based homophony of the very end at Fig. 73, and the 'quadrophony' of the link to that ending at Fig. 74. The way in which the three distinct paragraphs of this last part of the third section lead directly into the finale is perhaps the finest passage in the work.

The finale is much more directly concerned than the earlier movements with superimposing rhythmically distinct segments, and with juxtaposing temporal as well as textural contrasts. The main material at Fig. 82 is a duet in which the first violin and cello exchange material while the inner parts accompany. After that, and after the galvanizing reference to the *Grosse Fuge*, a much greater degree of uniformity sets in, and, by the very ease with which it seems to unfold and expand, it provokes the crucial discontinuity, at Fig. 95. The conflict here is short-lived to the extent that the new, slower material evolves an episode of its own (from Fig. 97). with its own internal contrasts. But this is to be no symmetrical arch-form, still less a palindrome like the central part of the third sonata's finale. The return of fast material at Fig. 105 provokes more persistent juxtapositions of 'medium slow' and 'very fast' (from Fig. 109), and when the initial material finally reappears at Fig. 122 the sense of recapitulation in reverse finally destroys the urge to assertive resolution.

Not only does the fourth quartet avoid the return to its own opening which 'winds down' the fourth symphony, it actually disperses its final-section recapitulation with completely new material, as a means of preparing the mediating coda. This material (Fig. 124) arose when Tippett was already beginning to plan his next work, the Triple Concerto, and it is referred to (not by exact quotation) during the concerto's first movement.

The Triple Concerto for violin, viola, cello and orchestra occupied Tippett from November 1978 to December 1979, and shares formal features with both the fourth symphony and the fourth quartet, beyond being a multi-sectioned single movement. Like the symphony, its main sections (three, not four) are linked by episodes which provide contrast rather than development (called Interludes in the concerto). Like the quartet, it has new finale material, although this eventually yields, not to more new material, but to a recapitulatory recall of material from the first movement of the concerto (from Fig. 148). Tippett may be no more successful in the concerto than in its two immediate predecessors in devising material of the breath-taking distinctiveness and spontaneity of which he was once capable; but the use of extended lyric melody in the first and central sections, as well as in the second half of Interlude II, permit the clearer use of focused harmonies which are not only higher consonances, but which hint at the old style of extended tonality. The slow central movement, in particular, refers to a potentially over-sweet F major to which strong clashes between major and minor thirds in the tonic triad bring a welcome dash of acid (Ex. 64). Initially, the finale may seem the least substantial section, but its progress towards a recall of the work's opening music and its use of that material shows that Tippett has lost none of his zest for jaundiced references to the goal-directed endings of the Great Tradition. The cadential motions from B flat to E are rhythmically decisive, but the kaleidoscopic prolongation of the E in a work which has already swung the balance away from thematic argument to textural by-play has little of the solemnity or solidity which attaches to 'true' tonics. The coda nevertheless clarifies the function of the E-based initial chord of the work, a 'benign' device in sharp contrast to the argumentative progression around E which opens the Symphony No. 3, and to the more equivocal opening and closing gestures of the fourth symphony and fourth quartet. There is no doubt that E is the central pitch, even if pitch itself seems more a property of colour than the crucial structural element. But the concerto has the first sharply defined ending composed by Tippett since the Piano Sonata No. 3, and both are exceptional in the degree to which they permit reminiscence of those much earlier certainties and more traditional processes on which his style and technique were founded.

Ex. 64 Tippett, Triple Concerto for violin, viola, cello and orchestra

Epilogue

Benjamin Britten died on 4 December 1976, less than two weeks after his sixty-third birthday. His last completed work was the *Welcome Ode* for young people's chorus and orchestra op. 95, and he had also sketched 'a significant portion' of a cantata for solo quartet, chorus and orchestra, setting Edith Sitwell's poem 'Praise we Great Men'.[1]

Britten's death was not unexpected. His illness had been protracted, and his rare public appearances left no doubt that the man whom Tippett described in a tribute as 'the most purely musical person I have ever met and I have ever known'[2] was cruelly weakened and diminished. The hopes expressed at the time of his sixtieth birthday that there might be another quarter-century of creative achievement were summarily dashed.

It was indeed fortunate, given his early death, that Britten should have achieved so much so young. Fluency and pessimism may have combined to determine the course, and term, of his development, but they facilitated the homogeneity of an *oeuvre* which is remarkably extensive and unfailingly resourceful in its exploration of its clearly defined and challenging territory. For Britten there were no sudden changes of direction, no sudden grasping for the security of an almost anonymous idiom, no sudden drying up of his own intensely personal reserves of invention and imagination. Tippett, too, in his later works, has been able to deepen his individuality most directly by reference to aspects of his own past which had seemed exhausted twenty years before. His expansiveness and confidence were such that, at seventy-five, he was able to contemplate a work concerned with the nature of creativity itself – to affirm, in the title of the poem by Shelley to which the text refers, 'The Triumph of Life'.

If Britten's triumph was to make powerful and satisfying images out of perceptions about things musical and extra-musical which could easily have yielded utterly negative responses, Tippett's has been to maintain, enhance and control his instinctive exuberance and spontaneity, so that the welter of ideas and influences which seem to hedge his work round like a museum of world culture are swept up into the one great, individual gesture of affirmation and clarification. The extent to which control and clarification are dominant in Tippett's music is, undoubtedly, a matter of opinion, since it is the essence of his modernity that codifiable pitch procedures comparable to those of traditional tonality are not offered – or have not so far been demonstrated by any commentator. To some, Tippett's music seems not so much free as functionless in its rejection of hierarchic or symmetric structuring in favour of apparently spontaneous combinations and juxtapositions of ideas whose only evident rationale is their 'instinctive rightness' in both character and context. But while some find the lack of evident 'logic' disconcerting, others praise Tippett's modernist willingness to treat harmony expressively and colouristically, without anxious backward glances to the very different priorities and procedures of earlier epochs.

Britten's genius never drove him to resist the unifying forces of pitch hierarchies, however extended his tonality, however all-thematic or proto-serial his textures: to this extent, the contrast between Britten and Tippett is clear and unambiguous. In Britten, progressive 'conservatism' remains triumphantly fresh and satisfying. With Tippett, evolutionary empiricism constantly skirts the perils of the arbitrary and the random, but the sheer force of personal conviction and a musical identity of great expressive vitality and depth ensure remarkable success. Common and contrasting literary and dramatic themes need not be further emphasized: and as for techniques, it is perhaps the Purcellian inheritance, the coherence of living, evolving counterpoint, which provides the essential key. Britten's single points of structural and textural focus are more immediately comprehensible than Tippett's spontaneous, shifting superimpositions. There is a rich variety in the way Britten exploits different scales, modes and goal-directed processes which Tippett's more radical spirit has sacrificed; to this extent, Tippett's later works (at least up to and including the String Quartet No. 4) are instinct with the spirit of atonality, even when their materials at times seem to struggle to rediscover tonal priorities. This music challenges the conventions of structural coherence in a way Britten's never does, and which explains the comparisons with Ives, as well as the occasional unsympathetic comments about 'agnostic' counterpoint. In much Tippett it is no easier to codify degrees of tension and relaxation purely in terms of pitch-relations and functions than it is in any other modern composer who has gone beyond tonal extension into tonal suspension or atonality.

Tippett's work would probably not seem so challenging if the composer had also abandoned such 'traditional' textural devices as clear-cut repetition, octave doubling or florid decoration of a tone; or if he had embraced comprehensive serial systems and rigorous transformation processes, to compensate for the loss of tonal goal-directedness. The wealth of reference and association in the music of Peter Maxwell Davies, reaching from Dunstable to Schoenberg and Babbitt, or the confidence with which Harrison Birtwistle builds from blocks after the manner of Stravinsky, Varèse or Messiaen, shows how a younger British generation has reacted to the need for a new synthesis and more determined progress. Tippett's exuberant freedom may therefore come to seem more poignant as time passes, and younger composers distance themselves still more either by greater strictness or by more direct associations with the styles of tradition. Nor will Britten's controlled yet lucid intensity be easily captured by composers who lack his self-questioning fluency. Yet an age to which the 'new' means 'neo-late-Romanticism' is certainly an age to which the styles and techniques of both Britten and Tippett could remain challengingly relevant.

In Britten, extended tonality and emancipation of the dissonance yield contrapuntal structures whose emotional force often belies their economy of means. In Tippett, emancipation of the consonance blurs the borderline between extended tonality and 'restricted atonality', so that rhythmic propulsion and the drama of familiar formal devices – variation, contrast – attain a special prominence. There is no overriding precompositional discipline in either case, and this permits the imaginative foreground departure from any scheme, so long as stylistic coherence permits.

Britten, with his abiding concern to 'tear all the waste away',[3] probably shared Tippett's admiration for Mahatma Gandhi, while shunning the relish of 'contracting in to abundance' and the confident self-dramatization which has led the older composer to declare that 'Hermes is the key-figure in my own artistic life, because he goes between the human world and the divine world, breaking through both inner and outer words, and the things that compose them. He stands for the artistic – for myself – the go-between between one world and another.'[4] The mediating role of the modern artist can take many forms, and with both Tippett and Britten one senses the distinctiveness and clarity with which they relate what is most personal in their own work to what is most vital in the great traditions of the past. This is the essential technical means to the expressive end whereby, as in all great art, a vision of positive perfection is opened out and, on occasion, embraced.

Notes

Prologue

1 London, 1959.
2 *Tolstoy or Dostoevsky* p. 7.
3 Ibid., p. 116.
4 Ibid., p. 10.
5 Benjamin Britten in *Michael Tippett. A Symposium on his sixtieth birthday*, ed. Ian Kemp (London, 1965), pp. 29-30.
6 'Britten at fifty', *Music of the angels. Essays and sketchbooks of Michael Tippett*, ed. Meirion Bowen (London, 1980), p. 81.
7 An article in *Horizon* (1944), quoted in Eric Walter White, *Tippett and his operas* (London, 1979), p. 21.
8 *Music in England*, rev. edn (Harmondsworth, 1947), p. 270.
9 *Music and society* (London, 1950), p. 181.
10 'Music in Britain 1916-1960', *The modern age 1890-1960,* ed. Martin Cooper, *The New Oxford History of Music*, vol. 10 (London, 1974), p. 540.
11 *Michael Tippett. An introductory study* (London, 1980), p. 17.
12 *Die romantische Harmonik und ihre Krise in Wagners 'Tristan'*, (Bern, 1920), p. 265.
13 *Structural functions of harmony*, 2nd rev. edn, ed. Leonard Stein (London, 1969), pp. 76–7.
14 Ibid., p. 113.
15 *Theory of harmony*, transl. Roy E. Carter (London, 1978), p. 128.
16 Ian Kemp, 'Rhythm in Tippett's early music', *Proceedings of the Royal Musical Association*, 105 (1978–9), p. 146.
17 Peter Evans, *The music of Benjamin Britten* (London, 1979), p. 547.
18 See Jonathan M. Dunsby, 'Schoenberg and the writings of Schenker', *Journal of the Arnold Schoenberg Institute*, 2 (1977), p. 26.
19 See Felix Salzer, *Structural hearing. Tonal coherence in music* (New York, 1952) and Roy Travis, 'Directed motion in Schoenberg and Webern', *Perspectives of New Music,* 4/2 (1966), pp. 85-9.
20 'Schoenberg and Schenker', *Proceedings of the Royal Musical Association*, 100 (1973–4), pp. 214–15.
21 Benjamin Britten, *On receiving the Aspen Award*, 2nd impr. (London, 1978), pp. 17-18.
22 Tippett, notes with the recording of *Songs for Dov* on Argo ZRG 703.
23 *Theory of harmony*, p. 287.
24 *The standard edition of the complete psychological works*, vol. 21 (London, 1973), p. 122.
25 *Flawed words and stubborn sounds* (New York, 1971), p. 61.

1 Britten: Four early works (1931-3)

1 Prefatory note, *String Quartet in D major (1931)* (London, 1975).
2 'Early influences: a tribute to Frank Bridge (1879–1941)', *Composer*, 19 (Spring 1966), p. 3.

3   Address at Hull University (1962). *The London Magazine*, 3/7 (1963), pp. 89-90.
4   Murray Schafer, *British composers in interview* (London, 1963), p. 119.
5   'A time to recall', *Moving into Aquarius*, 2nd edn (London, 1974), p. 101.
6   'Music and life' (1938), *Music of the angels*, pp. 31-2.
7   'Early influences', p. 2.
8   Prefatory note, *String Quartet in D major (1931)*.
9   *The Musical Times*, 75 (1934), p. 75.
10 References are to the score of the revised edn, published in 1958.
11 See Donald Mitchell, *Britten and Auden in the thirties* (London, 1981), p. 19.

2 Tippett: String Quartet No. 1, Piano Sonata No. 1 (1934-7)

1   'Benjamin Britten: first encounters', *Music of the angels*, p. 77.
2   Notes with the recording on Philips DSLO 10.
3   Alan Ridout, 'The String Quartets', *Michael Tippett. A Symposium*, p. 184.
4   Notes with the recording on Philips 6500 534.

3 Britten: *Our Hunting Fathers* to the Violin Concerto (1936-9)

1   The term coined by Samuel Hynes in his book *The Auden generation* (London, 1976).
2   *Britten and Auden in the thirties*, p. 25.
3   *Christopher and his kind* (London, 1977), p. 200.
4   Schafer, *British composers,* p. 115.
5   Peter Pears, 'The vocal music', *Benjamin Britten. A Commentary on his work from a group of specialists*, ed. Donald Mitchell and Hans Keller (London, 1952), p. 64.
6   George Dannatt, *Penguin Music Magazine*, 2 (1947), p. 84.
7   *Music and Letters*, 19 (1938), p. 360.
8   Henry Boys, 'The younger English composers V', *Monthly Musical Record*, 68 (1938), pp. 235-7.
9   E. and K. Stone (eds), *The writings of Elliott Carter* (Bloomington and London, 1977), pp. 84-5.

4 Tippett in 1939: The Concerto for Double String Orchestra

1   'Music and life', *Music of the angels*, pp. 31-2.

5 Britten in America: 1939-42

1   *Benjamin Britten. A Complete catalogue of his published works,* Boosey & Hawkes and Faber Music (London, 1973).
2   Schafer, *British composers,* p. 121.

6 Tippett: An oratorio, a string quartet and a cantata (1939-43)

1   'Poets in a barren age', *Moving into Aquarius*, p. 152.
2   'T. S. Eliot and *A Child of Our Time*', *Music of the angels*, pp. 117-19.
3   'Poets in a barren age', pp. 152-3.
4   'Sketch for a modern oratorio', *Music of the angels*, pp. 127-87.
5   Ibid., p. 174.
6   'The nameless hero', *Music of the angels*, pp. 192-3.

7 'T. S. Eliot and *A Child of Our Time*', p. 120.
8 'What do we perceive in modern art?', *Moving into Aquarius*, pp. 92-3.
9 'The vocal works', *Michael Tippett. A Symposium*, p. 141.
10 Notes with the recording on Philips DSLO 10.
11 Notes with the recording on Argo DA 34.
12 'Benjamin Britten: first encounters', *Music of the angels*, p. 78.

8 Tippett and symphonic form (1944-6)

1 Wilfrid Mellers, 'Four orchestral works', *Michael Tippett. A Symposium*, p. 168.
2 Anthony Milner, 'Style', *Michael Tippett. A Symposium*, p. 220.
3 Notes with the recording on Philips DSLO 10.
4 Notes with the recording on Philips DSLO 10.
5 'Benjamin Britten: obituary', *Music of the angels*, p. 82.

9 Britten: *Peter Grimes* (1944-5)

1 Introduction, *Peter Grimes*, Sadlers Wells Opera Books, No. 3 (London, 1946), p. 8.
2 'The birth of an opera', *Moving into Aquarius*.
3 *Benjamin Britten. A Commentary*, p. 347.
4 Introduction, *Peter Grimes*, p. 8.
5 Ibid.
6 Ibid.
7 J. W. Garbutt, 'Music and motive in *Peter Grimes*', *Music and Letters*, 44 (1963), p. 337.
8 *Benjamin Britten. His life and operas* (London, 1970), pp. 108-9.
9 'The search for simplicity', *Times Literary Supplement*, 15 February 1980, p. 182.

11 Britten: *The Rape of Lucretia* and *Albert Herring* (1946-7)

1 The quotations in this paragraph are from Schafer, *British composers*, p. 118.
2 See *Tempo*, 120 (March 1977), p. 11.
3 Ibid., pp. 11-12.
4 *The music of Benjamin Britten*, pp. 104-23.

12 Britten: From *Albert Herring* to *Billy Budd* (1947-51)

1 Schafer, *British composers*, p. 121.
2 Herman Melville (ed. F. Barron Freeman), *Billy Budd and other tales* (New York, 1961), pp. 61-2.
3 P. N. Furbank, *E. M. Forster. A Life,* 1-vol. edn (London, 1979), p. 284.
4 Melville, *Billy Budd*, p. 47.
5 Ibid., p. 17.
6 Ibid., p. 14.

13 Tippett: *The Midsummer Marriage* (1946-52)

1 'The birth of an opera', *Moving into Aquarius*, p. 51.
2 Ibid., p. 54.
3 Ibid., pp. 54-5.
4 Ibid., p. 59.
5 Ibid., p. 56.

6   See White, *Tippett and his operas*, p. 48.
7   'The birth of an opera', p. 60.
8   Ibid., p. 61.
9   Ibid.
10 'Sketch for a modern oratorio', *Music of the angels*, p. 174.
11 'Stravinsky and *Les Noces*', *Music of the angels*, pp. 89-90.
12 'Opera since 1900', *Music of the angels*, pp. 202-3.
13 'Music and life', *Music of the angels*, p. 32.
14 'The birth of an opera', p. 61.
15 Notes with the recording on Argo DA 34.

14 Britten: From Canticle II to *Winter Words* (1952-3)
1   *Benjamin Britten. His life and operas*, p. 162.
2   *The music of Benjamin Britten*, p. 201.

15 Tippett: From the *Corelli Fantasia* to the Piano Concerto (1953-5)
1   Notes with the recording on HMV ALP 2073.

16 Britten: *The Turn of the Screw* to *Noye's Fludde* (1953-7)
1   *Benjamin Britten. His life and operas*, p. 66.

17 Tippett: Symphony No. 2 (1956-7)
1   Notes with the recording on Argo ZRG 535.
2   Ibid.

18 Britten: The *Nocturne* to the *War Requiem* (1958-61)
1   Schafer, *British composers,* p. 121.

19 Tippett: *King Priam* (1958-61)
1   'The resonance of Troy', *Music of the angels*, p. 232.
2   'Music and poetry', *Recorded Sound*, 17 (January 1965), p. 292.
3   'The resonance of Troy', p. 230.
4   *King Priam*, Royal Opera House, Covent Garden, programme, 1967.
5   'The resonance of Troy', p. 234.
6   Ibid., p. 223.
7   Meirion Bowen, 'Illusion and actuality in the operas of Michael Tippett', in a pamphlet issued by the composer's publishers, Schott: *Michael Tippett's operas* (London, 1980), p. 3.

20 Tippett: After *King Priam* (1962-3)
1   Adam Bell in the *Evening Standard.* See *A Man of our time,* Tippett exhibition catalogue (London, 1977), p. 84.
2   Notes with the recording on HMV ALP 2073.

21 Britten: The Cello Symphony and *Curlew River* (1963-4)
1   'How great is Britten?' *Music and Musicians*, 12/3 (1963-4), p. 13.
2   'The world around Britten', *Tempo*, 66-7 (Autumn/Winter 1963), p. 33.
3   See above, p. 113.
4   *The music of Benjamin Britten*, pp. 491-5.

22 Tippett: The *Vision of Saint Augustine* (1963-5)

1   Tippett's remarks on *The Vision of Saint Augustine* quoted in this chapter are all from his note published with the recording on RCA SER 5620.
2   Gordon Leff, *Medieval thought* (Harmondsworth, 1958), p. 41.
3   Anthony Storr, *Jung* (London, 1973), p. 104.

25 Tippett: *The Knot Garden* and *Songs for Dov* (1966-70)

1   *Michael Tippett. A Symposium*, p. 11.
2   Stephen Spender, *Eliot* (London, 1975), pp. 232 and 235.
3   In the synopsis published with the libretto of *The Knot Garden* (London, 1971).
4   See Tom Sutcliffe, 'Tippett and *The Knot Garden*', *Music and Musicians*, 19/4 (1970-1), p. 54.
5   'Dov's journey', *Music of the angels*, pp. 237-8.
6   This and the following remarks of Tippett on *Songs for Dov* are taken from his note published with the recording on Argo ZRG 703.

26 Britten: From *Owen Wingrave* to *Death in Venice* (1970-3)

1   Leon Edel, *The life of Henry James*, 2-vol. edn (Harmondsworth, 1977), vol. 2, p. 668.
2   'Benjamin Britten: obituary', *Music of the angels,* p. 84.
3   Myfanwy Piper, 'Writing for Britten', *The operas of Benjamin Britten*, ed. David Herbert (London, 1979), p. 15.
4   Colin Graham, 'Staging first productions III', in Herbert (ed.) *The operas . . .* , p. 53.
5   Donald Mitchell and John Evans, *Benjamin Britten. Pictures from a life* (London, 1978), caption to no. 328.
6   Thomas Mann, *Death in Venice*, transl. H. T. Lowe-Porter (Harmondsworth, 1955), p. 15.
7   Ibid., p. 58.
8   *Literature as opera* (New York, 1977), p. 338.
9   Ibid., p. 330.
10. Ibid., p. 323.
11 *The music of Benjamin Britten*, p. 527.

27 Tippett: Symphony No. 3, Piano Sonata No. 3 (1970-3)

1   In an article published in *The Christian Science Monitor*, 27 May 1968; quoted in Richard E. Rodda, 'Michael Tippett's Symphony No. 3', *Music Review*, 39 (1978), pp. 111-12.
2   Notes with the recording on Philips 6500 662.
3   See Bayan Northcott, 'Tippett's Third Symphony', *Music and Musicians*, 20/10 (1971-2), p. 30.
4   *Michael Tippett. An introductory study*, p. 96.
5   With the recording on Philips 6500 534.
6   See Northcott, 'Tippett's Third Symphony'.

28 Britten: The final compositions (1974-6)

1   *Eliot's early years* (London, 1977), pp. 62 and 91-2.
2   'Introduction: operatic music and Britten', in Herbert (ed.) *The operas of Benjamin Britten,* p. xv.

29 Tippett: *The Ice Break*, and after (1973-80)

1 *Tippett and his operas*, p. 122.
2 See the synopsis published with the libretto of *The Ice Break* (London, 1976).
3 'Illusion and actuality in the operas of Michael Tippett', *Michael Tippett's operas,* p. 4.
4 White, *Tippett and his operas*, p. 114.
5 See Northcott, 'Tippett's Third Symphony', *Music and Musicians*, 20/10 (1971-2), p. 32.

Epilogue

1 Mitchell and Evans, *Benjamin Britten. Pictures from a life,* caption to no. 439.
2 'Benjamin Britten: obituary', *Music of the angels*, p. 83.
3 Schafer, *British composers,* p. 118.
4 'Music and poetry', *Recorded Sound*, 17 (January 1965), p. 292.

Suggestions for further reading

Selective Britten and Tippett bibliographies will be found in *The New Grove Dictionary of Music and Musicians* (London: Macmillan 1980). The most extensive study of Britten's music is:

Peter Evans, *The music of Benjamin Britten* (London: J. M. Dent 1979). As yet there has been no substantial biographical study, but a great deal of useful information and fascinating documentation will be found in:

Alan Blyth (ed.), *Remembering Britten* (London: Hutchinson 1981)

Michael Kennedy, *Britten* (London: J.M. Dent 1981)

Donald Mitchell, *Britten and Auden in the thirties* (London: Faber and Faber 1981)

Donald Mitchell and John Evans, *Benjamin Britten. Pictures from a life, 1913-76* (London: Faber and Faber 1978)

As far as Tippett is concerned, the following material is particularly valuable:

David Matthews, *Michael Tippett. An introductory study* (London: Faber and Faber 1980)

Michael Tippett, *Moving into Aquarius*, 2nd (enlarged) edition (London: Palladin 1974)

Michael Tippett, *Music of the angels* (London: Eulenburg Books 1980)

For catalogues of works, see

Benjamin Britten. A Complete catalogue of his published works (London: 1973) Boosey & Hawkes and Faber Music

and

A Man of our time. Michael Tippett, (London: Schott 1977) (Exhibition Catalogue)

Index

309

313

WITHDRAW